Chicago Entertains

KENILWORTH UNION CHURCH
KENILWORTH, ILLINOIS

First Edition

First Printing	August, 1982	5,000 copies
Second Printing	June, 1983	5,000 copies
Third Printing	September, 1986	5,000 copies

Illustrations by Barbara Kauffmann Locke

For additional copies, use order blanks in the
back of the book or write directly to:

CHICAGO ENTERTAINS
P.O. Box 145
Kenilworth, Illinois 60043

printed by
S.C. Toof & Company
Memphis, Tennessee

INTRODUCTION

The Kenilworth Union Church, located just north of Chicago, is the oldest community church in the United States. It was founded in 1892.

Several years ago we elected to produce a cookbook which would express the interests and abilities of its many members and friends. Accordingly, "Chicago Entertains" is offered for your enjoyment.

Our emphasis is on entertaining. Chicago and its North Shore boast many fine restaurants, but you are as likely to find hostesses serving elegant dinners for twelve or intimate suppers for six. Perhaps it is a picnic with the Chicago Symphony under the stars at Ravinia or an afternoon sail on Lake Michigan.

No matter what your interests or culinary capabilities may be, assembled herewith is a broad sampling of menus and recipes to suit every occasion or palate.

Well over 1100 recipes were submitted from all over the United States. Each one was "blind-tested" three times to guarantee both quality of taste and accuracy of ingredients. We have endeavored to present those which will have the broadest appeal to our most severe critics—you, whose support of this book has made it possible.

The Committee

The Kenilworth Union Church

CONTRIBUTORS

We would like to thank the members and friends who contributed so much to this book

Mrs. H. Wayne Aden
Mrs. Richard H. Aishton
Mrs. William H. Alger, Jr.
Mrs. William H. Alger III
Mrs. James H. Anderson
Mrs. Donald G. Andrew
Mrs. Albert E. Attebery
Mrs. Frank K. Badger
Kathy Balderston
Mrs. Stuart S. Ball
Mrs. Robert J. Balsley
Jeanne Banta
Mrs. Charles O. Barnes
Mrs. Curtis F. Barnett
Joan Bartlett
Mrs. Norman E. Baughn
Mrs. James R. Beall
Dr. Mary Higginbotham Beaven
Mrs. Robert C. Becherer
Mrs. David Bellamy, Jr.
Mrs. Arthur W. Bergman, Jr.
Mrs. Ronald Bess
Melissa Bishop
Mrs. Edward C. Blomeyer
Casey Bohnstedt
Mrs. Howard W. Bonnell
Mrs. Edwin B. Bosler
Mrs. H. Sheldon Bott, Jr.
Mrs. Edward S. Bottum
Mrs. Edrita F. Braun
Mrs. John W. Brice, Jr.
Mrs. Paul L. Brown
Mrs. William A. Brown, Jr.
Mrs. John P. Bruemmer
Mrs. John Bryan
Mrs. Alfred F. Buckman
Mrs. Curtis D. Buford
Mrs. Charles R. Bylsma
Mrs. Charles Campbell
Mrs. R. E. Carlson
Mrs. Frank Castellvi
Mrs. David M. Chamberlain
Mrs. Julien H. Collins
Mrs. Julien H. Collins, Jr.
Mrs. Stanton R. Cook
Mrs. E. David Coolidge III
Mrs. Solon B. Cousins
Mrs. William A. Cox, Jr.
Mrs. J. Wendall Crain
Mrs. Daniel N. Cross
Mrs. Robert J. Cunningham
Mrs. Albert E. Day
Mrs. Norman E. Deletzke
Mrs. John G. Dorrer
Mrs. Harry DuPrey

Jan Ellerman
Mrs. Samuel H. Ellis
Miss Anne Engelmann
Mrs. Reid O. Engelmann
Mrs. Harry C. Fehr
Mrs. Steven D. Fifield
Miss Anne Finger
Mrs. Moritz Finger
Mrs. John N. Fix
Mrs. William D. Folland
Mrs. Carl E. Fowler
Mrs. Jon R. Fowler
Mrs. Thomas A. Fraker
Mrs. Arthur A. Frank, Jr.
Mrs. Clair W. Furlong
Mrs. John H. Fyfe
Mrs. Andrew E. Good
Mrs. Bruce J. Gooden
Mrs. John B. Graham
Mrs. John Grainer
Mrs. Raymond C. L. Greer
Mrs. H. Thomas Griffith
Mrs. Dennis Gronek
Miss Joan V. Groves
Mrs. Geoffrey Gummersall
Mrs. Gus M. Hagenah
Mrs. Dane F. Hahn
Mrs. Walter Hallsteen
Mrs. H. H. Hanlon
Mrs. Harry F. Hartel
Mrs. Warren C. Haskin
Anis Hauseman
Mrs. Peter T. Haverkampf
Mrs. Howard R. Hayes
Mrs. Wilfred H. Heitmann
Mrs. Robert W. Higgins
Mrs. Gordon J. Hjalmarson
Mrs. Robert A. Hoaglund
Mrs. William R. Hodgson
Mrs. Mark T. Hogan
Miss Lee Horton
Mrs. Edward R. James
Mrs. A. B. Johnson
Mrs. Edward Q. Johnson
Mrs. Gene Johnson
Mrs. Joen B. Johnson
Mrs. Thomas Johnson
Miss Margaret Jones
Mrs. Phillip N. Jones
Mrs. H. W. Jordan
Mrs. Sibrand S. Jurriaans
Mrs. Emmett L. Kearney
Mrs. Robert P. Keith
Mrs. Harry M. Kelso III
Mrs. G. Preston Kendall

Mrs. Robert R. Kenyon
Mrs. John K. Kerr
Mrs. Dick O. Klein
Mrs. Morley C. Lautens
Mrs. William G. Lawrence
Mrs. Lawrence J. Lawson
M. Lay
Mrs. John R. Lee
Mrs. Thomas Leith
Mrs. Robert M. Levy
Lisa Lillard-Caldwell
Mrs. Thomas M. Lillard
Mrs. Steven E. Lindblad
Mrs. Barbara Kauffman Locke
Mrs. Scott Lockridge
Mrs. William R. Lyman
Mrs. James Lynch
Mrs. James D. Lyons
Jackie Maue
Mrs. James R. McClamroch
Mrs. Richard P. McClamroch
Mrs. Archibald McClure
Mrs. L. William McCrea
Mrs. James P. McGuffin
Mrs. Robert McLellan
Mrs. Preston J. McNurlen
Mrs. Sumner W. Mead
Mrs. Edith Michell
Mrs. L. Steven Minkel
Mrs. Lyman Missimer
Mrs. John M. Mitchell
Mrs. Douglas Moir
Kathleen Mollison
Mrs. Duane Molthop
Mrs. Gerard Moons
Mrs. William A. Morrell
Mrs. Geoffrey C. Murphy
Mrs. H. D. Murphy
Mrs. Alvin B. Nordhem
Paula Nordhem
Mrs. Gerald C. North
Mrs. James R. O'Brien
Mrs. David P. O'Donnell
Mrs. Lee E. Osborne
Mrs. L. Carl Oseland
Pat Palmer
Ruth Palmer
Mrs. Donald W. Patterson
Mrs. Ted Payseur
Mrs. Ellwood G. Peterson
Mrs. A. W. Phelps
Sally Pierce
Mrs. James W. Pierpont
Mrs. Adolph Pifko
Mrs. John E. Porta
Mrs. Bert R. Prall
Mrs. Thomas P. Price
Mrs. John W. Puth
Mrs. Richard C. Rastetter
Mrs. Thomas M. Ritchie, Jr.
Mrs. John C. Roberson
Mrs. David H. Robertson
Jody Robertson

Mrs. Peter J. Robinson
Mrs. Donald J. Ross
Mrs. Royce Rowe, Jr.
Mrs. Edward Ruegg
Mrs. Barnard A. Savage, Jr.
Mrs. David D. Schafer
Mrs. Bruce W. Schneidewind
Mrs. R. G. Schultz
Mrs. Gordon R. Scott
Mrs. John R. Scott
Mrs. Harvey A. Scribner
Mrs. David R. Seibel
Mrs. William H. Sethness
Mrs. Charles Shaw
Mrs. Charles W. Sherman
Mr. William Skinner
Mrs. George Sladoje
Mrs. Len Young Smith
Sallie Lillard Smith
Mrs. Robert A. Southern
Mrs. George W. Stamm
Mrs. David B. Sterrett, Sr.
Mrs. John Stettner
Mrs. Marion Stevens
Cheryl Stewart
Mrs. William P. Stewart
Mrs. John S. Stiles
Mrs. David M. Stone
Mrs. Fred L. Stone
Mrs. R. Scott Stratton
Mrs. J. William Straughan, Jr.
Mrs. James E. Sullivan
Mrs. Laurence F. Tidrich
Mrs. Timothy L. Tilton
Julie Thompson
Mrs. David Trickey
Mrs. Reed J. Tupper
Mrs. Allen Urbahns
Mrs. Franklin A. Urbahns
Patsy Vanatta
Mrs. Craig Vance
Mrs. Jaak van Elk
Mrs. Philip A. Van Vlack III
Mrs. C. M. Varde
Mrs. John E. Vette
Mrs. Victor J. Voorhis
Mrs. John Vratimos
Mrs. Eric Wagner
Mrs. Donald K. Warfield
Mrs. William W. Watts
Mrs. Carroll G. Wells
Miss Cheryl E. Wells
Mrs. F. Postin White
Carlyn Whitehand
Mrs. Paul S. Wise
Mary Wise
Mrs. Kenneth H. Wood, Jr.
Mrs. Milton M. Wood
Mrs. John M. Wolfe
Mrs. Kenneth T. Wright
Miss Kathleen Young
Mrs. Robert B. Young

TABLE OF CONTENTS

Appetizers and Beverages

ARTICHOKE TREE

Delicious eye-catcher!

1 styrofoam cone with
   7-inch base, trimmed
   to height of 13 inches
U-shaped florist pins
skewers
hammer
round serving tray at
   least 12 inches in
   diameter
3 large heads chicory
   or escarole
18 medium artichokes,
   cooked in water to
   which lemon juice has
   been added
16 to 18 large lemons

Cover cone completely with chicory or escarole, attaching with florist pins. Set cone on serving tray. Attach 6 artichokes around base of cone by skewering each straight through center and once on each side. Don't push skewers all the way into cone at this point. Attach one artichoke at very top of cone using 3 more skewers. Fill in sides with remaining artichokes, spacing evenly and leaving room between for lemons. Attach lemons as desired by skewering each lengthwise straight through center, but do not push skewers all the way into cone. Position artichokes and lemons with skewers exactly where you want them, then carefully hammer skewers into place. Remember, each artichoke must be secured with 2 or 3 skewers so the leaves can be removed easily. Can be assembled a day ahead, wrapped in damp towels and stored in a cool place (do not refrigerate). Serve with lemon cream for dipping.

LEMON CREAM

2 cups mayonnaise
2 cups sour cream
1/4 cup fresh
   lemon juice
1 T. finely grated
   lemon peel
1 T. white horseradish
1 T. Dijon mustard
1 tsp. salt

Combine all ingredients in a large bowl and blend. Cover and refrigerate. Adjust seasoning before serving. Can be made 2 or 3 days ahead.

Mrs. James Pierpont

ARTICHOKE HORS D'OEUVRES

Makes 30

Easy to make.

1 7-1/2-oz. can artichoke
  bottoms
1 cup mayonnaise
1 cup grated
  Parmesan cheese
Worcestershire sauce
  to taste
Tabasco sauce to taste
party or cocktail
  rye bread
paprika

Use steel blade on food processor (or blender). Feed artichoke bottoms until finely chopped. Add mayonnaise and grated cheese. Process until well mixed. Mix in Worcestershire and Tabasco to taste. Toast the bread slices. Spread artichoke mixture on toasted bread. Sprinkle with paprika. Broil until lightly browned.

VARIATION: Artichoke mixture may be baked in a shallow pan at 350 to 400 degrees until brown. Serve with crackers.

Mrs. Kenneth H. Wood, Jr.

APPETIZING AVOCADOS

Serves 6

Even avocado haters agree this is a delicious way to devour an avocado!

3 small or 2
  large avocados
salad greens

Halve or third and pit avocados. Nestle in a bed of greens.

SAUCE
4 T. butter
2 T. water
4 T. catsup
2 T. vinegar
3 T. dark brown sugar
2 tsp. Worcestershire
  sauce
1/4 tsp. salt
dash Tabasco

Combine all sauce ingredients in a small saucepan. Cook over low heat, stirring constantly, until butter and brown sugar are melted. Cook until sauce thickens slightly. Keep hot. Spoon hot sauce over avocados and serve immediately.

NOTE: Peeling avocado skin is optional. It depends on the type you have, size of portion and the appearance you want.

Mrs. Edwin B. Bosler

ASPARAGUS CANAPES

Serves 36

Delicious blend of flavors...

**2 1-lb. loaves thin-sliced
white bread
8 oz. Roquefort cheese,
crumbled
1 8-oz. pkg. cream
cheese
1 T. mayonnaise
1 egg, well beaten
2 15 oz. cans asparagus
spears
melted butter**

Preheat oven to 350 degrees. Cut all crusts off bread and discard. Flatten bread slices with a rolling pin. Mix cheeses, mayonnaise and egg. Spread cheese mixture on bread, topping each slice with an asparagus stalk. Roll up bread and cut into three pieces. Dip canapés in melted butter and place on ungreased cookie sheet. Bake 15 minutes, until well browned. Serve hot.

NOTE: Canapés may be made the day before or frozen, then baked before serving. Cheese mixture keeps well in refrigerator.

Mrs. Adolph Pifko

SPINACH DIP FOR FRESH VEGETABLES

Makes 3 cups

Luscious, colorful dip seasoned to taste.

**2 10-oz. pkgs. frozen
chopped spinach
1 8-oz. pkg. cream
cheese (room
temperature)
1 cup mayonnaise
2 T. Beau Monde
seasoning
2 T. finely chopped
onion
lemon juice, garlic
powder and/or
Tabasco to taste**

Defrost spinach and *drain well.* Mix all ingredients together and add extra seasonings to suit personal taste. Refrigerate. Can be made 3 to 4 days ahead. Serve with julienne cut zucchini, celery, and carrots, cauliflower and large quartered mushrooms.

Mrs. R. Scott Stratton

CAULIFLOWER ANTIPASTO

Serves 6

A great side dish or toothpick hors d'oeuvres.

1 medium head fresh
  cauliflower
1 fresh green pepper,
  cut into 1/2-inch strips
1/2 cup fresh carrots, cut
  into 1/2-inch pieces
1/2 cup fresh
  mushrooms, sliced
  lengthwise
1/2 cup fresh celery,
  sliced diagonally
1/2 cup halved stuffed
  green olives
1/2 cup wine vinegar
1/2 cup olive oil
1/4 cup fresh lemon juice
1/4 cup water
2 T. granulated sugar
1 tsp. salt
1/2 tsp. crumbled
  basil leaves

Break cauliflower into flowerets, slicing larger ones to bite size. Combine vegetables in a large skillet. Mix together the vinegar, oil, lemon juice, water, sugar, salt and basil leaves. Pour over vegetables. Bring entire mixture to a boil. Reduce heat and simmer covered *just 3 minutes.* Cool and store in jars. Refrigerate overnight or a day or so, but no longer than 3 days. Drain and serve chilled.

Mrs. Ellwood G. Peterson

COCKTAIL CASSEROLE MUSHROOMS

Serves 8 to 10

Hmm...herbs and mushrooms...hmm!

2 lbs. large fresh
  mushrooms
3 T. marjoram
1-1/2 tsp. salt
1 cup chicken bouillon
1 cup butter, melted
1 T. chives
freshly ground pepper
  to taste
1/2 cup dry white wine

Preheat oven to 350 degrees. Put washed mushrooms in casserole. Combine rest of ingredients, stir well and pour over mushrooms. Cover and bake for 20 minutes. Serve in chafing dish with toothpicks.

NOTE: Sauce will keep in refrigerator to be used again or it's delicious in homemade soup. Freezes well, too!

Mrs. Sumner W. Mead

MUSHROOM CANAPES

Makes 96

Wonderful hors d'oeuvres for a large crowd!

1/2 lb. finely chopped
  mushrooms
3 T. flour
3 T. butter
1/4 tsp. Accent
3/4 tsp. salt
1 cup half and half
2 tsp. finely chopped
  chives
1 tsp. lemon juice
1-1/2 lbs. sliced
  white bread

Preheat oven to 400 degrees. Sauté mushrooms in butter 5 minutes. Stir in flour, Accent, and salt. Add half and half, stirring to make a smooth paste and cook until thickened and bubbly. Stir in chives and lemon juice. Cool. Trim crusts from bread, cut into various canapé shapes. Mound a rounded teaspoonful of mushroom mixture on each round. Bake for 8 minutes.

NOTE: May be frozen and/or doubled.

Mrs. James R. McClamroch

HOT MUSHROOM CAPS

Makes 24

Fabulous finger food!

1 lb. fresh mushroom
  caps
1/4 cup butter
6 slices bread, crusts
  removed and cut
  into quarters
1 8-oz. pkg. cream
  cheese, softened
2 egg yolks
1/2 tsp. salt
1/2 clove garlic,
  crushed

Wash and stem mushrooms. Save stems for another use. Sauté mushroom caps in butter. Toast bread squares on both sides on a cookie sheet in the oven. Place a mushroom, cut side down, on each piece of toast. Large mushrooms may be cut in half. Whip cream cheese and add egg yolks, salt and garlic. Beat until smooth. Spoon mixture over each mushroom, completely covering it. Broil 8 inches from the heat until lightly browned. These can be assembled early in the day and refrigerated until ready to brown and serve. They also may be frozen.

Mrs. James R. McClamroch

MINIATURE MUSHROOM CUPS — *Makes 24*

Plan to serve these delicious hot appetizers at your next party.

24 slices thin bread,
  cut into 3-inch rounds
soft butter

FILLING
4 T. butter
3 T. finely chopped onion
1/2 cup chopped
  mushrooms
2 T. flour
1 cup whipping cream
1 tsp. salt
1/8 tsp. cayenne pepper
1 T. chopped parsley
1-1/2 T. chopped chives
1/2 tsp. lemon juice
2 T. grated Parmesan
  cheese

Preheat oven to 350 degrees. Grease 24 miniature muffin cups with soft butter and fit bread slices into the cups. Sauté mushrooms and onions in butter for 5 to 10 minutes—or until moisture evaporates. Sprinkle with flour and stir. Add cream, stirring constantly. Bring to a boil, turn down heat and simmer for 2 minutes. Remove from heat and stir in seasonings and lemon juice. Fill cups with mushroom mixture, sprinkle with Parmesan cheese. Bake for 10 minutes.

Mrs. Samuel H. Ellis

KATE'S STUFFED MUSHROOMS — *Makes 36*

Yummy blue cheese flavor...

36 medium (one-inch)
  mushrooms
2 tsp. grated onion
1/3 cup butter
2 T. chopped parsley
1-1/4 cups fine bread
  crumbs
1/4 cup crumbled
  blue cheese
1 T. lemon juice
1/2 tsp. salt
2 T. melted butter

Preheat oven to 450 degrees. Clean mushrooms; remove stems and chop. Sauté stems and onion in butter; cool. Add remaining ingredients except melted butter. Stuff mushroom caps with mixture; brush with melted butter. Place on cookie sheet and bake for 5 minutes, then broil until brown.

Mrs. David M. Stone

CHICKEN LIVER PATE

Makes 3 cups

An excellent paté...

1 lb. chicken livers
1 cup milk
1/4 cup cognac
1-1/4 cups butter,
  softened
1 cup sliced onion
1 small green apple,
  peeled, cored and
  sliced
1/4 cup sherry or
  applejack
1/4 cup whipping cream
1-1/4 tsp. salt
1 tsp. fresh lemon juice
touch of garlic
freshly ground green
  peppercorns (optional)

GARNISH
parsley
grated hard-cooked
  egg yolks

Combine livers, milk and cognac. Soak one hour. Melt 1/2 cup butter. Add onion and sauté until browned. Add apple and cook until softened—3 to 4 minutes. Transfer to food processor. Drain livers. Return skillet to high heat, sauté livers until pink—10 to 12 minutes. Add to mixture in processor. Add sherry to skillet and cook, scraping brown bits from bottom. Add sherry and cream to liver mixture in processor and purée until smooth. Let stand until lukewarm. Beat remaining butter until creamy. With machine running, add to liver mixture, blending well. Mix in salt, lemon juice and garlic. Pour into paté dish or crock and refrigerate. Decorate with parsley. Sprinkle egg yolks on top. Serve with crackers.

Mrs. Sibrand S. Jurriaans

PATE IN ASPIC

Serves 16 to 18

Lovely to look at...delightful to eat!

ASPIC
**3 envelopes unflavored
  gelatin
6 T. cold water
2 10-1/2 oz. cans
  consommé
2 T. sherry**

Dissolve gelatin in cold water. Add to heated consommé and sherry. Pour 1 inch deep in a 3-1/2 x 10 x 2-3/4-inch paté pan. Set in refrigerator.

PATE
**3/4 lb. Jones liverwurst
2 T. Worcestershire
  sauce
6 oz. cream cheese
2 T. sherry
1 small onion, minced
parsley**

Mix ingredients in a food processor until smooth. Place on top of chilled aspic leaving a space around sides and ends. Fill with remaining aspic and set in refrigerator. Unmold and garnish with parsley. Serve with crackers.

NOTE: May substitute a 4-1/2 x 8-3/4 x 2-1/2-inch loaf pan.

Mrs. Peter Haverkampf

LIVER SAUSAGE CHEESE SPREAD

Serves 12 to 16

Brings rave reviews—especially from the men!

**1 8-oz. pkg. liver sausage
1 8-oz. pkg.
  cream cheese
1 4-oz. pkg. blue cheese,
  crumbled
1/2 cup finely chopped
  celery
1-1/2 T. onion juice
1 T. lemon juice
1 tsp. Worcestershire
1/2 tsp. salt**

Beat ingredients in blender or food processor until smooth and thoroughly blended. Serve in a crock with crackers to the side.

Mrs. John S. Stiles

PATE MADRILENE

Serves 12

Exquisite colors and textures...

1 13-oz. can madrilene
1 envelope unflavored
  gelatin
1/4 cup water
14 oz. liver sausage
1 T. grated onion
1 tsp. Worcestershire
  sauce
2 T. lemon juice
1 T. prepared mustard
1 8-oz. pkg. cream
  cheese

Heat soup to boiling. Dissolve gelatin in water and add to soup. Pour half of the mixture into a 5-cup mold and refrigerate until set. Mash sausage; add remaining ingredients, including rest of soup. Mix with a hand beater. Pour on top of chilled layer. Refrigerate. Unmold onto a platter and serve with crackers.

Mrs. Carl Fowler

1-2-3 SNACK MEAT BALLS

Makes 36

Great hot hors d'oeuvres!

2 tsp. Worcestershire
  sauce
2/3 cup evaporated
  milk
1 envelope dry
  onion soup mix
1 lb. ground beef

Preheat broiler about 5 minutes. Add Worcestershire sauce to milk and mix. Add remaining ingredients and mix well. Allowing one tablespoon of meat mixture for each, shape into balls. Place on broiler pan about 4 inches below burner. Broil 6 to 10 minutes without turning. Watch carefully.

SNAPPY SAUCE
2 cups catsup
1 cup brown sugar
1 T. Worcestershire
  sauce

Mix catsup, sugar and Worcestershire sauce and heat thoroughly. Then add meatballs. May be prepared ahead, refrigerated and reheated.

NOTE: If meatballs are doubled, one sauce recipe is still enough.

Mrs. Bruce J. Gooden

PIQUANT MEATBALLS FOR A CROWD

Makes 70

Great for the cocktail hour...

MEATBALLS
2 lbs. ground round
1 cup cornflake crumbs
1/3 cup dried parsley or
  2/3 cup chopped fresh
  parsley
2 eggs
2 T. soy sauce
1/4 tsp. pepper
1 tsp. garlic powder or
  2 cloves finely
  chopped garlic
1 T. salt
1/3 cup catsup
3 T. finely minced onion

Preheat oven to 350 degrees. Mix meatball ingredients together and form into balls smaller than walnuts. Place in a single layer on a 15 x 11-inch jellyroll pan. Cover meatballs with sauce. Bake uncovered 30 minutes. Keep warm in a chafing dish.

SAUCE
1 1-lb. can jellied
  cranberry sauce
1 12-oz. bottle chili sauce
2 T. brown sugar
1 T. lemon juice

Combine ingredients in saucepan. Stir over low heat until smooth.

Mrs. David M. Stone

CHILI BEEF DIP

Makes 3 cups

Great for a big party...

1 lb. ground round
1/2 cup chopped onion
1 large clove garlic,
   minced
1 cup tomato sauce
1/4 cup catsup
3/4 tsp. oregano
1 tsp. Worcestershire
   sauce
1 tsp. granulated sugar
salt and pepper to taste
2 tsp. chili powder
1/4 tsp. cayenne
pinch powdered cumin
4 oz. cream cheese
1/4 cup grated
   Parmesan cheese

Brown beef, onion and garlic. Add remaining ingredients, except cheeses, and simmer together for 10 minutes. Then add the cream cheese and Parmesan cheese. Heat until melted. Serve with large tortilla chips.

Mrs. Donald J. Ross

CHICKEN NACHOS

Makes 32

A fast snappy appetizer.

8 tostadas
2 5-oz. cans white
   chicken, drained
1 6-oz. can enchilada
   sauce (hot or picante)
1 cup sour cream
4 jalapeño peppers,
   rinsed and sliced
6 to 8 oz. grated
   Monterey Jack cheese

Preheat oven to 300 degrees. Place tostadas on a cookie sheet and bake for 5 minutes. Break chicken up with a fork in a small pan; add enchilada sauce; stir and heat through. Heat broiler unit in oven. Spread chicken mixture carefully over crisped tostadas; then put one tsp. sour cream on each quarter of a chip. Mound with cheese and put a *thin* slice of jalapeño pepper on each quarter over sour cream spot. Broil until cheese melts; cut into quarters.

Casey Bohnstedt

MEXICAN MEDLEY

Makes 6 cups

Serve with taco or tortilla chips...

1 lb. ground chuck
salt, pepper, and
   minced garlic to taste
2 10-1/2-oz. cans
   bean dip
1/2 lb. sharp Cheddar
   cheese, grated
1 7-oz. bottle taco sauce
1 8-oz. frozen container
   guacamole, thawed
1 pint sour cream
4 green onions, sliced
1 4-1/2-oz. can black
   olives, drained
   and sliced

Preheat oven to 350 degrees. Brown chuck with seasonings and drain. Layer bean dip, chuck mixture, cheese and taco sauce in 9 x 13-inch casserole dish. Bake until cheese melts. Mix guacamole, sour cream, onions and olives. Spread on top of baked mixture. Let stand at room temperature 1-1/2 hours before serving.

Mrs. Robert J. Cunningham

TACO DIP

Makes 4 cups

Guaranteed to disappear quickly on a buffet table!

1 16-oz. can refried beans
1 4-oz. can tomatoes
   and chilies
4 oz. shredded Cheddar
   cheese
1 8-oz. can frozen
   guacamole, thawed
8 oz. sour cream
tortilla chips

Preheat oven to 400 degrees. In a 9-inch pie plate layer the beans, tomatoes and chilies and then the cheese. Bake 10 minutes or until bubbly. Remove from the oven and top with the guacamole and then sour cream. May be garnished with pimiento and olives, if desired. Serve with tortilla chips.

Mrs. Donald J. Ross

REUBEN ROLLUPS

Makes 24

Cream cheese pastry makes the difference!

PASTRY
1 cup flour
1/2 tsp. salt
1/4 cup butter
1 3-oz. pkg. cream
cheese
2 to 3 T. water

FILLING
1/2 cup sauerkraut
1 2-1/2 oz. pkg. sliced
pressed corned beef
4 oz. shredded Swiss
cheese
1/4 cup Thousand Island
dressing

To prepare pastry, mix flour and salt together in a bowl. With a pastry blender or two knives, cut in butter and cream cheese until mixture resembles coarse cornmeal. Sprinkle in water a tablespoon at a time and mix with a fork. Push dough together into a ball and let rest 10 minutes. May be refrigerated overnight at this point or rolled out. If refrigerated, remove dough and let it come to room temperature before rolling.

Drain sauerkraut *very well.* Finely chop corned beef. Mix sauerkraut, corned beef, cheese and dressing.

Roll out half the pastry into a 10 x 12-inch rectangle. Spread half of filling on pastry and roll up lengthwise. Repeat for second rollup. Refrigerate covered until needed. Keeps well for two days. When needed, cut rolls into one-inch pieces; place on a cookie sheet and bake in a preheated 400-degree oven for 10 to 15 minutes or until golden brown. Serve hot with Thousand Island dressing for dipping!

Mrs. Fred L. Stone

CORNED BEEF BALL

Serves 8 to 10

Tangy appetizer to serve with crackers...

1 8-oz. pkg cream
  cheese, softened
1 bunch scallions,
  finely chopped
7 large radishes,
  finely chopped
1 3-oz. pkg. smoked
  corned beef, finely
  chopped
Worcestershire sauce
garlic salt
radish flowers
parsley sprigs

Mix scallions, radishes and corned beef with cream cheese. Add Worcestershire sauce and garlic salt to taste. Shape into a ball and refrigerate. Garnish with radish flowers and parsley sprigs.

Mrs. Carroll G. Wells

PARTY STEAK TARTARE

Serves 30

No cooking required for this yummy hors d'oeuvre!

1 lb. mushrooms, halved
Italian salad dressing
1-1/2 lbs. ground sirloin
6 T. finely chopped onion
3 egg yolks, beaten
3 T. grated Parmesan
  cheese
1-1/2 tsp. garlic salt
3/4 tsp. oregano
3 loaves cocktail
  rye bread

Place mushrooms in bowl; add salad dressing to cover. Refrigerate, covered, several hours to marinate. Combine sirloin, onion, egg yolk, Parmesan cheese, garlic salt and oregano. Cover and chill. To serve, mound meat mixture in center of serving tray. Serve with marinated mushrooms and cocktail rye.

NOTE: For added zing, add 1 T. capers and 1/2 tsp. freshly ground pepper.

Mrs. James R. McClamroch

TRIANGULAR BREAD NIBBLERS

Makes 12 to 16

Great as cocktail snacks!

thin sliced bread (12 to
  16 slices)
1/2 cup soft butter
1/2 tsp. rosemary
1/2 tsp. thyme
1/2 tsp. celery salt
1/2 tsp. garlic salt
sesame seeds

Preheat oven to 325 degrees. Trim crusts off bread. Roll flat with a rolling pin. Mix butter, seasonings and seeds. Spread on bread. Roll from the corner making cornucopias. Bake 20 to 25 minutes. Watch so they don't burn.

NOTE: May be cut in triangular shapes and served with soups.

Mrs. Carroll G. Wells

GOURMET PIZZA TOAST

Makes 8 to 9 dozen

A great man pleaser!

2 lbs. ground beef
1 lb. hot Italian sausage
2 lbs. Velveeta cheese,
  cubed
2 tsp. oregano
3 loaves party rye bread
2 cups shredded
  mozzarella cheese

Brown meats together; pour off fat. Add cubed cheese and oregano to hot meat mixture. Stir until cheese melts. Spread on bread and sprinkle with mozzarella cheese. Place on cookie sheets. Can be made in morning and refrigerated. Bake at 400 degrees for 8 to 10 minutes and serve hot.

NOTE: Freeze on cookie sheets; remove and put in plastic bags. Bake frozen when needed.

Mrs. Dane F. Hahn

CHEESE SAVOURIES

Makes 24

Marvelous with soup or as an appetizer.

1/2 cup butter, softened
1/2 lb. very sharp
  Cheddar cheese,
  grated
1-1/2 cups flour
1 tsp. salt
1/4 tsp. red pepper or
  paprika
1-1/2 cups Rice Krispies

Preheat oven to 350 degrees. Cream butter and cheese. Sift flour, salt and red pepper or paprika together. Stir flour mixture into butter/cheese mixture. Add Rice Krispies and mix well. Make small balls and flatten until very thin on well-greased cookie sheet. Bake 12 minutes. Place in tin with a tight fitting cover to keep several days. Also may be made in advance and frozen.

Mrs. David M. Stone

CHEDDAR CHEESE PUFFS

Makes 72

Great to have in the freezer for unexpected guests...

1 1-1/2-lb. loaf unsliced
  white bread
6 oz. cream cheese,
  cubed
1 cup butter, cubed
8 oz. extra sharp
  Cheddar cheese,
  shredded
1 tsp. dry mustard
4 egg whites, beaten stiff

Trim crusts from bread, slice one-inch thick and cut into one-inch cubes. In a medium size saucepan, over low heat, melt cream cheese, butter, Cheddar cheese and dry mustard. Remove from heat; cool slightly. Gently fold in egg whites. Using a fork, dip cubes into cheese mixture, coating evenly on all sides but one. Arrange on wax paper-lined trays. Place in freezer until frozen. Place in plastic bags, seal and store in freezer. To serve, preheat oven to 400 degrees. Place puffs, uncoated side down, on lightly greased cookie sheet while still frozen. Bake 10 to 12 minutes, or until piping hot and golden brown. Serve at once.

Mrs. Adolph Pifko

CHEESE RIBBONS

Makes 240 straws

Delicious with cocktails or tea...

1-1/2 cups margarine
20 oz. sharp or extra
sharp cheese, finely
grated
4 cups sifted flour
1 tsp. salt
3/4 tsp. Tabasco

Preheat oven to 350 degrees. Cream margarine. Add finely grated cheese and cream by hand about 10 minutes or 3 minutes in food processor. Add flour and seasonings and mix well. Using a cookie press with star pattern, pipe 12-inch lengths of dough onto cookie sheets. Bake 10 to 15 minutes. Cut into 3-inch straws (or desired length) and cool slightly on sheet. Cool on brown paper and store in tins.

NOTE: Straws may be frozen.

Mrs. John W. Brice, Jr.

SWISS CHEESE TOASTS

Makes 24

Melt in your mouth...

3/4 lb. Gruyère cheese,
shredded
2 eggs, beaten
1/2 cup dry white wine
2 T. butter, softened
seasoning salt to taste
24 small squares toasted
bread, toasted melba
rounds or Triscuit
crackers

Preheat oven to 425 degrees. In blender or food processor, mix cheese with eggs, wine, butter and seasoning salt if desired. Spread on toast or crackers and place on cookie sheet. Bake for 15 minutes or until cheese melts and puffs. Serve hot.

NOTE: Cheese mixture will keep in the refrigerator for 7 to 10 days. For variety, a layer of flaked crab can be placed on toast before topping with cheese.

Mrs. Edwin B. Bosler

CHEESE COOKIES

Makes 60 cookies

Golden goodness!

1/2 lb. sharp cheese,
  grated
1/2 cup butter
1 cup flour, sifted
1 tsp. salt
1/2 tsp. cayenne pepper

Preheat oven to 350 degrees. Let cheese and butter soften, then mix all ingredients together. *Don't omit cayenne*—it's the most important ingredient. Roll out very thin and cut into desired shapes. Extra flour may be needed to flour board. Bake 10 minutes or until golden and firm. Good sprinkled with nuts or sugar before baking.

Mrs. Philip A. VanVlack III

CARRE AU FROMAGE

Serves 8

Cumin adds real zest to this cheese.

1 7-oz. pkg. French
  double cream cheese
8 oz. shredded French
  Port Salut, St. Paulin
  or Bonbel cheese
1 cup Biscotte crumbs
  (Melba toast)
2 tsp. cumin seeds

Warm cheeses to room temperature, and blend. Shape into a square block about 1-1/2-inches thick. Roll the block in the bread crumbs. Sprinkle with the cumin seeds, and garnish. Serve with Melba toast, fresh French bread or unsalted biscuits.

Mrs. R. Scott Stratton

GARNISH
radish roses and
** fresh chives**

RED CAVIAR AND
CREAM CHEESE SPREAD

Makes 1 cup

Elegant and easy appetizer...

1 8-oz. pkg.
  cream cheese
1/3 cup finely chopped
  onion
1 T. Worcestershire
  sauce
1 T. lemon juice
sour cream to blend
2 oz. red caviar
orange wedges
thin lemon slices
thin lime slices
parsley sprigs
assorted crackers

Blend cream cheese, onion, Worcestershire sauce and lemon juice with enough sour cream to bind. Form into a large ball. Place on hors d'oeuvre plate. Make a depression in the top of the ball and fill with red caviar. Garnish plate with parsley and fruit slices. Surround with assorted crackers.

Mrs. Carroll G. Wells

CHEESE MOUSSE

Makes one 3-cup mold

Different and delicious.

1 4-oz. pkg. Camembert
  cheese (domestic) at
  room temperature
1 4-oz. pkg. crumbled
  blue cheese
1 egg, separated
1 tsp. (or more)
  Worcestershire sauce
1 envelope unflavored
  gelatin
1/4 cup cold water
1/2 cup whipping cream,
  slightly whipped
chopped nuts and
  parsley

Cut Camembert, including rind, into small pieces. Combine with blue cheese, egg yolk and Worcestershire. Cream until well blended. Soften gelatin in water and dissolve over low heat. Beat into cheese mixture. Fold in stiffly beaten egg white and whipped cream. Pour into lightly oiled 3-cup mold and chill until firm. Unmold and garnish with nuts and parsley. Serve as an appetizer with crackers and celery sticks or apple and pear slices.

Mrs. Donald J. Ross

APRICOT CHEESE LOG

Serves 12

Sophisticated blend of flavors.

1 8-oz. pkg. cream
   cheese, softened
1/4 cup white wine
1/4 tsp. salt
1/2 cup finely chopped
   dried apricots
1 lb. sharp cheese,
   grated
1 T. caraway seeds

Beat cream cheese until soft; mix in wine and salt. Blend in apricots, cheese and caraway seeds. Put on aluminum foil and shape into roll. Chill. Serve with party rye or crackers.

Mrs. Lyman Missimer

BLUE CHEESE DIP

Makes 2-1/2 cups

Marvelous with raw vegetables!

1 cup Hellmann's
   mayonnaise
1 cup sour cream
4 oz. blue cheese
1 tsp. garlic salt
1 cup small curd
   cottage cheese

Blend first 4 ingredients. May be done a few days ahead. *Just before serving,* add cottage cheese.

Mrs. Geoffrey C. Murphy

CHUTNEY-CHEESE SPREAD

Serves 12

An Indian spread to relish...

2 8-oz. pkgs. cream
   cheese, softened
1/2 to 3/4 cup chopped
   chutney
1/2 cup toasted chopped
   almonds
2 tsp. curry powder
1/2 tsp. dry mustard

Mix all ingredients until creamy; refrigerate for several hours to blend flavors. Serve with whole wheat crackers.

Mrs. Julien H. Collins, Jr.

PINEAPPLE CHEESE BALL

Serves 16

Appetizer with a light, delicate flavor.

2 8-oz. pkgs. cream
  cheese, softened
1 8-1/4-oz. can crushed
  pineapple, drained
1/4 cup finely chopped
  green pepper
1 T. finely chopped onion
1 T. seasoned salt
2 cups chopped pecans

In a medium sized bowl, beat cream cheese with a fork until smooth. Gradually stir in crushed pineapple, green pepper, onion, salt and 1 cup nuts. Shape into a ball; roll in remaining nuts. Wrap in plastic wrap or foil. Refrigerate until well chilled or overnight. Serve with crackers.

Mrs. James R. McClamroch

DILL IN THE RYE

Makes 1-3/4 cups

Easy and tasty dip!

1 8-oz. carton sour cream
2/3 cup mayonnaise
1 T. green onion flakes
2 tsp. dill weed
1 tsp. Beau Monde
  seasoning
1 T. parsley flakes
2 round loaves dark
  seedless rye bread

Combine sour cream, mayonnaise and seasonings and blend until smooth. Refrigerate 2 hours before serving. To serve, cut top from one rye loaf and hollow out. Save top and soft center. Put dip in hollowed out loaf. Cut second loaf of bread plus remainder saved from first loaf into bite-size cubes. Serve bread cubes with dip. Leftover dip can be refrigerated about 2 weeks.

Julie Thompson

HOT CHEESE DIP

Serves 12 to 16

A very nice spicy dip.

**1 lb. Velveeta cheese,
cubed
1 lb. very sharp cheese,
grated
1 16-oz. can tomatoes,
undrained
4 strips bacon
1 small onion,
finely chopped
1 4-oz. can Mexican
green chili peppers,
chopped**

Melt cheeses with tomatoes in a large saucepan. In another pan, fry bacon crisp. Remove bacon and sauté onion in bacon drippings. To melted cheese mixture, add crumbled bacon and onion. Add peppers to taste as they are *very* hot! Stir well and simmer on *very low* heat for several hours. Serve in chafing dish with corn chips.

Mrs. Lyman Missimer

MOCK BOURSIN

Serves 8

A fine addition to your cheese board!

**1 8-oz. pkg. cream
cheese
1 large clove garlic,
crushed
1 tsp. basil
1 tsp. chives
1 tsp. caraway seed
1 tsp. dill**

Soften cream cheese. Mash and blend remaining ingredients. Mix cream cheese with the seasonings. Shape into a ball. Refrigerate for 24 hours before using. Serve at room temperature.

NOTE: Can be thinned by mixing in sour cream or yogurt if a dip consistency is desired.

Mrs. Wilfred H. Heitmann

SHRIMP ASPIC

Makes 2-2/3 cups

A spicy cold hors d'oeuvre!

1 3-oz. pkg. lemon jello
1 cup boiling water
1 6-oz. bag frozen small
  precooked shrimp,
  thawed
1 8-oz. bottle seafood
  sauce
1 T. horseradish or
  to taste

Dissolve jello in water. Add shrimp, sauce and horseradish and mix well. Put in a small mold and refrigerate. Serve with crackers.

NOTE: May also be served as a salad.

Mrs. Lyman Missimer

CREAMED SHRIMP AND ARTICHOKES

Serves 20 to 30

An elegant chafing dish appetizer on toast rounds.

4-1/2 T. butter
4-1/2 T. flour
1/2 cup milk
3/4 cup whipping cream
salt and freshly ground
  pepper to taste
1/8 tsp. nutmeg
  (optional)
1/4 cup dry vermouth
2 T. Worcestershire
  sauce
1-1/2 lbs. shrimp,
  cooked and deveined
5 cups artichoke
  bottoms, drained and
  quartered or 5 cups
  artichoke hearts (not
  marinated), drained
  and halved
1/4 cup freshly grated
  Parmesan cheese

Melt butter and stir in flour; cook 2 minutes. Gradually add milk and whipping cream, stirring constantly with a whisk. When mixture is thickened and smooth, season with salt, pepper and nutmeg, if desired. Add vermouth and Worcestershire sauce to the cream mixture. Combine with shrimp and artichokes. Heat through. Pour into chafing dish. Sprinkle Parmesan cheese on top. Serve with buttered toast rounds.

NOTE: 1/2 cup grated Gruyère cheese may be added to the cream sauce to make it similar to a Mornay sauce.

Mrs. James R. McClamroch

DILLED CRAB DIP

Makes 2-1/2 cups

A nice change...a great partner with fresh vegetables or English biscuits.

1 8-oz. pkg. cream
  cheese, softened
1 cup mayonnaise
1/4 cup sour cream
1/2 cup fresh dill
1 .13-oz. packet
  brown bouillon powder
  or 1 beef bouillon cube,
  crushed
1 tsp. red pepper sauce
1 6-1/2-oz. can
  crabmeat, drained,
  or more if desired

Whip cream cheese until light. Beat in the mayonnaise and sour cream. Stir in the remaining ingredients. Cover and refrigerate for at least 8 hours.

Mrs. Robert J. Cunningham

CREAMY CRABMEAT DIP

Serves 24

My secret recipe...

24 slices thin-sliced
  white bread
3 8-oz. pkgs. cream
  cheese, cut into cubes
1/2 cup mayonnaise
2 tsp. prepared mustard
dash garlic salt
2 tsp. confectioners
  sugar
1 tsp. grated onion
several dashes Lawry's
  seasoned salt
6 T. good quality
  Sauterne wine
1 lb. crabmeat, flaked

Preheat oven to 300 degrees. Remove crusts from bread slices; cut into triangles. Bake for 15 minutes or until lightly browned. Melt cream cheese in top of double boiler until it can be stirred; add mayonnaise and seasonings. Mix well. When hot, add wine and crabmeat. If dip is too thick, add a bit more wine. Pour into chafing dish and serve with toast triangles.

Mrs. Adolph Pifko

HOT CHEESE'N CRAB DIP

Makes 3 cups

Makes an excellent fondue, too.

1 6-1/2-oz. or 7-1/2-oz. can crabmeat, drained
10 oz. sharp Cheddar cheese, grated
1 8-oz. pkg. sliced sharp process American cheese, cubed
1/4 cup butter or margarine
1/2 cup Sauterne

Reserving a few pieces for garnish, shred crabmeat. Combine cheeses in saucepan with the butter and Sauterne. Stir over low heat until cheeses melt. Stir in shredded crabmeat and continue cooking to heat through. Pour into chafing dish; garnish with reserved crabmeat. Serve with Triscuits or chunks of crusty bread and fondue forks.

Mrs. Philip A. VanVlack III

CRABMEAT MOLD APPETIZER

Serves 24

Delicious hors d'oeuvre for a special cocktail party.

3 7-1/2-oz. cans crabmeat
3 8-oz. pkgs. cream cheese
6 T. mayonnaise
1/4 tsp. salt
1/4 tsp. curry powder
2 tsp. grated onion
1 T. fresh lemon juice
1 tsp. Worcestershire sauce

Flake crabmeat and mix with remaining ingredients. Press into a greased 1-1/2-quart mold. Chill. Unmold, garnishing with paprika if desired. Serve with Bremner wafers.

Mrs. Julien H. Collins, Jr.

HOT CRABMEAT

Makes 2 cups

Elegant hors d'oeuvre.

1/2 lb. fresh crabmeat
1 8-oz. pkg. cream
  cheese
1 tsp. chopped onion
1 tsp. horseradish
salt and pepper
1/3 cup slivered almonds
1 T. butter

Preheat oven to 375 degrees. Mix crabmeat, cheese, onion, horseradish, salt and pepper together. Brown almonds in butter; sprinkle over crabmeat mixture. Bake 15 minutes. Serve with chippers or bland crackers. Great in a chafing dish.

Mrs. John S. Stiles

SHRIMP AND MUSHROOM APPETIZER

Makes 24 to 30

Perfect for your next cocktail party or as the first course of a special dinner.

1/3 cup butter
1/3 cup dry vermouth
3 cloves garlic,
  finely chopped
1 T. chopped fresh
  parsley
1 tsp. salt
1/2 tsp. pepper
1/4 cup lemon juice
2 cups small whole
  fresh mushrooms
1 lb. raw medium
  shrimp, peeled,
  deveined

Melt butter over medium heat; stir in vermouth, garlic, parsley, salt, pepper, lemon juice and mushrooms. Cook 5 to 8 minutes. Add shrimp. Cook until tender, about 3 minutes. Serve hot with toothpicks.

Mrs. David H. Robertson

THE BELL INN SMOKIES

Serves 4

Exquisite!

**1/2 lb. smoked haddock
  (finnan haddie)
2 fresh tomatoes, peeled,
  seeded and minced
6 T. whipping cream
salt and pepper to taste**

Preheat oven to 400 degrees. Flake haddock and divide among four 1/2-cup ramekins. Arrange tomatoes on top of fish. Pour 1-1/2 T. cream into each dish or enough to barely cover the fish. Sprinkle with salt and pepper. Bake for 10 minutes or until mixture is bubbly and fish is opaque.

Mrs. Donald J. Ross

DAIQUIRI PUNCH

Serves 12

Potent enough to please your best beau, too...

**1 16-oz. bottle
daiquiri mix
6 T. superfine sugar
2-1/2 cups light rum
1/2 cup Curaçao or
Cointreau
24 ice cubes
1 12-oz. bottle club soda**

Thoroughly mix daiquiri mix, sugar, rum and Curaçao together. Pour over ice cubes in punch bowl. Add club soda.

NOTE: Easily doubled. Additional club soda may be added to taste to dilute mixture. Especially attractive when served with a strawberry ice ring instead of ice cubes. Arrange strawberries in the bottom of a 6-cup ring mold. Fill with water. Freeze overnight.

Mrs. Arthur W. Bergman, Jr.

FRESH FRUIT DAIQUIRIS

Serves 6

Pick your flavor— peach, strawberry or banana

**3/4 to 1 cup fresh fruit
purée, peach,
strawberry or banana
1 6-oz. can frozen
limeade
6-oz. rum (more
if desired)
3 oz. ginger ale
4 to 6 ice cubes**

Prepare purée. For peach: peel, pit and slice 2 peaches. For strawberry: core and slice 1/2 pt. of strawberries. For banana: peel and slice one large banana. Place *one* of the fruits in the blender with limeade, rum, ginger ale and ice cubes. Blend until frothy and thick. Serve immediately or can be made a couple of days ahead and frozen. Defrost about one half hour before serving.

Mrs. Robert J. Cunningham

SNOWMAN PUNCH

Serves 20

Great for holiday time...

1/4 cup granulated sugar
12 whole cloves
2 cinnamon sticks
4 qts. cranberry
  juice cocktail
1 12-oz. can frozen
  lemonade
1 12-oz. can frozen
  orange juice
bourbon (optional)

Place sugar, cloves, cinnamon sticks and 1 to 2 cups cranberry juice in a saucepan. Simmer 5 to 10 minutes; strain out spices. Pour spiced juice into remaining cranberry juice mixed with lemonade and orange juice. Stir. *Chill* well. Serve with pitcher of bourbon on the side.

Mrs. William P. Stewart

PIQUANT PUNCH

Makes 5 quarts

A delightful surprise!

1 cup granulated sugar
2 cups water
1 2-inch cinnamon stick
5 whole cloves
5 whole allspice
1 12-oz. can frozen
  limeade
1 12-oz. can frozen
  lemonade
frozen lemonade ring
  mold
2 28-oz. bottles tonic
  water
2 28-oz. bottles soda
  water
gin or vodka (optional)
1 lime, thinly sliced
strawberries, thinly
  sliced

Prepare syrup from the first five ingredients. Bring to a boil and let simmer 5 minutes. Remove from stove and strain. This can be made ahead and refrigerated. Mix limeade and lemonade into syrup. Just before serving, pour over ring mold or ice cubes. Pour in tonic water, soda water and gin or vodka to taste if desired. Garnish with lime and strawberry slices.

Mrs. Alvin B. Nordhem

CHAMPAGNE PUNCH

Serves 15 to 20

A refreshing, light punch— perfect for any occasion!

4 6-oz. cans frozen
   lemonade
2 qts. soda water,
   chilled
2 bottles dry champagne
1 qt. fresh strawberries
1 bottle dry white wine,
   chilled

Mix together in a punch bowl, and add an ice mold to keep the mixture well chilled.

Mrs. Robert J. Cunningham

RED CHAMPAGNE PUNCH

Serves 24

A sparkler!

1 block ice or ice ring
1 bottle Sauterne
1 bottle dry champagne
1 bottle sparkling
   burgundy
2 T. grated lime rind
juice of 1 lime
1 lime, sliced
1 12-oz. pkg. frozen
   strawberries

Place ice in the bottom of a punch bowl. Pour in liquids. Mix in remaining ingredients gently. Serve immediately.

Mrs. Lee E. Osborne

BLOODY MARY MIX

Makes 2 quarts

Deliciously tangy and less spicy than the usual. Terrific for brunches!

2 to 3 tsp. Worcestershire
   sauce
1 small onion, peeled
   and minced
1 green pepper, seeded
   and finely chopped
juice of one orange
juice of two lemons
1 8-oz. can tomato sauce
1 tsp. salt
1/4 tsp. freshly ground
   pepper
1 46-oz. can V-8 juice

Place all ingredients except V-8 juice in blender and blend until smooth. Pour into pitcher and chill. To serve, stir in V-8 juice.

NOTE: For a hot and spicy version add jalapeño pepper and more salt and pepper.

Mrs. Arthur W. Bergman, Jr.

GENE'S RUM PUNCH

Serves 8 to 10

Refreshing, colorful summer drink...

2 cups pineapple juice
2 cups lime juice, made
   from reconstituted
   frozen concentrate
4 cups orange juice
1/4 cup Curaçao
light rum to taste

Whirl fruit juices and Curaçao in blender until foamy. Add rum, if desired. Serve ice cold in punch bowl or tall glasses, garnished with orange slices and maraschino cherries.

NOTE: Pineapple-grapefruit juice may be substituted for pineapple juice.

Mrs. Julien H. Collins, Jr.

SPICED TEA

Makes 7-1/2 cups

Good for caroling parties...

2-1/2 cups boiling water
2 T. tea or 2 tea bags
1-1/2 cups water
1/2 cup orange juice
1/3 cup lemon juice
2 cups cranberry juice
3/4 cup granulated sugar
1/4 tsp. nutmeg
1/4 tsp. allspice
1/4 tsp. cinnamon

Pour boiling water over tea. Let stand 5 minutes. Remove tea. Cook remaining ingredients together until sugar is dissolved. Combine 2 liquids. Serve hot.

Mrs. Arthur W. Bergman, Jr.

MULLED CITRUS TEA

Makes 10 cups

Great on a cold, snowy day by a warm fire!

1 cup granulated sugar
1 T. whole cloves
2 cinnamon sticks
4 cups water
4 cups boiling water
2-1/2 tsp. tea leaves
juice of 4 oranges
juice of 1 lemon

Put first four ingredients in pan and bring to boiling. Soak tea leaves in another pan of boiling water for 10 minutes. Strain cloves and cinnamon from first mixture and tea leaves from second mixture. Combine strained liquids with fresh citrus juices. Serve hot. Will store in refrigerator.

Mrs. Edward Ruegg

SUMMER COOLER

Serves 12

Refreshing punch for the younger set...

1 6-oz. can frozen
  limeade
1 6-oz. can frozen
  lemonade
1 6-oz. can frozen
  orange juice
1 28-oz. bottle 7-Up

Reconstitute juices according to directions; mix together. Pour over ice in a large punch bowl; add 7-Up. If desired, garnish with strawberries.

Mrs. Alvin B. Nordhem

KOOL SHERBET

Serves 8

Great for children's parties!

1 .23-oz. pkg. lime
  Kool-Aid
2 cups pineapple juice
8 scoops lime sherbet

Mix Kool-Aid as directed. Add pineapple juice and chill. Place sherbet in glasses; fill with juice.

NOTE: Other flavors may be substituted.

Mrs. Robert P. Keith

CRANBERRY COOLER

Makes 3 quarts

A refreshing, colorful punch to serve on Christmas or Valentine's Day.

1 qt. cranberry juice
  cocktail
2 6-oz. cans frozen
  lemonade concentrate
4 cups water
1 qt. lemon/lime
  carbonated beverage
lemon slices

Mix first 3 ingredients. Chill. Just before serving, add ice cubes and lemon/lime beverage. Garnish with lemon slices. When making large quantities, make an ice ring from the first 3 ingredients so punch doesn't become diluted.

Mrs. Arthur W. Bergman, Jr.

CRIMSON-APPLE GLOGG

Makes 3 quarts

A long-time favorite at Kenilworth Union, our own Holly Room punch!

2 qts. apple juice
1 qt. cranberry juice
   cocktail
2 cinnamon sticks
4 whole cloves
1/4 tsp. allspice
2 T. lemon juice
thin slices of orange
   and lemon
red food coloring
   (optional)

Heat juices and spices; add lemon juice when mixture is heated through. Float slices of orange and lemon on top before serving. Add red food coloring for brightness and festive look.

Mrs. Donald W. Patterson

THE DICKENS WASSAIL

Serves 20

Delicious beverage to serve at a tea or open house.

6 oranges
6 lemons
2 cinnamon sticks
1 T. ginger, chopped fine
1 T. allspice
1 T. whole cloves
1 T. nutmeg
1 qt. water
1 lb. granulated sugar
1 cup pineapple juice
1 gallon cider
1 qt. dry sherry
cored apples

Squeeze oranges and lemons and set juices aside. Add the outer peel of oranges and lemons to spices in a quart of water. Brew for one hour but do not boil. These steps can be done the day before the party. Combine sugar, the juice of the oranges and lemons, pineapple juice and cider. Add brewed spices and heat again. Strain, add sherry and serve hot. Float cored apples in punch bowl. If desired, stud apples with additional cloves.

Mrs. Philip A. VanVlack III

EGG NOG

Fluffy and beautiful!

1 dozen eggs
1-1/4 cups granulated
　sugar
1-1/2 tsp. vanilla
2 qts. milk
24 oz. bourbon
8 oz. Jamaica rum
nutmeg

Separate eggs. Beat yolks well, then mix with sugar. Add milk and mix well. Slowly pour liquor in, stirring constantly. Beat egg whites until stiff and fold into milk mixture. Serve with nutmeg.

Mrs. David M. Stone

MEXICAN CHOCOLATE

Serves 4

Nice after paddle tennis or cross country skiing...

1 qt. milk
1/4 cup unsweetened
　cocoa
1/4 cup confectioners
　sugar
1 cup coffee liqueur
whipped cream
4 cinnamon sticks

In a medium saucepan, heat milk to simmer. Stir in cocoa and sugar; cook and stir until sugar dissolves. Stir in coffee liqueur; taste and adjust sweetness. Pour into warmed mugs; garnish with whipped cream and cinnamon sticks.

Mrs. James R. McClamroch

DUTCH TREAT

Serves 1

A hint of mint makes this special...

1/2 cup plus 2 T.
　hot coffee
1 tsp. granulated sugar
2 T. brandy
2 T. chocolate mint
　liqueur
1 strip lemon zest

Preheat 8-ounce mug; pour in coffee. Stir in sugar. Add brandy and liqueur, stir again. Twist lemon zest over top before adding to coffee.

Mrs. Franklin A. Urbahns

CAFE A LA RUSSE

Serves 4

Perfect for a snowy evening...

3/4 cup boiling water
1 oz. semi-sweet
  chocolate
1-1/2 T. granulated
  sugar
1/2 cup whipping cream
1/2 cup milk
1-3/4 cups hot coffee
1/4 cup cognac
1/4 cup Crème de Cacao
4 cinnamon sticks
nutmeg

Combine water, chocolate and sugar in top of double boiler. Place over hot but not boiling water. Stir for 2 to 3 minutes, until chocolate is melted and sugar is dissolved. Scald cream and milk. Add coffee, cream, milk, cognac and Crème de Cacao to chocolate mixture, stirring. Pour into four preheated mugs; add cinnamon sticks and sprinkle with nutmeg to taste.

Mrs. Franklin A. Urbahns

COFFEE DIABLO

Serves 8 to 10

Lovely way to top off a special dinner!

1 orange peel
1 cinnamon stick
1 tsp. whole cloves
1/3 cup orange liqueur
2/3 cup brandy
1/3 cup granulated sugar
4 cups strong coffee

Cut peel off orange in a continuous strip and place in a 2-cup jar. Add cinnamon stick, cloves, liqueur, brandy and sugar. Close tightly and refrigerate overnight. When ready to serve, combine liqueur mixture with hot coffee and heat. Strain out solids and serve hot in demitasse cups.

Mrs. A. W. Phelps

Soups, Sauces and Condiments

GAZPACHO

Attractive, spicy summer soup...

4 T. fresh lemon juice
1 46-oz. can V-8 juice
2 T. instant bouillon
    granules dissolved in
    2 cups water
3/4 cup minced
    green onions
2 large fresh tomatoes,
    peeled and diced
2 cups minced celery
2 green peppers,
    finely chopped
2 cucumbers, peeled,
    seeded and finely
    chopped
1/4 tsp. Tabasco
    (or more to taste)
Worcestershire sauce
    to taste
pepper and salt
    to taste
1 4-oz. can ripe olives,
    drained and chopped

Mix all ingredients together and chill to blend flavors, preferably a day ahead.

Mrs. Roger W. Tinney

SOUP AVGOLEMONO

Serves 6 to 8

Enjoy this cold, light, lemony soup...:

6 cups good chicken
    stock
1/4 cup uncooked rice
1 tsp. salt
3 eggs
1/4 cup fresh lemon
    juice
lemon slices
fresh parsley

Pour stock into a saucepan. Add rice and salt. Simmer for 15 to 20 minutes, or until rice is tender. Cool slightly. Beat eggs well and add lemon juice. Slowly beat broth into egg and lemon mixture, mixing slowly and well. Soup will thicken as it cools. Decorate with lemon slice and parsley.

Mrs. David M. Stone

SENGALESE SOUP

Serves 6

Sends sweltering summer days scurrying.

2 T. minced onion
2 T. butter
2 tsp. madras curry
  powder
1 T. flour
3-1/2 cups chicken stock
4 egg yolks
1/4 cup finely diced
  cooked chicken, beef
  or shrimp
2 cups cold whipping
  cream

Sauté onion in butter until soft. Add curry and cook 1 minute. Stir in flour; cook 2 minutes. Stir in stock and bring to boil. Stir some of the hot sauce into the egg yolks, then whisk the egg yolk mixture into the sauce and cook 1 minute. Put through sieve and chill. May be frozen at this point or add the chicken and cream to the chilled mixture and serve cold.

Casey Bohnstedt

BULGARIAN CUCUMBER SOUP

Serves 4 to 5

Great texture and taste!

1-1/2 cups peeled, diced
  cucumbers
1 tsp. salt
1/4 tsp. pepper
1/3 cup chopped
  walnuts
2 T. olive oil
2 T. chopped fresh dill or
  1 T. dried dill
1 small clove garlic,
  minced
1 cup yogurt or
  sour cream
2 cups cold
  chicken stock

Combine cucumbers, salt, pepper, walnuts, oil, dill and garlic. Chill for 4 to 6 hours. Add yogurt or sour cream and cold chicken stock. Serve immediately. If weather is especially warm, serve with an ice cube in the bowl. Recipe is easily doubled.

Paula Nordhem

GAZPACHO STYLE CUCUMBER SOUP

Serves 8 to 10

Prepare this soup the day before serving.

4 cups chicken broth
6 medium cucumbers,
  peeled and chopped
1 medium yellow onion,
  peeled and chopped
3 cups sour cream
4 T. white vinegar
2 cloves garlic,
  peeled and chopped
salt to taste
3/4 tsp. white pepper

Combine chicken broth, cucumbers, onion, sour cream, vinegar, garlic, salt and pepper. Whirl in blender in small batches. Refrigerate in a glass or enamel container. Serve with bowls of almonds, parsley or chives, green onions and tomatoes so guests can garnish their soup gazpacho style. Serve very cold!

Mrs. Robert J. Cunningham

GARNISHES
chopped almonds
chopped parsley or
  chives
chopped green onions
chopped tomatoes

SERENDIPITY SUMMER SOUP

Serves 6

A winner!

1 10-oz. pkg. frozen peas
1 medium onion, thinly
  sliced
1 cup water
1 T. minced *fresh* mint
3 cups chicken stock
2 T. flour
1/2 cup whipping cream
salt and pepper to taste
sour cream
mint sprigs

Cook peas and onions in water until soft. Purée in blender with mint. In saucepan, blend flour and 1/2 cup stock until smooth. Add rest of stock and cook until thickened. Add pea mixture and bring to a boil. Cool. Stir in cream, salt and pepper and chill. Serve with dollop of sour cream and sprig of mint.

Mrs. Peter T. Haverkampf

ARCTIC ASPARAGUS SOUP

Serves 8

Refreshing chilled summer soup.

2 large leeks, chopped
1/4 cup butter
3 cubes chicken bouillon
   or 1 T. instant
   chicken broth
3 cups water
2 10-oz. boxes frozen
   asparagus
1/4 cup flour
1 tsp. salt
1/8 tsp. pepper
2 cups half and half
1 cup whipping cream
salt to taste
parsley

Sauté leeks in butter until soft. Heat chicken bouillon and water in sauce pan until cubes are dissolved. Add asparagus and cook 5 minutes. Remove asparagus and add asparagus to leeks. Stir flour into leek mixture, until absorbed. Add chicken broth, salt and pepper. Simmer 3 minutes. Pour small batches of soup into blender and blend until smooth. Pour into large bowl and stir in half and half. Chill 4 hours. Whip cream; add salt to taste. Serve soup with dollop of cream and sprinkle chopped parsley on top.

Mrs. Thomas M. Ritchie, Jr.

CREAMY AVOCADO SOUP

Serves 4 to 6

Interesting flavor...very pleasant!

1 large ripe avocado,
   peeled and pitted
1 cup chicken stock
1/2 cup dry white wine
   or white rum
1 cup whipping cream
2 tsp. lemon juice
1 tsp. dried dill or 2 tsp.
   fresh dill
dash Tabasco
salt and pepper to taste

Cut avocado into 1-inch cubes; put cubes into blender or food processor and purée. Heat stock to boiling; slowly blend stock into avocado. Mix in wine and cream. Pour avocado mixture into a container and stir in lemon juice, dill and Tabasco. Season to taste. Chill thoroughly before serving.

Casey Bohnstedt

CHILLED SALMON BISQUE

Serves 4 to 6

Delicious first course for a summer luncheon...

1/2 cup chopped green
   pepper
1/2 cup grated carrot
1/2 cup chopped onion
1-1/2 T. butter
1 tsp. curry powder
1 cucumber, peeled and
   chopped
1 7-3/4-oz. can salmon,
   undrained
1-1/2 cups chicken broth
1 T. lemon juice
1/2 tsp. salt
1/8 tsp. pepper
2 cups buttermilk
snipped chives

Sauté green pepper, carrot and onion in butter. Add curry powder and cucumber. Cook one minute. Place salmon, vegetables, broth, lemon juice, salt and pepper in blender or food processor. Blend until smooth. Add buttermilk and chill at least 8 hours. Garnish with snipped chives.

Mrs. Robert J. Cunningham

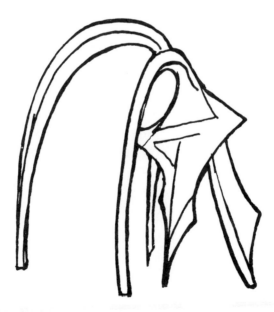

CREAM OF BROCCOLI SOUP

Serves 4 to 6

Reminiscent of a French or Swiss peasant soup.

3 T. butter
1/2 cup white wine
1/3 cup finely chopped leek
1/3 cup finely chopped onion
1/3 cup finely chopped celery
1 cup chopped broccoli, fresh or frozen
3 T. flour
3 cups chicken broth
salt and pepper to taste
1/4 tsp. thyme
1/2 cup half and half
1/2 cup whipping cream

Melt butter. Add wine. Cook vegetables 5 minutes over low heat. Blend in flour, and then chicken broth. Let boil 1 minute. Season and simmer for 20 to 30 minutes or until vegetables are tender. Add half and half and cream and serve.

Kenilworth Union Church

MICROWAVE BROCCOLI SOUP

Serves 6

Speedy and good...

1-1/2 lbs. fresh broccoli, cut in 1/4-inch pieces
1 cup chicken broth
1/2 cup chopped onion
2 T. butter
2 T. flour
1/2 tsp. dry mustard
1/4 tsp. salt
1/4 tsp. thyme
1/8 tsp. white pepper
1/8 tsp. cayenne
2 cups half and half

Combine broccoli, chicken broth, onion and butter in 3-qt. casserole. Cover and microwave on high 10 to 20 minutes or until broccoli is tender. Sprinkle flour over broccoli; stir until blended. Stir in seasonings. Blend in half and half. Cover and microwave on high until simmering and slightly thickened, about 8 to 10 minutes. Stir several times.

Mrs. Donald J. Ross

POTAGE CREOLE

Serves 4

A hot and spicy tomato soup.

2 T. finely chopped onion
1 T. butter
2-4 T. chopped pimiento
1-1/2 T. flour
2 cups canned tomatoes
   (28-oz. can tomatoes,
   drained)
1-1/2 to 2 pts. chicken
   stock
salt and pepper to taste
dash cayenne
1 T. grated horseradish
1/2 tsp. sugar
2 T. cream or sour
   cream per serving

Soften onion in butter. Add pimiento and after a few minutes, the flour. Add tomatoes and stock; bring to a boil, season and simmer 20 to 25 minutes. Put in blender. Stir cream or sour cream into hot soup.

Mrs. Alfred F. Buckman

VERMONT CHEDDAR CHEESE SOUP

Serves 6 to 8

A hearty wintertime soup.

3 T. butter
3 scallions, finely
   chopped
1 small onion, finely
   chopped
1 rib celery, finely
   chopped
3 T. flour
2 cups chicken broth
1 qt. milk, at room
   temperature
2 cups grated Cheddar
   cheese
dash nutmeg, white
   pepper and salt
shake of Worcestershire

In large pot, melt butter; sauté vegetables until soft. Sift in flour; cook 2 to 3 minutes, stirring. Whisk in broth, bring to boil, reduce heat and simmer. Add milk, bring just to boil, reduce heat and add cheese *slowly*, stirring until melted. Return to boil, stirring often. Remove from heat. Adjust seasonings. Serve with croutons.

Casey Bohnstedt

CREAM OF FRESH ASPARAGUS SOUP

Serves 4 to 6

So much better than canned and so easy!

**1-1/2 lbs. fresh
    asparagus**
1/2 cup water
2 T. chopped onion
1-1/2 tsp. salt
1/4 cup butter
1/4 cup flour
2 tsp. chicken stock base
1/4 tsp. pepper
3-1/2 cups milk, scalded
sour cream

Wash asparagus well, trim off bases. Cut off tender tips and set aside. Cut remaining stalks into 1/2-inch pieces. Put in saucepan with water, onion and salt. Heat to boiling. Reduce heat and simmer, covered, 10 minutes or until tender. Do not drain. Purée in blender or food processor. Simmer tips in small amount of salted water until just tender. Drain, saving liquid to thin soup if desired, and set aside. Melt butter in heavy saucepan. Blend in flour, stock base and pepper. Gradually add scalded milk and cook, stirring until thickened and smooth. Stir in puréed asparagus. Heat thoroughly. Serve with asparagus tips (and sour cream dollop if desired) on top.

Mrs. Edwin B. Bosler

CREAM OF MUSHROOM SOUP

Serves 4 to 6

Delicious herb flavor...

1/2 cup chopped green
  onions
1/2 lb. sliced fresh
  mushrooms
1/2 cup butter
1/3 cup white or whole
  wheat *pastry* flour
1 T. chopped rosemary
  or to taste
1 T. chopped parsley
5 beef bouillon cubes
  dissolved in 2 cups
  water (or tamari sauce
  or soy sauce to taste in
  2 cups water)
2 cups milk
1/2 cup whipping cream
nutmeg and pepper to
  taste
sherry to taste (optional)

Sauté onions and mushrooms in butter. Slowly add flour, rosemary, parsley and bouillon water. Reduce heat to low and add the milk. When soup thickens, add cream. Turn heat off and flavor with nutmeg, pepper and sherry if desired. Soup may be frozen before milk and cream are added.

Lisa Lillard-Caldwell

HAMBURGER SOUP

Serves 8

Vary the flavor of this delicious soup with seasonings of your choice!

1-1/2 lbs. ground chuck
  in 3-4 large pieces
4 beef bouillon cubes
1 cup chopped celery
1 cup chopped onion
1/4 cup chopped green
  pepper
1 tsp. salt
2 tsp. oregano
1 bay leaf
1 46-oz. can V-8 or
  tomato juice
1 20-oz. pkg. frozen
  mixed vegetables
2 cups cooked macaroni,
  noodles or rice

Combine all ingredients except pasta and simmer for one hour. Break up pieces of meat and add cooked noodles or rice before serving.

NOTE: This is a great way to clean out the refrigerator—anything you have can go into this soup. It freezes well.

Mrs. Charles R. Bylsma

WILLY'S CHILI

Serves 12 to 14

Probably the best chili you'll ever introduce to your taste buds.

5 lbs. chopped meat—
  2-1/2 beef, 2-1/2 pork
1/4 cup olive oil
3 medium onions,
  chopped
2 medium green peppers,
  seeded and chopped
2 large celery stalks,
  diced
1 T. Jalapeño peppers,
  seeded and chopped
2 14-1/2 oz. cans stewed
  tomatoes with liquid
  (chopped)
1 16-oz. can tomato
  sauce with mushrooms
1 6-oz. can tomato paste
1 tsp. chili powder or
  to taste
1/2 cup water
1/2 cup beer
3 crushed bay leaves
1 tsp. to 1 T. Tabasco
  sauce
2 tsp. ground cumin
salt, pepper to taste
2 tsp. coriander

Brown meat in 2 tablespoons olive oil. Drain excess fat. Sauté onions, green peppers and celery in remaining oil. Combine all ingredients in large pot. Simmer for 3 hours. Add water if needed.

William Skinner

58

SPAGHETTI CHILI

Serves 8

After paddle tennis or cross country skiing—wonderful!

6 T. butter or margarine
1 lb. mushrooms, sliced
1 cup chopped onion
1 clove garlic, crushed
2 lbs. ground beef
1 28-oz. can tomatoes
1 20-oz. can red kidney
  beans
1 T. chili powder
2 tsp. salt
1 tsp. cumin
2 cups cooked spaghetti,
  cut up
shredded sharp cheese

Melt 3 T. butter and add mushrooms. Sauté 5 minutes. Melt remaining butter, add onion and garlic. Sauté 3 minutes. Add beef 1/3 at a time. Cook and stir until brown. Drain off excess fat. Add tomatoes, beans, chili powder, salt and cumin. Stir well and bring to boil. Cover and simmer 20 minutes. Add mushrooms and spaghetti and simmer 2 minutes longer. Serve with shredded cheese.

Mrs. Steven E. Lindblad

MRS. MURPHY'S CHOWDER

Serves 6

No overalls here...just wonderful flavor!

1 qt. water
1 tsp. salt
1/4 tsp. pepper
1 bay leaf
8 whole cloves
1 lb. frozen haddock or
  cod filets
1 lb. bacon, diced
2 medium onions,
  chopped
3 cups diced potatoes
4 saltines
2 cups milk
1 cup whipping cream
chopped parsley

Bring water to a boil with spices. Add fish and simmer 15 minutes or until tender. Drain, reserving liquid. Separate fish into large pieces. Cook bacon until crisp and set aside. Reserve 1 T. bacon fat. Sauté onions in fat until golden. Combine onions, strained fish liquid and potatoes. Bring to a boil; cover and simmer 15 minutes. Add fish, crumbled saltines, milk and cream. Heat thoroughly, but do not boil. Season to taste with salt and pepper. Garnish with bacon and parsley.

Mrs. Geoffrey C. Murphy

CASTELLVI'S SOUP

Serves 8

A wonderful, authentic Cuban black bean soup.

1 lb. black beans
10 cups water
1 green pepper
1 large onion, chopped
4 cloves garlic, mashed
1 green pepper, chopped
2/3 cup olive oil
4 tsp. salt
1/2 tsp. pepper
1/4 tsp. oregano
1 bay leaf
2 T. sugar
2 T. vinegar
2 T. sherry
2 T. olive oil
1 medium onion,
   finely diced

Wash, rinse and drain beans. Place in large pot, cover with water, add green pepper and soak overnight. Cook 45 minutes or until soft. Discard green pepper. Sauté onions, garlic and chopped green pepper in oil 5 minutes. Mash 1 cup of beans in skillet with onion/oil mixture then transfer onion/bean mixture to bean pot. Add spices and sugar. Cover and bring to boil. Lower heat and simmer slowly 1 hour. Add vinegar and sherry and simmer for another hour. If beans look too watery, cook beans uncovered for a few minutes during the last hour. Just before serving add the 2 T. olive oil. Garnish with minced onion. Make at least a day before serving.

VARIATION: As a vegetable side dish, serve over rice.

Mrs. Frank Castellvi

DEEP SOUTH BRUNSWICK STEW

Serves 10

It's a zinger!

1 4-lb. stewing chicken
2 lbs. pork shoulder,
  cubed
2 lbs. stewing beef
3-1/2 quarts cold water
1 16-oz. can tomatoes
10 oz. drained canned
  corn or frozen corn
10 oz. drained canned
  okra or frozen okra
1/4 cup catsup
1 T. Worcestershire sauce
2 tsp. Tabasco sauce
3 T. parsley flakes
3 T. celery seed
1 tsp. chili powder
1 tsp. mustard seed
1 tsp. curry powder
1 tsp. thyme
2 bay leaves
1/4 tsp. cayenne pepper
1 15-1/2-oz. can butter
  beans

Place meats in an 8-quart stockpot and cover with water. Bring to a boil over medium heat. Reduce heat to simmer and cook meats until chicken and pork are tender, about 1-3/4 hours. Remove scum as it rises to the top of the pot during first hour of simmering. Shred meat by hand, removing as much fat and gristle as possible; place in large bowl. Strain stock through cheesecloth and pour over meats. Cool, cover and refrigerate overnight. Place meats and stock in stockpot, removing fat if desired. Add remaining ingredients, except butter beans. Simmer, partially covered, for 6 to 8 hours. Add butter beans during last hour of cooking time. Stir soup frequently. Remove bay leaves before serving.

Mrs. Geoffrey C. Murphy

BEEF AND SAUERKRAUT SOUP

Serves 6 to 8

Creative conventional or crockpot cookery...

4 beef shanks (2-1/2 to 3
  lbs.) or 2 lbs. lean
  stew meat
1 T. butter
1 T. vegetable oil
1 large onion, finely
  chopped
1 1-lb. can sauerkraut,
  undrained
4 cups water
1 lb. solid pack tomatoes,
  undrained
10 whole black peppers
1 bay leaf
1 tsp. salt
sour cream

Brown beef in butter and oil in large soup pot. Reduce heat, add onion, and cook until limp. Add sauerkraut, water and tomatoes. Tie peppers and bay leaf in cheese cloth; add to pot. Bring to a boil; reduce heat, cover and simmer about 2-1/2 hours or until meat is very tender. If beef shanks are used, after cooking remove meat from bones and return to soup. Discard seasonings. Add salt. Serve with sour cream.

NOTE: To use crockpot, put beef/sauerkraut mixture, using *only 2 cups of water,* into 2-1/2-qt. crockpot and set at low for 8 to 10 hours.

Mrs. Paul S. Wise

SHRIMP LA MAIZE SAUCE

Makes 3 cups

A sweet remoulade...

1 pt. salad dressing
  or mayonnaise
4 rounded T. chili sauce
4 rounded T. prepared
  mustard (Gulden's)
1 T. Worcestershire
  sauce
1 tsp. vinegar
1 medium onion, grated
1 T. India relish
2 T. granulated sugar
salt and pepper to taste
2 diced hard boiled eggs
  (optional)

Mix all ingredients. Sauce will keep for one month in refrigerator. Serve with shrimp or lobster. Garnish with eggs if desired.

Mrs. Adolph Pifko

CHAMPAGNE MUSTARD

Makes 2 cups

Delicious with ham or vegetables.

**2/3 cup white
  champagne vinegar
2/3 cup dry mustard
  (Colman's)
3 eggs
3/4 cup granulated sugar**

Mix together vinegar and mustard. Beat eggs, add sugar and add to mustard mixture. Put in top of double boiler over boiling water and stir until thickened. Refrigerate in covered jar.

NOTE: Mix with sour cream to taste for broccoli, asparagus, etc.

Mrs. Carl Fowler

PARMESAN SAUCE

Makes 1 cup

Versatility plus!

**1/4 cup Parmesan
  cheese
1/4 cup sour cream
1/4 cup mayonnaise
1/4 to 1/2 tsp. salt
3 scallions, sliced
1 T. red wine vinegar
3 drops Tabasco**

Mix all the ingredients together. Spoon over 2 pounds fish filets. Bake in a preheated 350-degree oven 25 to 30 minutes. This sauce is wonderful with chicken, too.

Mrs. Carroll G. Wells

SWEET AND SOUR SAUCE

Makes 2 cups

A good addition to Oriental recipe files...

1/4 cup brown sugar
2 T. cornstarch
1 tsp. salt
3/4 cup water
1 cup pineapple juice
1/3 cup vinegar
1 T. soy sauce

Mix sugar, cornstarch and salt; add water gradually while stirring. Stir in juice, vinegar and soy sauce. Cook mixture over medium heat until thickened, stirring constantly.

Mrs. Fred L. Stone

GREAT BAR-B-Q SAUCE

Makes 2 cups

Great with ribs or chicken.

2 T. butter
1/4 cup chopped onion
2 T. dark brown sugar
1 tsp. salt
1/2 tsp. dry mustard
3/4 cup catsup
1/2 cup pineapple juice
1/4 cup fresh lime juice
1-1/2 tsp. soy sauce

In a small pan, melt butter. Add onion and cook until tender, but not brown. Blend in brown sugar, salt and mustard. Stir in catsup, pineapple juice, lime juice and soy sauce. Heat to boiling.

NOTE: Do not substitute lemon juice for lime juice.

Mrs. Edwin B. Bosler

CHICKEN BARBEQUE SAUCE

Makes 1-1/3 cups

Can be doubled or tripled and made ahead of time.

1/2 cup chopped onion
1/2 cup catsup
1/2 cup cold water
1 T. Worcestershire sauce
1 T. vinegar
1 tsp. salt
1/2 tsp. chili powder
1/4 tsp. black pepper

Combine all ingredients in a saucepan and simmer for about 15 minutes. Store in refrigerator.

Mrs. A. E. Attebery

CREAM CHEESE SPAGHETTI SAUCE

Makes 2 cups

Can't stop eating it!

2 T. basil
2 T. parsley flakes
1/4 cup butter, softened
1 8-oz. pkg. cream
　cheese, softened
1/3 cup freshly grated
　Parmesan cheese
1/4 cup olive oil
1 clove garlic, minced
1/2 tsp. pepper
1-1/3 cups boiling water

Add basil and parsley to butter. Blend in cream cheese, Parmesan, olive oil, garlic and pepper. Stir in water. Let flavors blend 1/2 hour, then reheat gently. Enough sauce for one lb. cooked, drained spaghetti.

Mrs. Geoffrey C. Murphy

SPAGHETTI SAUCE

Makes 2 quarts

Easy to make. Freezes well.

1 lb. ground round
1/2 lb. hot sausage
1 medium green pepper,
　chopped
1 medium onion,
　chopped
1 6-oz. can tomato paste
1 6-oz. can sliced
　mushrooms
2 15-oz. cans tomato
　sauce
1 10-oz. can whole
　tomatoes
oregano, garlic, Italian
　seasoning, to taste
1/2 cup water

Brown beef and sausage; drain. Combine all ingredients in large pot. Add spices to taste. Add water. Bring to boil; then turn to low heat and cook covered for 4 to 5 hours. Stir occasionally. Additional water may be needed during cooking.

Mrs. Barnard A. Savage, Jr.

MUSHROOM WINE SAUCE

Makes 2 cups

Serve this tarragon flavored sauce with chicken or veal.

**1/4 lb. fresh mushrooms,
  sliced
3 T. butter
2 T. flour
1 cup rich chicken stock
1/2 cup dry white wine
1/2 tsp. tarragon
salt and white pepper
  to taste
1/2 cup half and half
1 egg yolk**

Sauté mushrooms in 1 T. butter and set aside. Melt 2 T. butter; add flour. Cook, stirring constantly, for one minute. Slowly add stock, wine and spices. Simmer several minutes. Add mushrooms and simmer 5 minutes; remove from heat. Mix cream and egg yolk; stir into mushroom mixture. Cook, stirring constantly, until mixture is heated through, but do not boil. Sauce may be made a day ahead and reheated.

Mrs. Lyman Missimer

CUCUMBER SAUCE

Makes 2-1/2 cups

Serve warm over boiled or baked chicken breasts...

**1/2 T. finely chopped
  onion, or more to taste
1 large cucumber, peeled,
  seeded and chopped
1 T. butter
2 cups sour cream at
  room temperature, or
  Crème Fraiche
salt and pepper to taste
1-1/2 T. fresh lemon juice
dill weed to taste**

Sauté onions and cucumber in butter until soft. Mix other ingredients and add to onions. Warm over low heat but do not boil.

Mrs. H. H. Hanlon

BEURRE BLANC

Makes 1-1/2 cups

Savory sauce for broiled fish or steamed vegetables...

4 shallots, finely chopped
1/3 cup white wine
1 T. fresh lemon juice
**1-1/2 cups unsalted
  butter**
1/2 tsp. salt
1/8 tsp. white pepper

Combine shallots, wine and lemon juice in heavy 2-quart saucepan. Simmer over high heat until only 2 tablespoons of liquid remain. Strain out shallots; return liquid to pan. Continue simmering until only one teaspoon liquid remains. Cut butter into tablespoon-size pieces. Remove saucepan from stove and reduce heat to low. Rapidly whisk one tablespoon butter into liquid; swirl in another 2 or 3 tablespoons butter. Return pan to low heat. Continue to add butter, 3 tablespoons at a time, until all butter is used and a light sauce is formed. Remove from heat; continue stirring until sauce is smooth. Add salt and pepper and serve immediately.

NOTE: Sauce may be held for a few minutes by placing over a bowl of slightly warm water. It will separate if kept on stove. Extra sauce may be refrigerated. Remove desired amount from refrigerator about one half hour before serving to soften.

Mrs. Donald J. Ross

BUTTERSCOTCH SAUCE

Makes 1 pint

Versatile...

1-1/4 cups brown sugar
2/3 cup white corn syrup
4 T. butter
1/2 cup half and half

Combine sugar, syrup and butter. Cook to soft ball stage. Remove from heat and cool. Stir in cream. Serve warm. Keeps well in refrigerator. Reheat when serving.

Mrs. Fred L. Stone

GRAND MARNIER SAUCE

Makes 5 cups

Delicious over fresh fruit...

8 egg yolks
1 cup granulated sugar
1/2 cup Grand Marnier
2 cups whipping cream

Whip egg yolks until very thick and lemon colored. Gradually add sugar and beat well. Add Grand Marnier, beat again and set aside. Whip cream until thick. Fold into egg mixture until blended. Best when served the day it's made. Keep refrigerated.

Mrs. Gerald C. North

BLENDER FUDGE SAUCE

Makes 1-3/4 cups

This bittersweet sauce keeps well in the refrigerator.

4 1-oz. squares
   unsweetened chocolate,
   quartered
2/3 cup hot milk
1 cup granulated sugar
dash salt
1 tsp. vanilla
2 T. soft butter

Place all ingredients in blender and mix until smooth. Store in refrigerator and reheat in the top of double boiler. Delicious on top of ice cream or cream puffs.

NOTE: Semisweet chocolate may be substituted for unsweetened chocolate.

Mrs. Arthur W. Bergman, Jr.

APRICOT BUTTER

Delicate and delicious.

**3 11-oz. pkgs. dried
  apricots
6 cups granulated sugar
2 cups orange juice
2 T. allspice**

Check apricots, one at a time, removing black specks. Wash thoroughly in a colander with spray of cold water. Place in a 3 or 4-quart heavy-bottomed sauce-pan and fill with cold water to cover. Let soak, covered, at least 3 hours or over-night. Bring mixture to a simmer. Continue to simmer, uncovered, stirring frequently with a long-handled wooden spoon until apricots are soft and mushy. Turn off heat. Mash with potato masher. While still warm, sieve through a food mill, a cup at a time, scraping the residue from outside of sieve. Discard pith and use only the purée, put-ting it into another 3 or 4-quart heavy-bottomed saucepan. Add sugar to purée, plus a little of the orange juice. Return saucepan to heat and bring to a simmer. Stir constantly, scraping bottom of pan frequently, and gradually add more orange juice until the desired consistency is ob-tained. Remember, the jam will thicken on cooling. Add the allspice and stir until well mixed. Remove from heat. Spoon at once into hot sterilized jars and seal.

NOTE: Recipe may be halved or doubled. Delicious as a spread, this purée also may be used in dessert recipes, mixed with whipped cream or in a meringue.

Mrs. Curtis D. Buford

RHUBARB PRESERVES

Makes 3 pints

A different, tangy jam.

1 20-oz. bag frozen
  rhubarb
3 cups granulated sugar
1 3-oz. pkg. strawberry
  jello
1 tsp. lemon juice
  (optional)

Put rhubarb in a large bowl. Add sugar and mix. Cover bowl and put in refrigerator. Let stand overnight. Transfer rhubarb and sugar to a kettle and cook until rhubarb is tender (about 10 minutes simmering time). Remove from heat and add jello. Stir until jello is dissolved. Pour into clean jelly glasses and seal.

Mrs. Charles W. Sherman

VIVIAN'S SPICED RHUBARB

Makes 4 cups

Sophisticated sweet-sour taste...

5 cups fresh or frozen
  rhubarb
1 cup vinegar
4 cups granulated sugar
1 tsp. cinnamon
2 scant tsp. cloves

Wash rhubarb and cut in cubes without peeling. Place in large saucepan and add vinegar. Cook very slowly until rhubarb is soft but unbroken. Add sugar and spices. Cook, uncovered, very slowly until the consistency of marmalade.

NOTE: Lasts indefinitely in the refrigerator. Delicious on toasted English muffins or as an accompaniment to chicken or pork.

Joan V. Groves

JALAPENO PEPPER JELLY

Makes 6 6-oz. jars

Colorful Christmas classic...

1 6-oz. can jalapeño peppers, hot or mild, drained, rinsed and seeded
1 lb. fresh green peppers, seeded
1-1/2 cups white vinegar
6-1/2 cups granulated sugar
4 or 5 drops green food coloring
1 6-oz. bottle Certo

Using either blender or food processor, purée all peppers. Place in a large kettle with vinegar and sugar. Bring to a hard boil for 6 minutes, stirring constantly. Add food coloring and Certo and blend thoroughly. Pour into sterilized jars and seal. Serve with cream cheese and crackers as an hors d'oeuvre or as a meat condiment. Small old-fashioned glasses make nice gift containers.

Mrs. Edwin B. Bosler

SPICED PLUMS

Makes 4 pints

A nice hostess gift...

5 lbs. purple plums
3 lbs. granulated sugar
1/2 pint vinegar
1 T. allspice
1 T. cloves
1 T. cinnamon

Combine ingredients and cook uncovered until thick, about 30 to 45 minutes. Put into jelly jars and seal.

NOTE: Wash plums but do not pit. The pits fall out as the plums cook.

Mrs. Dane F. Hahn

GREEN TOMATO MINCEMEAT

Makes 4 pints

A super condiment which also makes a super pie!

4 lbs. finely chopped
   green tomatoes (skins
   on)
2 lbs. brown sugar
1 cup water
1 quart boiled cider
1 lb. kidney suet, finely
   chopped
1 cup hot water
6 lbs. peeled apples,
   finely chopped
2 lbs. seeded raisins
1/2 lb. dried currants
1 lb. citron
finely chopped rind of
   one orange
finely chopped rind of
   one lemon
1/2 tsp. cinnamon
1/2 tsp. nutmeg
1/2 tsp. cloves
1/2 tsp. salt

Drain tomatoes overnight in a muslin bag. Next day, in a large pot, cook tomato juice, brown sugar and water for one hour. Add the boiled cider, suet and hot water and boil for 1/2 hour. Add tomatoes and remaining ingredients and boil for 15 minutes more. Place in sterilized jars and seal.

Mrs. Dane F. Hahn

CORN RELISH

Makes 2 cups

A streamlined version of a classic...

1/4 to 1/3 cup granulated
   sugar
1 T. cornstarch
2 T. finely chopped onion
1 tsp. ground turmeric
1/2 tsp. celery seed
1/4 cup vinegar
1/4 cup water
1 12-oz. can whole kernel
   corn, drained
2 T. finely chopped green
   pepper
1 T. chopped pimiento

In saucepan, combine sugar, cornstarch, onion, turmeric, celery seed, vinegar, water and corn. Cook and stir until the mixture thickens and bubbles. Stir in green pepper and pimiento. Chill. Keeps several weeks in refrigerator.

Mrs. Bruce J. Gooden

SAUERKRAUT RELISH

Makes 3-1/2 cups

Makes a good winter salad, too.

1 1-lb. can sauerkraut, drained
1/2 cup granulated sugar
1/2 cup chopped celery
1/2 cup chopped green pepper
1/2 cup chopped carrots

Chop sauerkraut coarsely. Mix in sugar and let stand 1/2 hour. Add celery, green pepper, and carrots; mix. Cover and chill for at least 12 hours.

Mrs. Preston J. McNurlen

SEASONED SALT

Makes 3/4 cup

Nice to sprinkle on meats before broiling or roasting. Makes a good salad dressing with vinegar and oil.

6 T. salt
2-1/2 tsp. paprika
1 tsp. dry mustard
1/2 tsp. thyme
1/2 tsp. majoram
1/2 tsp. garlic salt
1/2 tsp. curry powder
1/2 tsp. celery salt
1/4 tsp. onion salt
1/8 tsp. dill seed

In a small bowl, mix together. Store in covered jar. Let set several days before using. Equally good without curry powder and/or garlic salt depending on personal taste. Makes a nice Christmas gift in a pretty shaker or jar.

Mrs. Edwin B. Bosler

SWEET PICKLES

Makes 1 gallon

Easy and fun to have on hand...

1 gallon sliced cucumbers
2 large sliced onions
3 cups granulated sugar
1/3 cup salt (not iodized)
1 tsp. turmeric
1 tsp. celery seed
1 tsp. mustard seed
3 cups vinegar

Put all ingredients in large gallon jar and shake. Keep in refrigerator. Ready to eat in 3 days. Will keep refrigerated indefinitely.

Mrs. Fred L. Stone

MARY'S MARINATED CUCUMBER SLICES

Makes one quart

Keep for several weeks in the refrigerator...

1-1/2 cups water
1-1/2 cups cider or white
  vinegar
1-1/2 cups granulated
  sugar
3/4 tsp. salt
3/4 tsp. celery seeds
1/2 tsp. onion salt
1/2 tsp. celery salt
4 medium unwaxed
  cucumbers, washed,
  thinly sliced
2 medium onions, thinly
  sliced

Shake all marinade ingredients in a one-quart jar until sugar dissolves. Add thinly sliced cucumbers and onions in alternating layers. Refrigerate.

NOTE: The slices can be served many ways: as a "pickle" garnish with a sandwich, "as is" in a big bowl as a salad or mixed with sour cream. The marinade also may be mixed with oil as a salad dressing, using the cucumber slices as part of a tossed vegetable salad.

Mrs. Julien H. Collins, Jr.

HOHEISEL SWEET PICKLES

Makes 2 pints

Can't stop eating them!

1 1-quart jar small
  Kosher dills
2 cups granulated sugar
1/4 cup vinegar
1 heaping tsp. celery seed
1 heaping tsp. mustard
  seed

Drain and thinly slice pickles, reserving liquid. Mix with rest of ingredients. Let stand overnight at room temperature. Stir and place in jars. Seal.

Mrs. Moritz Finger

Breads

WALNUT CRUNCH CAKE

Serves 10 to 12

Morning coffee treat...

CAKE
1 cup butter
1 cup granulated sugar
1 tsp. vanilla
2 eggs
2 cups sifted flour
1 tsp. baking powder
1 tsp. baking soda
1/2 tsp. salt
1 cup sour cream

Preheat oven to 350 degrees. Beat butter, sugar and vanilla until light and fluffy. Add eggs one at a time, beating after each. Sift dry ingredients together and add in thirds alternately with sour cream, beating well after each addition.

FILLING
1/3 cup firmly packed
  brown sugar
1/2 cup granulated sugar
1 tsp. cinnamon
1 cup chopped walnuts

Mix sugars, cinnamon and nuts. Grease and flour a 9-inch tube pan. Sprinkle layer of filling in pan. Spread layer of batter on top. Repeat, totaling 3 layers. Bake one hour. Cool 15 to 30 minutes and then carefully invert pan.

Mrs. Steven E. Lindblad

BREAKFAST BREAD

Makes 1 loaf

A fantastic quick bread with a hint of molasses.

2 cups buttermilk
1/2 cup honey
1/4 cup molasses
1 tsp. salt
2 tsp. baking soda
1-1/2 cups whole
  wheat flour
1 cup unbleached
  white flour
1/2 cup wheat germ
1/2 to 3/4 cup raisins
  (optional)

Preheat oven to 400 degrees. Mix buttermilk, honey, molasses, salt and baking soda. Combine flours and wheat germ and add. Stir in raisins, if desired. Pour into greased 9 x 5-inch loaf pan. Reduce oven temperature to 350 degrees. Bake for one hour; turn loaf out onto wire rack and cool. Wait one day before slicing and toasting.

Mrs. Arthur W. Bergman, Jr.

THANKSGIVING COFFEECAKE

Serves 9

Something different for cranberry lovers.

2 cups flour
1 cup granulated sugar
1 T. baking powder
1/2 tsp. salt
2 eggs, beaten
1 cup sour cream
1 tsp. grated orange rind
1 cup cranberry sauce,
   canned or fresh

Preheat oven to 350 degrees. Sift dry ingredients. Blend eggs, sour cream and orange rind. Mixture will be stiff. Add all at once to flour mixture. Mix until smooth. Pour half of the batter into a greased 9-inch square baking pan. Spread cranberry sauce over the batter. Spread remaining batter. Top with streusel topping. Bake for 40 to 45 minutes.

STREUSEL TOPPING
3 T. flour
1/2 cup brown sugar
1 tsp. cinnamon
2 T. softened butter
   or margarine

Mix flour, brown sugar and cinnamon. Cut in butter until mixture resembles coarse crumbs.

Joan V. Groves

LAYERED APPLE CAKE

Serves 12 to 15

A delicious fresh coffee cake.

4 cups apples, pared,
   cored, sliced thin
2 tsp. cinnamon
5 T. granulated sugar
3 cups unsifted flour
3 tsp. baking powder
2-1/2 cups granulated
   sugar
1/2 tsp. salt
4 eggs
1 cup salad oil
2-1/2 tsp. vanilla
1/2 cup orange juice

Preheat oven to 350 degrees. Grease and flour a 9 x 13-inch pan. Mix apples, cinnamon and 5 tablespoons sugar. Set aside. Mix together flour, baking powder, sugar and salt in a large mixing bowl. Add eggs, oil, vanilla and orange juice and mix on medium speed until smooth. Layer as follows: 1/2 of batter, 1/2 of apples, 1/2 batter, top with apples. Bake for 1-1/2 hours.

Kenilworth Union Church

CINNAMON CRISPS

Makes 24

A homemade version of those old bakery favorites, "Elephant Ears."

3-1/2 cups sifted flour
1 pkg. active dry yeast
1-1/4 cups milk
1/4 cup granulated sugar
1/4 cup shortening
1 tsp. salt
1 egg
4 T. butter or margarine, melted
1/2 cup granulated sugar
1/2 cup brown sugar
1/2 tsp. cinnamon
4 T. butter or margarine, melted
1 cup granulated sugar
1/2 cup chopped pecans
1 tsp. cinnamon

In large mixer bowl, combine 2 cups of flour and the yeast. In saucepan, beat together the milk, 1/4 cup granulated sugar, the shortening and salt just until the shortening melts. Add to dry ingredients in mixer bowl; add egg. Beat at low speed for 1/2 minute, scraping sides of bowl constantly. Beat 3 minutes at high speed. By hand, stir in enough of remaining flour to make a moderately soft dough. Place in greased bowl; turn once to grease surface. Cover and let rise until double (1 to 1-1/2 hours). Turn out onto lightly floured surface. Divide dough in half. Roll out each section to a 12-inch square. Combine the first 4 T. butter, granulated sugar, brown sugar and cinnamon. Spread 1/2 of mixture over dough. Roll up jelly-roll fashion, pinch to seal edges. Cut into 12 pieces. Place on greased baking sheets 3 inches apart. Flatten each to 3 inches in diameter. Repeat with remaining dough and sugar mixture. Allow to rise about 30 minutes. Preheat oven to 400 degrees. Cover rolls with waxed paper. Flatten to 1/8-inch thickness with rolling pin or palm of your hand. Remove paper and brush with remaining melted butter. Combine remaining sugar, nuts and cinnamon; sprinkle on rolls. Cover with waxed paper and roll flat again. Bake for 10 to 12 minutes. Remove immediately from baking sheets. Rolls can be frozen.

Mrs. Donald J. Ross

CARAMEL CINNAMON TWISTS

Melt in your mouth...

1 cup butter, melted
1 cup sour cream
1 tsp. salt
1 tsp. vanilla
1 pkg. active dry yeast
2 egg yolks
1 egg
3-1/2 cups flour
1-1/2 cups granulated
  sugar
2 tsp. cinnamon

Blend together hot butter, sour cream, salt and vanilla. The mixture should be luke-warm. Sprinkle in yeast. Beat egg yolks and egg until blended. Stir into yeast mixture. Stir in enough of the flour to make a soft dough. Beat until smooth. It is not necessary to knead this dough. Cover bowl with plastic wrap and chill for at least 2 hours. Mix sugar and cinnamon. Spread half of mixture on a board or counter. Divide dough in half. Roll each piece to a rectangle about 1/4-inch thick. Fold each piece over three times, as you would a letter, coating each side with the sugar mixture. Repeat the rolling and folding process three times for both dough pieces, until sugar mixture is almost used. Roll each piece into a rectangle about 1/4-inch thick. Cut dough into strips 1/2-inch by 4 inches. Twist strips; dip in remaining cinnamon mixture. Place on baking sheet and cover with a towel. Let rise in a warm place until light and fluffy, about 30 minutes. Bake in a preheated 375-degree oven for 15 minutes, or until golden. Great hot or at room temperature.

Mrs. Dennis Gronek

ALMOND COFFEE PUFF

Serves 8 to 16

Rich and absolutely delicious!

CRUST
1 cup sifted flour
1/2 cup butter
1 T. cold water

To prepare crust, mix flour and butter as for pie crust, adding cold water. Form 2 long strips about 3 inches wide and 3 inches apart on a cookie sheet or jelly roll pan. Preheat oven to 350 degrees while preparing filling.

FILLING
1 cup water
1/2 cup butter
1 cup sifted flour
salt, if desired
3 eggs
1 tsp. almond extract

Heat water and butter to boiling. Toss in flour (and salt if desired). When mixture forms a big ball, remove from heat. Add eggs, one at a time, beating well after each addition. Add almond extract. Spread over crust and bake for 55 to 60 minutes.

FROSTING
1-1/3 cups confectioners
   sugar
1 T. soft butter
1 tsp. almond extract
hot coffee to thin
1/4 cup toasted
   blanched almond slices

Stir butter and sugar together. Add almond extract and thin with coffee to desired consistency. Spread frosting over hot puffs. Decorate with slivered almonds.

NOTE: Puff does not freeze well and should be eaten within a day or two.

Mrs. Alvin B. Nordhem

MINIATURE BLUEBERRY MUFFINS

Makes 24

These yummy muffins can be frozen and reheated.

1 cup granulated sugar
1 T. butter
1/2 cup milk
1 egg
1-1/2 cups flour
2 tsp. baking powder
pinch of salt
1/2 tsp. cinnamon
1/2 tsp. allspice
1 cup blueberries, lightly
   dusted with flour

Preheat oven to 425 degrees. Cream sugar and butter. Add milk and egg. Mix flour, baking powder, salt and spices; add to above mixture. Stir in blueberries. Bake in greased miniature muffin tins for 15 to 20 minutes. Serve hot. To reheat, place in new paper bag, close tightly. Place in oven for 5 minutes.

NOTE: If desired, dip tops of muffins in melted butter, then in mixture of 1/3 cup sugar and 1 tsp. grated orange peel after baking.

Mrs. Stuart S. Ball

NEVER FAIL DROP BISCUITS

Makes 12

Rich and delicious...great for strawberry shortcakes, too!

2 cups self-rising flour
2 T. granulated sugar
1 egg
1/2 cup oil
3/4 cup milk

Preheat oven to 400 degrees. Mix flour and sugar together. Mix egg, oil and milk together. Stir liquids into flour mixture just until mixed. Drop by spoonfuls onto 2 ungreased cookie sheets. Bake 20 minutes.

VARIATION: May substitute 2 cups flour, 1 T. baking powder and 1 tsp. salt for self-rising flour.

Mrs. Harry DuPrey

RHUBARB MUFFINS

Makes 20 to 24

A good way to use extra rhubarb from your garden...

1-1/4 cups brown sugar
1/2 cup oil
1 egg
2 tsp. vanilla
1 cup buttermilk
1-1/2 cups diced raw
rhubarb
1/2 cup chopped walnuts
2-1/2 cups flour
1 tsp. baking soda
1 tsp. baking powder
1/2 tsp. salt

TOPPING
1 T. butter, melted
1/3 cup granulated sugar
1 tsp. cinnamon

Preheat oven to 400 degrees. Combine brown sugar, oil, egg, vanilla and buttermilk in large bowl. Beat well. Stir in rhubarb and walnuts. In separate bowl, combine flour, soda, baking powder and salt. Stir into rhubarb mixture just until blended. Spoon batter into muffin cups, filling 2/3 full. Scatter topping mixture over the muffin cups and press lightly into the batter. Bake for 20 to 25 minutes, until a toothpick comes out clean. Muffins are best when served warm.

NOTE: They freeze well. For variety, the muffins can be topped with a mixture of 1/4 cup granulated sugar and one tsp. cinnamon instead of the streusel topping.

Mrs. L. Steven Minkel

ICEBOX BRAN MUFFINS

Makes 60

Batter may be stored in the refrigerator for six weeks!

2 cups All-Bran cereal
2 cups boiling water
1 heaping cup
   shortening
3 cups granulated sugar
4 eggs, beaten
1 qt. buttermilk
5 cups sifted flour
5 tsp. baking soda
1 tsp. salt
5 cups All-Bran cereal

Preheat oven to 400 degrees. Soak All-Bran in boiling water; set aside. Cream shortening and sugar; add eggs, buttermilk and soaked bran. Sift together flour, baking soda and salt. Add all at once with bran, folding until ingredients are moistened. Spoon into greased muffin tins and bake for 20 to 25 minutes. Batter recipe may be cut in half.

NOTE: Variations are endless: add blueberries, dates, currants, raisins, nuts, orange marmalade, etc. to batter.

Mrs. Lawrence Lawson

FIBER RICH FRUIT BREAD

Makes 2 loaves

Moist and crunchy...

2 cups boiling water
1-1/2 cups chopped
   prunes
1/2 cup chopped raisins
3 eggs
3/4 cup brown sugar
2 cups whole wheat flour
2 tsp. baking powder
1 tsp. baking soda
1 tsp. cinnamon
1/2 tsp. cloves or nutmeg
2 cups bran
1 cup chopped nuts

Preheat oven to 350 degrees. Pour boiling water over prunes and raisins. Set aside. Beat eggs until light. Continue beating while adding brown sugar. When light and creamy, add 1 cup whole wheat flour sifted with baking powder, soda, cinnamon and cloves. Stir in half the prune/raisin mixture and then the rest of the whole wheat flour and bran. Stir in remaining prune/raisin mixture and nuts. Pour into 2 well greased and floured 9 x 5-inch loaf pans. Bake for 45 minutes.

Mrs. Robert B. Young

BRAN BREAD

Naturally delicious...

2 cups bran
2/3 cup granulated sugar
1 cup flour
1 tsp. soda
1-1/2 cups buttermilk
1/2 cup raisins

Preheat oven to 350 degrees. Mix bran, sugar, flour and soda together. Stir in buttermilk and raisins just until mixed. Put in greased 9 x 5-inch loaf pan. Bake for 35 to 40 minutes or until done.

Mrs. Fred L. Stone

BANANA PECAN BREAD

Makes 1 loaf

Spread with whipped cream cheese for elegant tea sandwiches.

1/2 cup butter
  or margarine
3/4 cup granulated sugar
2 eggs
2 cups flour
1 tsp. baking soda
1/2 tsp. salt
2 very ripe bananas,
  mashed
1 tsp. vanilla
1 cup chopped pecans

Preheat oven to 350 degrees. Cream butter and sugar well. Add eggs one at a time, beating well. Mix flour, baking soda and salt. To butter-sugar mixture, add flour and mashed bananas alternately. Start and end with flour and stir after each addition. Add vanilla and pecans. Bake in greased 9 x 5-inch pan for 30 minutes; then reduce heat to 325 degrees and bake 20 to 30 minutes more. Cool completely before slicing.

Mrs. Paul S. Wise

PLUM-NUT BREAD

Makes 2 loaves

Cake-like texture, delicate flavor...

1 cup butter
2 cups granulated sugar
1 tsp. vanilla
4 eggs
3 cups flour
1 tsp. salt
1 tsp. cream of tartar
1/2 tsp. baking soda
3/4 cup plain yogurt
1 tsp. grated lemon rind
2 cups purple prune
   plums, cut into
   1/2-inch pieces
1 cup chopped nuts

Preheat oven to 350 degrees. Cream butter with sugar and vanilla until fluffy. Add eggs, one at a time, beating well after each addition. Sift flour, salt, cream of tartar and baking soda. Blend yogurt and lemon rind; add to creamed mixture alternately with dry ingredients. Stir until well blended. Add chopped plums and nuts; mix well. Divide batter between 2 greased and floured 9 x 5-inch loaf pans. Bake for 50 to 55 minutes or until bread tests done. Freezes beautifully.

Mrs. Timothy Tilton

PENNSYLVANIA APPLESAUCE BREAD

Makes 1 loaf

Can be made at a moment's notice from ingredients in the cupboard.

2 cups sifted flour
1 tsp. baking powder
1 tsp. salt
1 tsp. cinnamon
1 tsp. baking soda
1/2 tsp. nutmeg
1/2 cup butter
3/4 cup granulated sugar
1/2 tsp. vanilla
2 eggs
1-1/4 cups applesauce
1/2 cup chopped walnuts

Preheat oven to 350 degrees. Sift dry ingredients together. Cream butter and sugar. Add vanilla and eggs. Beat well. Blend in the dry ingredients. Mix well. Add applesauce and chopped walnuts. Pour into a well-greased 9 x 5-inch loaf pan. Push the batter up into the corners leaving the center hollowed. For a well-rounded loaf, allow it to stand 20 minutes before baking. Bake 45 to 55 minutes. Cool before slicing.

Mrs. Robert B. Young

LEMON NUT BREAD

Makes 1 loaf

Tangy lemon glaze makes this tea bread extra special.

1 cup granulated sugar
6 T. butter
1 tsp. salt
grated rind of 1 lemon
2 eggs
1 tsp. baking powder
1-1/2 cups flour
1/2 cup milk
1/2 cup finely chopped
   pecans

Preheat oven to 325 degrees. Cream sugar and butter in electric mixer. Add salt, lemon rind and eggs one at a time, beating well after each addition. Sift baking powder and flour. Sprinkle a little flour over nuts. Alternately add flour and milk to butter mixture, one third at a time. Add floured nuts. Bake in a well-greased 9 x 5-inch loaf pan for one hour. Keep in pan until cool.

GLAZE
1/3 cup granulated sugar
juice of 1 lemon

Dissolve sugar in lemon juice and spoon over the loaf while piping hot. Be sure the sugar is dissolved!

Lee Horton

CARROT TEA CAKE

Serves 12 to 18

This spicy treat freezes well.

3/4 cup plus 2 T. corn oil
2 cups granulated sugar
4 eggs, beaten
2 cups finely grated
   raw carrots
2 cups flour
1 tsp. salt
2 tsp. baking soda
3 tsp. cinnamon
1 tsp. nutmeg
confectioners sugar

Preheat oven to 350 degrees. In a large bowl mix oil, sugar, eggs and carrots together. Add flour, salt, baking soda, cinnamon and nutmeg; mix well. Bake in a greased Bundt pan or spring form pan for one hour. Cool for 25 minutes and remove from pan. Dust with confectioners sugar and slice very thin.

Mrs. Donald J. Ross

DATE BREAD

Makes one loaf

Tea time treat.

1 cup chopped dates
1 tsp. baking soda
1 cup boiling water
1 T. butter
1 cup granulated sugar
1 egg
1/2 tsp. salt
2 scant cups flour
1/2 cup chopped walnuts

Preheat oven to 300 degrees. Mix dates, baking soda and boiling water. Let stand until cool. Mix butter, sugar and egg. Add flour and salt; stir to mix. Stir in walnuts. Add date mixture; blend together. Pour into a greased and floured 9 x 5-inch pan. Bake one to 1-1/2 hours.

NOTE: Makes good cream cheese sandwiches.

Mrs. Fred L. Stone

MOTHER'S DATE NUT BREAD

Makes 2 loaves

Revives childhood reveries...

1 cup chopped dates
1-1/2 cups boiling water
3 T. butter, softened
3 cups sifted flour
2-1/2 tsp. baking powder
1 tsp. baking soda
2 eggs
2/3 cup granulated sugar
2 tsp. vanilla
2/3 cup chopped nuts

Preheat oven to 325 degrees. Chop dates, add boiling water and butter; allow mixture to cool. Sift flour, baking powder and baking soda together. Beat eggs slightly and add sugar. Add flour mixture to egg mixture and stir well. Add vanilla, nut meats and date/butter mixture and mix thoroughly. Place in 2 greased and floured 8 x 4-inch loaf pans. Bake for 40 minutes or until done.

Mrs. Adolph Pifko

BEER BREAD

Makes 1 loaf

A crusty, coarse loaf— perfect for casual entertaining.

3 cups self-rising flour
3 T. granulated sugar
1 12-oz. can beer

Preheat oven to 350 degrees. Mix ingredients together and place in greased 9 x 5-inch loaf pan. Bake for one hour. Don't peek!

NOTE: If desired, drizzle 2 T. melted butter over batter before baking.

Mrs. Donald J. Ross

FRENCH BREAD

Makes 4 loaves

Flavor's built right in!

1 T. granulated sugar
2/3 cup warm water
2 pkgs. active dry yeast
2 cups warm water
1/2 tsp. instant
   minced garlic
2 tsp. dill seed
1 T. salt
6 to 7 cups sifted
   unbleached flour

Add sugar to 2/3 cup warm water and sprinkle in yeast. Set aside for 5 minutes. Pour 2 cups warm water into large mixing bowl; add garlic, dill seed and salt. Beat 2 mixtures together. Sift in 2 cups flour and beat with electric mixer. Stir in another 2 cups sifted flour. Continue to add 1 cup of flour at a time until there is enough to make a sticky dough. Knead dough on well-floured pastry cloth. Keep kneading at least 10 minutes, adding flour to the dough and your hands as needed until the dough becomes smooth and elastic. Drop dough into a floured bowl and cover with Saran Wrap. Let rise until double, 1-1/2 to 2 hours. Punch down and place on a floured pastry cloth, knead several times and place back in clean floured, covered bowl. Let rise again about 1-1/2 hours. Punch down and place on a floured pastry cloth. Divide into 4 equal parts. Roll one part into a 6 to 8-inch oval. Fold the oval over itself into thirds. Roll it back into an oval. Do this twice more to get out bubbles. Roll dough up tightly and shape into a 14-inch roll that fits into half of a 15-inch French bread mold. Repeat with 3 other parts of dough. Let rise until double, about 1 hour. Preheat oven to 500 degrees. Fill a spray bottle with cold water. Place loaves in oven and spray every 2 minutes for 20 minutes. Remove from pans and bake another 3 minutes for crusty loaves. Cool completely and freeze if you are not going to use within 3 hours.

Mrs. Arthur W. Bergman, Jr.

POPPY SEED BREAD

Makes 2 loaves

A sweet bread perfect for morning coffee or brunch.

1/4 cup poppy seeds
1 cup buttermilk
1 cup butter
1-3/4 cups granulated
  sugar
4 eggs, separated
1/2 tsp. almond extract
1 tsp. vanilla extract
2-1/2 cups plus 2 T. flour
1 tsp. baking powder
1/2 tsp. baking soda
1/4 tsp. salt
1/4 cup granulated sugar
2 tsp. cinnamon

Preheat oven to 350 degrees. Put poppy seeds in buttermilk and let them soak. Cream butter and 1-3/4 cups sugar. Add egg yolks and almond and vanilla. Beat well. Sift flour, baking powder, soda and salt together. Add dry ingredients alternately with buttermilk mixture. Beat egg whites until stiff peaks form. Fold beaten egg whites into batter. Grease two 9 x 5-inch pans. Mix 1/4 cup sugar and cinnamon. Pour small amount of batter into pans and sprinkle half the cinnamon sugar over it. Add remaining batter and then remainder of cinnamon sugar. Bake for 45 minutes.

Mrs. Milton M. Wood

LAMPKIN BREAD

Makes 2 loaves

An easy yeast bread that only rises once—in the pans.

2 pkgs. active dry yeast
1/2 cup warm water
1 egg
1/3 cup oil
2 cups milk
7 cups flour
1/2 cup granulated sugar
2-1/2 tsp. salt

Dissolve yeast in warm water. Combine with egg, oil and milk. Sift in flour, sugar and salt and stir until mixed. Turn onto floured board; knead for 10 minutes. Put into 2 greased 9 x 5-inch loaf pans. Let rise 1-1/2 hours. Preheat oven to 350 degrees. Bake 35 to 45 minutes or until golden brown.

Mrs. Phillip A. VanVlack III

CINNAMON RAISIN BREAD

Makes 3 loaves

Splendid!

1-1/2 cups milk
1/4 cup granulated sugar
1 T. salt
1/4 cup butter
1 tsp. granulated sugar
1/2 cup warm water
2 pkgs. active dry yeast
3 eggs
7-1/4 to 7-1/2 cups flour
2 cups raisins
3 T. butter, softened
2/3 cup granualted sugar
2 T. cinnamon

Heat milk, 1/4 cup sugar, salt and butter until butter melts. Cool to 110 degrees. Mix 1 tsp. sugar in warm water and sprinkle in yeast. Let stand 5 minutes. Pour cooled milk mixture in mixing bowl. Beat in eggs and then yeast mixture. Sift in 3-1/2 cups flour and beat until smooth. Mix in raisins and sift in enough of the remaining flour to make the dough easy to handle. Knead dough on floured pastry cloth until smooth and elastic—about 5 minutes. Place in greased bowl. Turn greased side up. Cover and let rise in warm place until double (2 to 2-1/2 hours). Punch down dough and cut into 3 equal pieces. Cover and let pieces rest 10 minutes. Preheat oven to 375 degrees. Roll each third into a rectangle 18 x 9-inches. Spread a tablespoon of very soft butter on rectangle and sprinkle with 3 heaping tablespoons of sugar/cinnamon mixture. Roll up, beginning at short side. Seal seams and fold ends under. Place seam side down in greased 9 x 5-inch pans. Let rise until double, about 1 hour. Bake 30 to 35 minutes until loaves are golden brown and sound hollow when tapped. Immediately remove from pans and cool. Brush with melted butter if desired.

Mrs. Arthur W. Bergman, Jr.

HONEY BRAN BREAD

Makes 4 small loaves

Delicious and nutritious...

2 cups milk
2 tsp. salt
1/2 cup oil
1/3 cup warm water
**   (110 degrees)**
1 tsp. granulated sugar
2 pkgs. active dry yeast
1/2 cup honey
2 eggs
6 to 7 cups flour, sifted
1-3/4 cups bran

Scald one cup milk, salt and oil. Stir sugar into warm water and sprinkle with yeast; set aside for 5 minutes. Remove scalded milk mixture from heat and stir in honey; pour milk mixture into large mixing bowl and stir in remaining milk. Let cool to 110 degrees, then pour yeast/water into milk. Stir until all yeast is *dissolved* with mixer. Beat in eggs, one at a time. Sift 2 cups flour into liquids and beat one minute. Stir in bran; cover and let it stand for 20 minutes if using bran buds (30 minutes for long bran). Stir in 2 more cups of sifted flour. Stir in enough additional flour to make a moderately stiff dough. Knead on floured surface until smooth (6 to 10 minutes). Shape in ball; place in greased bowl turning once. Cover; let rise until doubled (around 1-1/2 hours). Punch down; cut into 4 equal pieces; cover and let rest for 10 minutes. Place each piece in a greased 7 x 5-inch loaf pan. Push down into pan; pierce every 1/2-inch with a fork. Cover and let rise until rounded —about one hour. Preheat oven to 325 degrees. Bake for 45 minutes. Turn immediately out onto cooling rack.

Mrs. Paul S. Wise

RUSSIAN BLACK BREAD

Makes 2 loaves

A rich, full-bodied, dark bread.

2-1/2 cups water
1/4 cup dark molasses
1/4 cup vinegar
4 T. butter or margarine,
  softened
1 square unsweetened
  chocolate
1 tsp. salt
2 tsp. instant coffee
2 tsp. onion flakes
2 T. caraway seeds,
  crushed
1 tsp. granulated sugar
2 pkgs. active dry yeast
7 cups rye and wheat
  flour (50/50)
2 cups bran flakes
1 egg white,
  slightly beaten

Heat 2 cups water, molasses, vinegar, butter, chocolate, salt, coffee, onion flakes and caraway seeds until warm, stirring constantly until butter and chocolate almost melt. Cool to 110 degrees. Warm 1/2 cup water and mix with sugar. Sprinkle in yeast and let stand 5 minutes. Mix cooled liquid into yeast mixture in large mixing bowl. Sift half of flour into liquid mixture. Add bran flakes. Beat at low speed for 1/2 minute. Scrape sides of bowl constantly. Beat 2 minutes on high. By hand, stir in enough sifted flour to make a moderately stiff dough. Knead until smooth—6 to 8 minutes. Shape in ball in greased bowl. Cover and let rise until double—1 to 1-1/2 hours. Punch down. Divide in half on floured surface. Cover and let rest 10 minutes. Shape into loaves and place in 2 greased 9 x 5-inch pans. Let rise until double—1 to 1-1/2 hours. Preheat oven to 350 degrees. Bake 25 minutes. Brush with egg white. Return to oven and bake 20 minutes more. Turn out immediately on cooling racks.

Mrs. Robert B. Young

OATMEAL BREAD

Makes 2 loaves

Subtly flavored with molasses and ginger.

2 cups milk
1/4 cup molasses
2 T. butter
2 tsp. salt
1/3 cup warm water
1 tsp. granulated sugar
2 pkgs. active dry yeast
5 to 5-1/2 cups
   unbleached flour, sifted
1/2 tsp. ginger
1 cup old fashioned oats

Heat milk, molasses, butter and salt until warm and butter melts. Cool to 110 degrees. Mix warm water and sugar, sprinkle in yeast and let stand 5 minutes. In large mixing bowl, mix yeast mixture into cooled liquid. Sift 3 cups flour and ginger into liquids; add oats. Beat at low speed 1/2 minute and at high speed for 2 minutes. Stir in enough sifted flour for a soft dough. Knead 4 to 5 minutes. Place ball of dough in greased bowl, cover and let rise until double—45 minutes to 1 hour. Divide dough in half and let rest 10 minutes. Shape into loaves and place in two greased 9 x 5-inch pans. Let rise until double—45 minutes to 1 hour. Preheat oven to 375 degrees. Bake 35 to 40 minutes. Immediately remove from pans and cool.

Mrs. Arthur W. Bergman, Jr.

HERB BREAD

Makes 1 loaf

An easy way to "dress up" French bread!

1/2 cup butter, softened
1 tsp. marjoram
1 tsp. basil
1 tsp. thyme
1 tsp. crushed rosemary
1/8 tsp. garlic salt
1 loaf French or Vienna
   bread, sliced

Preheat oven to 350 degrees. Blend butter and herbs; spread on bread. Wrap in foil and bake for 30 minutes. Serve at once.

Mrs. Laurence F. Tidrick

CORNMEAL MINI-LOAVES

Makes 6 loaves

Small loaves for small families.

2 pkgs. active dry yeast
1/2 cup warm water
1 cup scalded milk
1/2 cup shortening
1/2 cup granulated sugar
1 T. salt
1/2 cup cold water
5-1/2 to 6 cups flour
2 eggs
1 cup cornmeal
2 T. cornmeal

Dissolve yeast in warm water. Pour scalded milk over shortening, sugar and salt, stirring occasionally until shortening melts. Add cold water and cool to *lukewarm*. Beat in eggs and dissolved yeast. Stir in 2 cups flour and 1 cup cornmeal. Add rest of flour or enough to make a soft dough. Turn dough onto a lightly floured surface. Knead 8 to 10 minutes or until smooth and elastic. Shape into a ball. Put in a greased bowl; turn to coat surface of dough. Cover, let rise in warm place about one hour or until double. Preheat oven to 400 degrees. Punch down; form 6 individual loaves, about 6 inches long, shaped like French bread. Generously grease 2 large cookie sheets and sprinkle each with 1 T. cornmeal. Put 3 loaves on each cookie sheet. Cut three 1/2-inch deep slashes across top of each loaf. Cover; let rise about 45 minutes, or until nearly double. Bake 18 to 20 minutes or until golden brown. This bread freezes very well.

Paula Nordhem

ENGLISH MUFFINS

Makes 12

Fun to make! Especially easy with a Cuisinart.

3/4 tsp. salt
1 T. granulated sugar
1-1/2 cups lukewarm
   water
1 pkg. active dry yeast
3 T. shortening
3-1/2 to 3-3/4 cups flour

Mix salt, sugar, water and yeast until yeast is dissolved. Add shortening. Then mix flour in two additions. Knead until smooth and elastic. Place in greased bowl and let rise until double in bulk—about 1-1/2 to 2 hours. Roll out 3/4 to 1-inch thick and cut with a 2-1/2-inch cutter. Place on a lightly greased, cornmeal sprinkled cookie sheet about 1 inch apart. Cover with a damp cloth and let rise until light, about 1 hour, removing cloth during last 10 minutes. Preheat oven to 375 degrees. Cover with an ungreased cookie sheet. Bake 20 to 25 minutes. Cool on rack.

Mrs. Timothy L. Tilton

CHEESE BREAD

Makes 2 loaves

Hot and cheesy French bread.

1/4 lb. butter or
   margarine, softened
1 cup grated Cheddar
   cheese
1 cup mayonnaise
Worcestershire sauce
   to taste
dried minced onions
   to taste
2 medium loaves French
   bread

Cream butter. Beat in cheese, mayonnaise, Worcestershire and onions. Horizontally slice top crust off bread. Discard crust (or use for crumbs). Slice bread into 3/4-inch slices. Spread each piece thinly with mix on the sides and top. Wrap in foil, leaving top open. Preheat oven to 350 degrees. Bake for 30 minutes or until top is golden brown.

NOTE: Mixture may be made up to one week before use and refrigerated; spread only one hour before baking.

Jan Ellerman

HERB BREAD STICKS

Be creative! Season them with fresh herbs of your choice...

3-1/4 cups flour
1 pkg. active dry yeast
1-1/4 cups water
1 T. granulated sugar
1 T. oil
1-1/2 tsp. salt
1 garlic clove, minced
1 cup grated *fresh*
  Parmesan cheese
2 tsp. finely chopped
  fresh herbs; dill,
  parsley and/or basil
melted butter

Stir together 1-1/4 cups flour and yeast in large bowl of electric mixer. Heat water, sugar, oil, salt and garlic in small saucepan over low heat until warm — 120 degrees. Add liquid ingredients to flour mixture and beat until smooth, about 3 mintues on medium speed. Add cheese, combination or single herb desired and remaining flour. Turn out onto lightly floured board; knead until smooth and satiny, about 3 minutes. Divide dough in half. Roll half to 15 x 6-inch rectangle about 1/2-inch thick. Cut crosswise into 18 bread sticks. Twist sticks, place on greased baking sheets and brush with melted butter. Repeat. Let rise until double, about 45 minutes. Preheat oven to 400 degrees. Bake 12 to 15 minutes until lightly browned. Cool. Serve with your favorite summer salad or soup.

Paula Nordhem

Salads and
Salad Dressings

APRICOT SALAD WITH FRUIT DRESSING

Serves 10

Delightful for dessert, too...

1 6-oz. pkg. lemon jello
1 17-oz. can whole peeled
  apricots
1 3-oz. pkg. cream cheese

Dissolve the jello in 3-1/2 cups liquid—all the apricot juice in can plus water. Pour mixture into a 6-cup ring mold, and refrigerate. Stuff apricots with small balls of cheese in place of apricot stones. When jello thickens, slightly press apricots into mixture. Refrigerate mold until firm. To serve, unmold. Garnish with strawberries.

FRUIT DRESSING
1 cup mayonnaise
1 cup whipped cream
1 banana, cut in small
  cubes
1 cup diced canned
  pineapple
1 cup small marsh-
  mallows, chopped
1/2 cup pineapple juice
strawberries

Fold mayonnaise into whipped cream. Marinate banana, pineapple, and marsh-mallows in 1/2 cup of pineapple juice. Mix drained fruit and marshmallows with mayonnaise/cream. Put dressing in center of ring mold.

Mrs. Lawrence J. Lawson

PINEAPPLE CHEESE SUPREME

Serves 6 to 8

A rich molded salad.

1 16-oz. can crushed
  pineapple, undrained
1 cup granulated sugar
1/2 cup water
2 T. unflavored gelatin
1 cup grated Cheddar
  cheese
juice of 2 lemons
1/2 pt. whipping cream,
  whipped

Heat pineapple and sugar. Soften, then dissolve gelatin in water. Add gelatin to pineapple mixture. Add cheese and lemon juice. When slightly cool, add whipped cream. Place all in ring mold and refrigerate until set. Allow several hours.

Mrs. Charles O. Barnes

FROZEN CHEESE AND CRANBERRY SALAD

Serves 6

Different do-ahead salad...

**2 3-oz. pkgs. cream
cheese, softened
3/4 cup salad dressing
1 1-lb. can jellied
cranberry sauce
1 8-1/4-oz. can crushed
pineapple, drained
1/2 cup ripe olives,
drained and chopped
1/4 cup chopped celery
1 cup whipping cream,
whipped**

Blend cream cheese and salad dressing until smooth. Thoroughly blend in cranberry sauce. Fold in pineapple, olives, celery and whipped cream. Put mixture in an 8 x 8-inch pan and freeze until solid. Cut into 6 squares.

Mrs. Lawrence F. Tidrick

HOLIDAY CRANBERRY MOLD

Serves 8 to 10

Fix-ahead salad for your turkey feast...

**2 3-oz. pkgs. dark
raspberry or
blackberry jello
1 cup boiling water
1 16-oz. can cranberry
sauce with whole
berries
3/4 cup port wine
1/4 cup wine vinegar
1/4 cup lemon juice
1/4 tsp. salt
1/2 cup chopped walnuts
1 cup finely chopped
celery**

Dissolve jello in water. Stir in cranberry sauce, wine, vinegar, lemon juice and salt. Chill until mixture thickens. Fold in nuts and celery. Pour into a greased 6-1/2-cup mold or hollowed out orange shells. Chill until firm. Can be made 2 days ahead. Delicious with turkey, chicken, duck or pork.

Mrs. R. Scott Stratton

ORANGE-APRICOT RING

Serves 6 to 8

A super salad with endless garnish variations!

**2 1-lb. cans peeled
  apricots
2 3-oz. pkgs. orange jello
dash salt
1 6-oz. can frozen orange
  juice
2 T. lemon juice
1 7-oz. bottle lemon/
  lime carbonated
  beverage**

Drain apricots, reserving 1-1/2 cups syrup. Purée apricots in blender. Combine syrup, jello, and salt. Heat to boiling to dissolve jello. Remove from heat; add puréed apricots, orange juice and lemon juice. Stir to melt orange concentrate. Slowly pour beverage down side of pan. To keep bubbles, mix gently with up and down motion. Pour into a 6-cup ring. Chill overnight. Decorate with grapes, pineapple, lemon dipped avocado slices, strawberries, blueberries and/or mint sprigs. Serve with mixture of 1/2 mayonnaise and 1/2 whipped cream or all whipped cream.

Lee Horton

STRAWBERRY RHUBARB MOLD

Serves 8 to 10

This colorful, refreshing mold also may be served as a dessert.

**2 10-oz. pkgs. frozen
  sliced strawberries
1 lb. pkg. frozen sliced
  rhubarb
1/2 cup cold water
1/4 cup granulated sugar
2 3-oz. pkgs. strawberry
  jello
1 cup crushed
  unsweetened pine-
  apple, undrained**

Thaw frozen strawberries at room temperature for at least one hour. Cook rhubarb in water and sugar until just done — do *not* follow package directions — about 8 to 10 minutes. Add jello and mix well; add pineapple and juice. Add strawberries and mix well. Place in a well greased 9 x 9-inch pan or 2-quart mold. Refrigerate until firm, at least one day. Serve with mayonnaise thinned to desired consistency with milk. Recipe can be doubled but use a 20-oz. can of pineapple.

Mrs. Dan N. Cross

MANDARIN WALDORF SALAD

Serves 6

Pecans and ginger make it different.

**5 cups diced apples,
  not peeled
3 T. frozen orange juice
  concentrate, thawed
1/2 tsp. salt
2 stalks celery, thinly
  sliced
1 11-oz. can mandarin
  oranges, drained
1/2 cup pecan halves
lettuce leaves**

In a large bowl, combine apples, orange juice concentrate, salt, celery, oranges and pecans. Stir well. Chill until serving time. Arrange salad on lettuce. Top with desired amount of dressing.

**GINGER-YOGURT
DRESSING
1/2 cup mayonnaise
1 8-oz. carton mandarin
  orange yogurt
3/4 tsp. ginger**

Combine ingredients, blending well.

NOTE: Plain yogurt could be substituted for mandarin orange yogurt for a less sweet dressing.

Mrs. Julien H. Collins, Jr.

FRESH PEACH SALAD

Serves 6 to 8

A beautiful salad with a special crunch.

**1 head lettuce
4 peaches
1 tsp. garlic powder
1/4 cup lemon juice
2 T. confectioners sugar
1 T. butter
1/4 tsp. salt
1 3-oz. pkg. slivered
  almonds**

Discarding outer leaves of lettuce, separate and crisp lettuce heart in refrigerator. Peel peaches and slice; sprinkle with garlic powder, lemon juice and sugar. Cover tightly and place in refrigerator. Put butter and salt on almonds and brown in low oven; keep hot. At last minute toss peaches and lettuce; pour hot nuts over salad and toss lightly. Serve immediately.

Mrs. Carl Fowler

MARGE'S MANDARIN ORANGE SALAD

Serves 6

Try the variations too!

1 11-oz. can mandarin oranges, drained and juice reserved
1 ripe avocado, sliced
1 bunch endive, torn into bite-size pieces
1 head iceberg lettuce
1/4 cup toasted slivered almonds

Wash salad greens and refrigerate. Place avocado slices in reserved mandarin orange juice. At serving time, toss greens, drained mandarin oranges and avocado slices with almonds. Serve with desired amount of poppy seed dressing.

POPPY SEED DRESSING
1 cup granulated sugar
2 tsp. dry mustard
2 tsp. salt
2/3 cup cider vinegar
3 T. onion juice
2 cups salad oil
3 T. poppy seeds

Mix ingredients together and refrigerate.

VARIATIONS: Use grapefruit or orange sections instead of mandarin oranges. Include a small amount of shredded red cabbage. Substitute spinach for lettuce and endive. Add cooked shrimp for an entrée salad.

Mrs. Julien H. Collins, Jr.

MANDARIN TOSSED SALAD

Serves 6 to 8

Interesting!

Bibb or other lettuce
1 11-oz. can mandarin
oranges, drained
1/2 cup chopped
green onions
1/2 cup green grapes
1/2 cup toasted almonds

Break lettuce into salad bowl. And oranges, onions, grapes and almonds. Just before serving, toss.

DRESSING
2/3 cup salad oil
1/3 cup orange juice
1/4 cup granulated sugar
3 T. vinegar
1/2 tsp. salt
1/4 tsp. dry mustard

Mix ingredients and pour over salad after tossing.

Mrs. Carroll G. Wells

TANGY TOMATO ASPIC

Serves 6 to 8

Easy! Can be served as a light luncheon dish or an accompaniment salad.

3-3/4 — 4 cups V-8 juice
2 3-oz. pkgs. lemon
jello
salad oil

Heat 2 cups V-8 juice and dissolve gelatin in hot juice. Add remaining cold V-8. Pour into lightly oiled 1 quart mold. Chill until set.

VARIATION #1: Add one box thawed crab meat to aspic before chilling. Good main dish salad.

VARIATION #2: Add 1 small minced onion and 12 pitted and chopped ripe olives to aspic before chilling.

Mrs. Reid Engelmann

PAM'S PERFECTION

Serves 6 to 8

Colorful contrast of flavors and textures...

1 medium head lettuce
4 green onions and stems,
  chopped
1 cup chopped celery
1 T. minced fresh parsley
1 11-oz. can mandarin
  oranges, drained
1 avocado, diced
1/4 cup slivered toasted
  almonds

Break lettuce in pieces into salad bowl. Top with remaining salad ingredients, except almonds. Refrigerate. To serve, toss salad and dressing together. Garnish with almonds.

DRESSING
1/4 cup oil
2 T. tarragon vinegar
1/2 tsp. salt
1/4 tsp. Tabasco
2 T. granulated sugar
freshly ground pepper

Mix ingredients and chill.

Mrs. James R. McClamroch

LAYERED OVERNIGHT SALAD   *Serves 6 to 8*

A favorite recipe of many hostesses because it's completely prepared ahead of time! Simply layer your favorite salad ingredients in your best glass bowl, top with mayonnaise and refrigerate overnight. Don't toss the salad before serving...just remind guests to "dig deep" as they serve themselves. Below is a basic recipe plus suggestions for variety.

BASIC SALAD
**small head iceberg
  lettuce, shredded**
**5 oz. frozen petite peas,
  uncooked**
**4 stalks celery, thinly
  sliced**
**1 large green pepper,
  diced**
**7 oz. raw spinach,
  shredded**
**1 bunch green onions,
  chopped**
**1 large cucumber, peeled
  and chopped**
**1 6-oz. can water
  chestnuts, drained
  and thinly sliced**
**salt, pepper and sugar
  to taste**

Wash all vegetables and dry thoroughly before cutting. Layer vegetables in order listed, sprinkling each layer with salt, pepper and a small amount of sugar.

DRESSING
**2 cups Hellmann's
  or homemade
  mayonnaise**
**1/2 to 3/4 lb. crisp,
  crumbled bacon**
**1/3 cup freshly grated
  Parmesan cheese**

Spread mayonnaise on salad and sprinkle with bacon and Parmesan cheese. Cover and refrigerate until serving time. Garnish with tomatoes and eggs.
SUBSTITUTIONS: Thinly sliced red onions for green onions, shredded Swiss or sharp Cheddar cheese for Parmesan cheese. Add a layer of cubed cooked chicken or turkey for a meal-in-one bowl. Use fruits such as seedless grapes and pineapple tidbits in place of some vegetable layers. Create *your own* version!

The Committee

COLD VEGETABLE MEDLEY

Serves 8 to 10

Colorful and crunchy...

· 1 cup thinly sliced carrot
   curls (or radishes for
   added color)
2 medium heads cauli-
   flower, broken into
   flowerets
1-1/2 lbs. fresh green
   beans
1 large sweet onion,
   thinly sliced and
   broken into rings
1 4-oz. can pitted and
   drained black olives
2 to 3 14-oz. cans
   drained and halved
   artichoke hearts
salt and pepper to taste
Seven Seas Caesar
   Salad dressing
mayonnaise

Blanch beans and cauliflower in boiling water for 5 to 8 minutes or until still crunchy. Rinse in cold water. Toss all vegetables, except olives, together and cover with dressing made in proportions of 1/3 Seven Seas dressing to 2/3 mayonnaise. At serving time, add olives and sprinkle with freshly ground pepper. Serve on lettuce as a salad or in a large bowl for buffet of picnic. Keeps 2 to 3 days in refrigerator.

NOTE: You can add chunks of salami for a nice summer main dish salad. You can substitute frozen peas or blanched pea pods for the beans.

Mrs. R. Scott Stratton

SPINACH SALAD

Serves 12

Dynamite combination!

2-3 bunches fresh
   spinach
1/3 cup granulated sugar
1 T. dry mustard
1 T. salt
1 T. celery seed
1/4 cup grated onion
1 cup salad oil
1/3 cup tarragon or wine
   vinegar
1 small can salted
   Spanish peanuts

Clean spinach, remove stems and tear into pieces. Put next five ingredients in blender with a little of the vinegar. Then blend in oil and slowly add the rest of the vinegar. Add peanuts to the salad just before tossing with dressing and serving.

Mrs. Gordon R. Hjalmarson

MY BEST SPINACH SALAD

Serves 8 to 10

Oriental vegetables make this salad special.

1/2 lb. bacon, diced
1 16-oz. can bean sprouts,
   drained
1 lb. fresh spinach
1 5-oz. can water chest-
   nuts, drained, sliced
4 hard cooked eggs,
   chopped

Fry bacon until crisp. Drain on paper toweling. Wash spinach; dry thoroughly. Remove stems, tear leaves into small pieces. Chill. Chill remaining ingredients until serving time.

DRESSING
1 cup safflower oil
1/4 cup white wine
   vinegar
1 small onion, grated
2 tsp. salt
3/4 cup granulated sugar
1/3 cup catsup
1 T. Worcestershire sauce

Place all ingredients in electric blender and mix until emulsified—about 30 seconds. Refrigerate. At serving time, gently toss vegetables and eggs with enough dressing to coat greens. Top with bacon.

NOTE: The dressing recipe is enough for two or three recipes of salad. Try using peanut oil for variety.

Mrs. Edwin B. Bosler

BEET DELIGHT

Serves 6 to 8

Bonanza!

1 3-oz. pkg. raspberry
   jello
1 16-oz. can julienne
   beets
1 cup crushed pineapple
1/4 cup sweet relish
   (piccallili)

Measure drained beet and pineapple juice and add water to make 1-3/4 cups liquid. Heat juice, add jello and stir until jello is dissolved. Cool to warm before adding the remaining ingredients. Pour into 6-cup greased mold.

Mrs. William Alger, Jr.

ESQUIRE SALAD

Serves 8 to 10

Cosmopolitan combination...

1 15-1/2-oz. can
   garbanzo beans
wine vinegar
your choice of mixed
   greens to equal 2 large
   heads iceberg lettuce
   (fresh spinach,
   Romaine, Boston
   lettuce)
3 tomatoes, cut in eighths
1 lb. fresh mushrooms,
   thinly sliced
1 14-oz. can hearts of
   palm, drained, sliced
6 slices bacon, crisply
   cooked and crumbled

The night before serving, drain juice from can of garbanzo beans and refill with vinegar. Refrigerate overnight. Drain beans and mix with other salad ingredients before serving.

DRESSING
1 cup oil
1/2 cup wine vinegar
juice of 1/2 lemon
2 cloves garlic, minced
1/2 tsp. Worcestershire
   sauce
2 T. chili sauce
1 tsp. prepared mustard
4 T. Parmesan cheese
dash oregano
salt and pepper to taste

Combine ingredients and toss with salad.

Mrs. James R. McClamroch

ZUCCHINI SALAD

Serves 6

Topped with a tart lemon sauce...it's terrific!

3 medium zucchini
lettuce leaves
3 tomatoes, peeled, sliced
3 hard cooked eggs,
   quartered
1 green pepper, diced
3 green onions, sliced,
   including some green
   tops
2 T. chopped dill weed

Cook zucchini in boiling salted water until tender. Drain and cut in 1/3-inch thick slices; chill well. Arrange lettuce leaves on a large serving platter. Place zucchini slices at the center and tomato slices around the zucchini. Top tomatoes with egg quarters. Mix green pepper, green onions and dill and sprinkle over zucchini.

LEMON SAUCE
1/4 cup vegetable or
   olive oil
5 T. fresh lemon juice
salt and pepper to taste
1/4 cup chopped *fresh*
   parsley

Prepare sauce by beating oil, lemon juice, salt and pepper together with a wire whip. Add parsley and mix well. Spoon sauce over vegetables.

Mrs. Julien H. Collins, Jr.

CHILLED LIMA BEAN SALAD

Serves 6 to 8

Nutty flavor with a hint of dill.

3 cups baby lima beans,
   cooked and drained
1 cup diced celery
1/4 cup minced parsley
1/4 cup snipped chives
2 tsp. dill seed
1/2 cup mayonnaise
1/2 cup sour cream
1 tsp. lemon juice
1/2 tsp. salt or to taste
1/4 tsp. pepper
paprika

Combine lima beans, celery, parsley, chives and dill seed. Make a dressing of mayonnaise, sour cream, lemon juice, salt and pepper. Carefully fold in lima bean mixture. Sprinkle paprika on top. May be prepared the night before.

Mrs. James R. McClamroch

BROCCOLI AND SPINACH SALAD

Serves 8

Different and delicious...

1 10-oz. pkg. frozen
  chopped broccoli
1 10-oz. pkg. frozen
  chopped spinach
1/2 cup mayonnaise
1/2 cup sour cream
1 envelope unflavored
  gelatin
1 10-1/2-oz. can
  consommé
1 T. Worcestershire sauce
1/2 tsp. Tabasco
1 T. lemon juice
tomato wedges
hard cooked egg slices

Cook and drain broccoli and spinach. Mix mayonnaise and sour cream together. Soak gelatin in part of consommé, then heat to dissolve. Add rest of consommé, seasonings and lemon juice. Mix and put in a greased 6-cup ring mold. Chill until firm. To serve, unmold and garnish with tomato wedges and egg slices.

NOTE: For a smoother texture, blender may be used.

Mrs. Duane Molthop

CAULIFLOWER AND APPLE SALAD

Serves 6 to 8

Tangy, change of pace salad...

1 small head cauliflower
3 red apples
lemon or orange juice
1 cup sliced celery
3 green onions, sliced,
  including tops
1/4 cup chopped fresh
  parsley or 1 small
  bunch watercress,
  chopped
1/2 teaspoon salt
1/4 cup red wine vinegar
1/4 cup olive or salad oil
freshly ground pepper
  to taste

Thinly slice cauliflower. Dice apples but do not peel; dip in juice to prevent discoloration. Mix cauliflower, apples, celery, onions and parsley; thoroughly chill. Mix vinegar, salt, oil and pepper vigorously. Pour dressing over salad and serve after tossing gently. The above mixture can also be mixed with torn greens and additional dressing to extend the salad or to cut down on the "bite" of the cauliflower.

Mrs. Julien H. Collins, Jr.

BEET SALAD

Serves 6

An attractive, uniquely flavored salad which is super fast to make!

1 16-oz. can julienne
   beets
1 3-oz. pkg. lemon gelatin
1/4 cup granulated sugar
1/4 cup vinegar
1 T. horseradish

Drain beets and save liquid. Add enough water to beet liquid to make 1-1/2 cups; bring to boil and add gelatin. Stir until gelatin is dissolved. Mix in sugar, vinegar and horseradish. Add beets and pour in 5-cup mold. Refrigerate until firm. Serve on lettuce bed with mayonnaise dressing.

Mrs. Fred L. Stone

INSALATA TRICOLORE

Serves 4 to 6

Colorful chilled salad...

1 lb. red potatoes
1/2 lb. fresh green
   beans, cut, or 1 9-oz.
   pkg. frozen
2 T. red wine vinegar
2 large tomatoes
3/4 tsp. salt
1/4 tsp. pepper
1 medium red onion or
   4 green onions
2 T. olive or salad oil
1/4 tsp. dried oregano

Cook potatoes in their jackets in boiling salted water until just tender; drain. Steam green beans until just tender; drain and chill quickly in cold water; drain again. Cool, peel and dice potatoes; place in large bowl and sprinkle with vinegar. Peel tomatoes and cut in eighths. Add green beans and tomatoes to potatoes; season with salt and pepper. Toss and chill for 2 hours. Add thinly sliced red onion or sliced green onions and tops. Add olive oil mixed with oregano. Toss well and chill for one more hour. Salad can be made in the morning but the beans will lose some of their "green-ness."

Mrs. Julien H. Collins, Jr.

THE POTATO SALAD

Serves 4 to 6

Tangy and terrific and can be tripled!

2 cups diced, cooked,
  pared potatoes
1/3 cup chopped celery
1/3 cup sliced radishes
1/4 cup sliced green
  onions, including tops
1/4 cup sweet pickle
  relish
1/4 cup mayonnaise
1/4 cup sour cream
1 tsp. French's prepared
  mustard
1/2 tsp. each: salt, celery
  seed, freshly ground
  pepper
2 hard cooked eggs,
  sliced

Combine vegetables. Blend relish, mayonnaise, sour cream, mustard and seasonings together. Add to vegetables. Mix well. Gently stir in eggs, saving a few slices for garnish. Refrigerate at least one hour to blend flavors.

Mrs. Edwin B. Bosler

HOT TARRAGON POTATO SALAD

Serves 8

Tasty with baked ham...

10 medium size red
  potatoes, boiled and
  peeled
6 T. salad oil
3 T. tarragon wine vinegar
3 T. fresh lemon juice
3 green onions, chopped,
  including tops
1 tsp. salt
3 T. chopped fresh
  parsley
freshly ground pepper
  to taste
4 slices crisp bacon,
  crumbled (optional)

Dice or slice potatoes into a 2-quart casserole. Heat oil, vinegar, lemon juice, onions and salt, stirring occasionally. Pour mixture over potatoes. Sprinkle with parsley and pepper. For a change of flavor, bacon may be added. Heat in a 350 degree oven for 20 minutes. Toss and serve.

Mrs. Julien H. Collins, Jr.

BLUE CHEESE TURKEY SALAD *Serves 4 to 5*

Blue cheese gives it a special flavor.

**3 cups diced turkey
  or chicken
1 cup mayonnaise
3 T. tarragon vinegar
2 T. chili sauce
1/4 cup chopped green
  pepper
1/2 cup chopped celery
1/2 cup crumbled blue
  cheese or according
  to taste
lettuce cups
cherry tomatoes**

Mix all ingredients. Let marinate at least 6 hours. Serve in lettuce cups. Garnish with tomatoes.

Mrs. John C. Roberson

CHEESE AND OLIVE SALAD *Serves 8 to 10*

A change of pace...

**1-1/2 lbs. Romaine
  lettuce, trimmed and
  torn into pieces
8 scallions, chopped
4 oz. green olives, sliced
4 oz. Mozzarella cheese,
  grated
4 oz. Swiss cheese, grated**

Place salad ingredients in large bowl and toss.

**DRESSING
1 T. vinegar or lemon
  juice
1 T. Dijon mustard
1/4 cup salad oil
1/4 cup olive oil
salt and pepper to taste**

Blend vinegar and mustard; gradually add oils. Season to taste, remembering that olives and cheeses are salty. Pour dressing over salad just before serving and toss.

Kathleen Young

TROPICAL CHICKEN SALAD

Serves 8

Exotic luncheon entrée with a hint of curry.

2 fresh pineapples
2-1/2 cups cubed cooked
   chicken (3 large
   breasts)
3/4 cup diced celery
3/4 cup mayonnaise
2 T. chopped chutney
1 tsp. curry powder
1 medium banana, sliced
1/3 cup salted skinless
   peanuts
1/2 cup flaked coconut
1 11-oz. can mandarin
   orange slices

Cut each pineapple into four sections, boat style. Remove pineapple centers and cube, excluding core. Combine chicken, pineapple cubes and celery. Mix mayonnaise, chutney and curry powder. May refrigerate the above overnight. Just before serving, drain juice from the chicken mixture; add banana slices and peanuts. Toss with mayonnaise mixture. Fill pineapple boats. Sprinkle with coconut and garnish with orange slices. Recipe can be doubled easily. For a buffet luncheon, serve on a platter covered with red leaf lettuce, an exotic flower in the center.

VARIATION: Four avocados, split in half lengthwise just before serving, and two 20-oz. cans drained pineapple cubes may be substituted for fresh pineapples.

Mrs. Robert M. Levy

CHICKEN SALAD A LA CHINOIS

Serves 6 to 8

A perfect salad for a summer luncheon!

SALAD
8 cooked chicken breasts*
2 cups chopped fresh
  pineapple
3 T. chopped green onion
1 cup chopped cucumber
1 cup chopped celery
3 T. toasted sesame
  seeds**
1 cup mayonnaise

Remove skin and bones from chicken breasts and cut into one-inch pieces. Combine chicken with rest of salad ingredients. Set aside to chill. Spoon salad into lettuce cups, top with sweet-sour sauce and won-ton crispies.

SWEET AND SOUR SAUCE
1/4 cup vinegar
1/4 cup water
1/4 cup catsup
6 T. granulated sugar
1 T. soy sauce
1 T. cornstarch
2 T. water

Mix first 5 ingredients in sauce pan and simmer until sugar is dissolved. Add cornstarch mixed with water and stir until thickened. Cool.

Paula Nordhem

GARNISH
6-8 lettuce cups
2 cups won-ton crispies
  (julienne strips of won-
  ton sheets deep fat
  fried)

* Chicken breasts may be poached 45 minutes in water with 1 cup each of coarsely chopped carrots and celery, one chopped onion, a bay leaf and 3 pepper corns. Save the broth for other recipes.

** Spread sesame seeds on a cookie sheet in a single layer. Bake at 350 degrees for 5 to 10 minutes. Watch carefully.

CELESTIAL CHICKEN SALAD

Serves 6 to 8

Men are particularly fond of this!

4 cups diced cooked
  chicken
2 cups diagonally sliced
  celery
1 4-1/2 oz. jar whole
  mushrooms, drained
1/2 cup toasted pecan
  halves
4 slices crisp bacon,
  crumbled
1 cup mayonnaise
1 cup sour cream
2 T. lemon juice
salt to taste

Combine chicken, celery, mushrooms, pecans and bacon in large bowl. Blend mayonnaise with remaining ingredients and add to chicken mixture. Chill well before serving.

Mrs. Edward C. Blomeyer

MOLDED CHICKEN SALAD

Serves 6

Chilled chicken à la king...

2 T. unflavored gelatin
1 cup cold water
1 10-3/4-oz. can
  condensed cream of
  celery soup
1/2 tsp. salt
2 T. lemon juice
1 tsp. instant minced
  onion
1 cup salad dressing
2 T. diced pimiento
1 cup diced celery
2 cups diced cooked
  chicken

Sprinkle gelatin over water in medium saucepan. Place over low heat. Stir constantly until gelatin dissolves. Remove from heat. Stir in soup, salt, lemon juice, onion and salad dressing. Beat with a rotary beater until smooth. Chill, stirring occasionally, until mixture mounds when dropped from a spoon. Add pimiento, celery and chicken. Turn into a 6-cup loaf pan or mold. Chill until firm.

Mrs. Robert A. Southern

EGG SALAD

Serves 4 to 6

The egg salad with a fresh herb flavor.

**10 large hard cooked
  eggs, chopped**
**1 medium Bermuda or
  Spanish onion,
  chopped**
**1-1/2 T. *fresh* dill leaves,
  chopped fine (or 2 tsp.
  dry dill weed)**
**1 T. chopped *fresh* chervil
  (or 1-1/2 tsp. dry
  chervil)**
3/4 tsp. dry mustard
**1-1/2 T. chopped fresh
  Italian parsley (or 2 tsp.
  dehydrated parsley
  flakes)**
1 tsp. celery salt
**1/3-1/2 cup mayonnaise
  (Hellmann's or
  homemade)**
**salt and freshly ground
  pepper to taste**

Combine all ingredients and mix together lightly. Serve on lettuce leaf. Can be used as a filling for tiny cream puffs and served as appetizers.

Mrs. Warren C. Haskin

SHRIMP AND RICE SALAD

Serves 6

Fix-ahead supper for a hot summer evening...

1-1/2 lbs. peeled, cooked
  shrimp
3-1/2 cups cooked rice
1/2 cup thinly sliced
  celery
1/3 cup sliced pimento-
  stuffed olives
1/3 cup chopped green
  pepper
1/3 cup sliced green
  onions
1/4 tsp. salt
1/4 tsp. pepper
1/4 cup mayonnaise
Romaine lettuce leaves
2 large tomatoes, cut in
  wedges
1 lemon, cut in wedges

Combine shrimp, rice, celery, olives, green pepper and onions in large bowl. Chill for at least one hour. Mix mayonnaise with salt and pepper; stir into shrimp mixture. Chill one more hour. Spoon salad onto lettuce leaves; garnish with tomato and lemon wedges. Be sure to tell guests to squeeze lemon on top of their portion of salad!

Mrs. Julien H. Collins, Jr.

SHRIMP MOLD

Serves 6 to 8

Most attractive when prepared in a fish mold...

1 lb. shrimp, cooked and
  dried
3/4 cup diced celery
1/4 cup minced onion
1 8-oz. pkg. cream
  cheese, softened
1 cup mayonnaise at
  room temperature
1 T. unflavored gelatin
1/3 cup cold water
1 10-3/4-oz. can tomato
  soup, undiluted

Have shrimp, celery and onion ready. Beat cream cheese and mayonnaise together with electric mixer. Add water to gelatin and dissolve. Bring soup to a boil and add gelatin mixture. Beat soup mixture into cream cheese mixture. Fold in celery, onion and shrimp. Pour into greased mold. Refrigerate overnight.

Mrs. John Grainer

SOLE SALAD SUPREME

Serves 4

Supremely delicious...

1 T. lemon juice
1/2 tsp. salt
1/8 tsp. cayenne pepper
3 T. olive oil
2 T. finely chopped
   scallions
2 tsp. dill weed
2 cups chilled poached
   sole, cut into 1 or
   2-inch pieces
1 cup Hellmann's
   mayonnaise
2 to 3 cups shredded
   Romaine lettuce
2 hard cooked eggs,
   sliced
4 small tomatoes, peeled
   and sliced
2 T. capers, drained,
   washed and dried

Mix first 5 ingredients together with 1 tsp. dill. Pour over fish; marinate one hour, gently turning the fish. Combine fish, marinade and 1/2 cup mayonnaise. Arrange mixture on shredded lettuce. Blend remaining mayonnaise with remaining 1 tsp. dill and spread over fish, masking it completely. Garnish with eggs, tomatoes and capers.

Mrs. Geoffrey C. Murphy

MOLDED CORNED BEEF OR TUNA SALAD

Serves 15

A very compatible blend of ingredients.

2 beef bouillon cubes
1 cup boiling water
1 3-oz. pkg. lemon jello
1 cup salad dressing
11 oz. cream cheese
1-1/2 cups chopped
   green pepper
1/2 cup diced celery
3 T. chopped onion
4 hard cooked eggs,
   chopped
1 12-oz. can corned beef,
   coarsely chopped

Dissolve bouillon cubes in boiling water. Add jello and cool. Soften cream cheese and mix with salad dressing. Add chopped ingredients and beef. Add jello mixture and allow to set. This will fit into an 11-cup ring mold or an 11 x 9-inch pan. French dressing may be used when serving on a lettuce bed.

VARIATION: Substitute tuna fish for the corned beef and add juice of one lemon.

Mrs. Frank Badger

AVOCADO SALAD WITH CRAB DRESSING

Serves 8

Elegant luncheon dish.

watercress
8 crustless toasts
  or Holland Rusks
8 3/4-inch slices of
  avocado, in shape
  of a ring
8 3/4-inch slices
  of tomato
4 deviled eggs,
  cut lengthwise

Form a mound with watercress. Layer other salad ingredients on top.

DRESSING

1 green pepper, chopped
2 hard cooked eggs,
  chopped
onion juice to taste
2 T. catsup
4 T. chili sauce
2 tsp. Worcestershire
  sauce
2 cups mayonnaise
1 7-oz. can crabmeat,
  flaked
salt to taste
paprika

Mix all ingredients except mayonnaise, crabmeat and paprika. Add crabmeat and mayonnaise and blend. Pour dressing over each serving of salad. Dust with paprika.

Mrs. Sumner W. Mead

CRANBERRY TUNA MOLD

Serves 8 to 10

Even non-tuna lovers love it!

1 envelope unflavored
　gelatin
1/4 cup cold water
1/4 cup boiling water
2 6-1/2 oz. cans tuna,
　drained
1 cup mayonnaise
1 cup chopped celery
1 onion, chopped

Soften gelatin in cold water and dissolve in boiling water. Add all remaining ingredients and spoon into an 8 x 8-inch dish. Chill until firm. Mix topping and spoon over chilled tuna mixture. Chill eight hours or overnight.

TOPPING
1 3-oz. box lemon jello
3/4 cup boiling water
1 16-oz. can whole
　cranberry sauce
1/4 cup orange juice

Dissolve jello in boiling water. Add remaining ingredients and stir well.

Mrs. Lyman Missimer

TUNA ASPIC MOLD

Serves 12

Tasty luncheon dish...

FIRST LAYER
1 3-oz. pkg. lemon jello
1 cup boiling water
1 cup mayonnaise
2 6-1/2-oz. cans tuna,
　drained
2 cups diced celery
6 hard cooked eggs,
　chopped

Dissolve lemon jello in boiling water. Cool slightly and beat in mayonnaise. Break up tuna. Add celery and hard cooked eggs. Pour jello mixture over tuna mixture and let set in a 9 x 12-inch Pyrex pan.

SECOND LAYER
2 3-oz. pkgs. orange jello
4 cups hot tomato juice
2 T. lemon juice
2 tsp. horseradish
1/4 tsp. salt
few drops Tabasco

Mix orange jello in hot tomato juice. Add remaining ingredients and let set slightly. Pour second layer over first layer.

Mrs. Philip Jones

TUNA MOUSSE

Pretty pink color...

MOUSSE
5 7-oz. cans water-
  pack tuna
1-1/2 cups chopped
  celery
1/4 cup minced onion
4 T. unflavored gelatin
1 cup cold water
1 cup catsup
1/2 cup vinegar
2 cups mayonnaise
salt and pepper to taste

SAUCE
2 cups sour cream
1/2 small cucumber,
  minced
4 tsp. dried dill weed
1 tsp. onion juice or
  1/4 cup snipped chives
salt and pepper to taste

Drain tuna, reserving liquid. Mix tuna, celery and onion. Soften gelatin in water. Combine reserved tuna liquid, catsup and vinegar; bring to a boil and add gelatin. Stir until dissolved. Gently blend hot liquid into tuna mixture. Stir in mayonnaise and season to taste with salt and pepper. Turn into a large fish mold which has been coated with mayonnaise.

NOTE: Recipe may be cut in half to serve 5 to 6. Mold could also be served as an appetizer with crackers.

Combine ingredients and refrigerate until serving time.

Anne Engelmann

MRS. RAND'S CRABMEAT COLD LUNCHEON

Serves 12

Spectacular salad for a hot summer day...

VEGETABLES
12 tomatoes
3 medium cucumbers
12 large carrots
12 stalks celery
1-1/2 lbs. fresh green beans, blanched
3 16-oz. cans julienne-cut beets, drained
Bibb or leaf lettuce
watercress
paprika

Cut tomatoes in quarters; peel, seed and chop cucumbers; cut carrots, celery and beans into shoestring-sized pieces. Chill well. Salad may be served on large platter or individual plates. Line plate with lettuce. Place tomato in center of plate; top with cucumber. Arrange bunches of carrots, celery, green beans and beets as spokes around tomato. Top with watercress and paprika.

CRABMEAT SAUCE
1 pt. mayonnaise
1 7-oz. can crabmeat, flaked
6 hard cooked eggs, chopped
1/2 cup chopped sweet pickles or relish
salt to taste
1 pt. whipping cream

Mix together all ingredients except cream and refrigerate. Just before serving, whip the cream and gently fold into crab sauce. Let guests pour the sauce themselves. Serve with hot rolls.

Mrs. L. Steven Minkel

CRAB SALAD

Different and delectable...

4 fresh pears
lemon juice
1 7-oz. can or 1 6-oz.
    pkg. frozen crabmeat
1/2 cup mayonnaise
1 T. chopped parsley
1 T. catsup
1 tsp. vinegar
dash of Worcestershire
    sauce
dash of Tabasco sauce
lettuce
lemon wedges or slices
    for garnish

Halve and core pears. With small melon ball cutter, cut out balls from each pear half, forming a boat. Sprinkle cut halves with lemon juice to prevent browning. Place pear balls in bowl. Rinse, drain and flake crab meat. Add to pear balls. Mix mayonnaise, parsley, catsup, vinegar and spices. Toss lightly with crabmeat and pear balls. Spoon into pear boats. Chill. Serve on lettuce-lined plates with lemon garnish.

NOTE: To cut cost, substitute part or all crab with salad shrimp. To cut calories, substitute 1/2 the mayonnaise with Wishbone Low Calorie Creamy Italian Dressing.

Mrs. R. Scott Stratton

STEAK SALAD

Nifty combination of colors, flavors and temperatures!

DRESSING
1 cup mayonnaise
1/4 cup chopped dill
  pickles
2-1/2 T. chopped onion
1-1/2 T. Rhine wine
1 T. chopped cooked
  spinach
1-1/2 tsp. prepared
  mustard
1 tsp. lemon juice
1/2 tsp. granulated sugar
1/2 tsp. Worcestershire
  sauce
1 egg yolk
salt and pepper to taste

Combine ingredients, mixing with a blender or food processor if a smooth sauce is preferred. Chill.

SALAD
1 lb. beef sirloin or
  tenderloin, cut into
  1-inch cubes
salt to taste
1/2 tsp. each: black
  pepper, thyme,
  oregano, basil leaves
1/8 tsp. garlic powder
2 T. butter
salad greens, watercress,
  curly or Belgian endive
sliced avocado or
  cantaloupe
pitted black olives

Place meat seasonings in a plastic bag; add meat and shake to coat evenly. Quickly brown meat in hot butter to doneness you prefer. Cool 1 to 2 minutes. Arrange greens on serving dishes. Add avocado or canta-loupe slices. Divide steak cubes among salads. Garnish with olives. Serve dressing over salad or on the side.

Mrs. Sumner W. Mead

COLD ROAST BEEF SALAD

Serves 4

A great main-course for a welcomed change of pace.

SALAD
1 lb. cooked, rare roast
  beef
4 green onions
2 stalks celery
1 green pepper
1/4 lb. fresh mushrooms
1 boiled potato
1 dill pickle

Cut all salad ingredients into julienne strips. Pour dressing on mixed salad and marinate for 4 hours or more to blend flavors. Serve in lettuce cups with garnishes. Makes a nice summer luncheon or supper when served with a hot bread and a cool dessert.

DRESSING
2/3 cup oil
1/3 cup wine vinegar
1 tsp. lemon juice
1 tsp. salt
1 tsp. dry mustard
1 tsp. chives
1 tsp. tarragon
1 tsp. dried parsley or
  2 tsp. fresh parsley
1/2 tsp. Worcestershire
  sauce
1/4 tsp. pepper
1/4 tsp. thyme

Put all ingredients into a jar and shake to mix.

Mrs. Donald J. Ross

GARNISH
lettuce cups
asparagus spears
pickled beets
hard cooked eggs

HERBED BUTTERMILK SALAD DRESSING

Makes 1-1/2 cups

At last a homemade ranch dressing!

1 egg
1 egg yolk
1 T. white vinegar
2 tsp. Dijon mustard
1 small clove garlic,
   crushed
3/4 tsp. salt
3/4 tsp. dill
1/2 tsp. thyme
1/2 tsp. marjoram
1/2 tsp. basil
1/2 tsp. celery salt
1/2 cup vegetable oil
1 cup buttermilk
white pepper to taste

Place eggs, vinegar, mustard, garlic, and seasonings except white pepper in food processor. Make one on/off turn. With motor running, add vegetable oil and buttermilk. Add white pepper to taste — dressing will be thin.

Kenilworth Union Church

HERB SALAD DRESSING

Makes 1-1/2 cups

Also a great dip.

1 cup salad dressing
   or mayonnaise
2 T. lemon juice
1/4 tsp. salt
1/4 tsp. paprika
1 tsp. salad herbs
2 T. grated onion
2 T. Plochman's mustard
   with added
   horseradish
2 T. chopped chives
1 clove garlic, minced
1/8 tsp. curry powder
1/2 tsp. Worcestershire
   sauce
1 cup sour half and half

Mix all ingredients together except half and half. When well mixed, gradually fold in the sour half and half.

Mrs. Norman E. Baughn

LIZ'S FRENCH DRESSING

Makes 1-1/2 cups

Good and easy with creative options.

1/2 cup salad oil
1/2 cup wine vinegar
1/2 cup chili sauce
granulated sugar to taste

Combine oil, vinegar and chili sauce and shake to blend. Add sugar to taste. Season to taste with all or any combination of the optional ingredients.

Mrs. Edwin B. Bosler

OPTIONS
seasoned salt
grated onion
paprika
lemon juice
crumbled blue cheese

SPINACH SALAD DRESSING

Makes 1-1/2 cups

Scrumptious...

1/2 cup salad oil
1/4 cup catsup
1/4 cup white vinegar
3 to 4 T. granulated sugar
1 small onion, chopped
1/2 tsp. salt

Place all ingredients in blender and mix until onion is puréed. Put in a jar and refrigerate.

Mrs. Stanton R. Cook

FRUIT SALAD DRESSING

Makes 1-1/2 cups

Refreshing boiled dressing...

2 T. flour
2/3 cup granulated sugar
2 eggs, well beaten
juice of 1 lemon
juice of 1 orange
1 cup canned pineapple
   juice (or mixed fruit
   juices)
1/2 cup Cool Whip
rum or liqueur to taste,
   if desired

Mix together flour and sugar; blend with eggs. Add fruit juices. Cook in top of double boiler, stirring constantly, until mixture thickens. Cool and refrigerate. When ready to serve, add Cool Whip and rum, if desired.

Mrs. Norman Baughn

HONEY OF A DRESSING

Makes 2 cups

Goes well with fresh fruit.

1 T. paprika
1/2 tsp. salt
1 tsp. celery seed
1 tsp. onion flakes
1/2 cup granulated sugar
1 tsp. dry mustard
1/4 cup vinegar
1 cup corn oil

Mix dry ingredients. Add tablespoon vinegar alternately with tablespoon of oil slowly in electric mixer. Pour rest of oil in *very* slowly while mixing fast. Dressing should be thick. Keeps well in refrigerator.

NOTE: Can be emulsified in blender if dressing separates.

Mrs. Donald J. Ross

VEGETABLE MARINADE

Makes 2-1/2 cups

This tangy blend can be poured on a combination of vegetables of your choice.

1-1/2 cups wine vinegar
1 tsp. granulated sugar
1-1/2 tsp. salt
1 tsp. Lawry's salt
1/2 tsp. pepper
2 tsp. oregano
1/2 cup salad oil
1/2 cup olive oil

Mix all ingredients and heat for 3 minutes. Mix in broccoli, cherry tomatoes, black and green olives, mushrooms, artichokes, blanched green beans or whatever vegetables you desire. The marinade recipe can be doubled or tripled. Very attractive when served in a glass bowl.

Mrs. Robert J. Cunningham

MUSTARD SALAD DRESSING

Makes 2 cups

Sensational for slaw, too!

1/2 cup red wine vinegar
1/2 cup Dijon mustard
2 tsp. salt
1/4 tsp. white pepper
1 tsp. granulated sugar
1 clove garlic, crushed
   (optional)
1 cup olive or
   vegetable oil

Place all ingredients except oil in blender. Beat well. Add oil very slowly while beating (or processing). Strong mustard flavor.

Mrs. Edward R. James

ANNA'S LOURENZE DRESSING

Makes 2 cups

Tart, sophisticated flavor...

2/3 cup salad oil
1/3 cup vinegar
1 tsp. salt
1 tsp. paprika
1 cup chili sauce
1 cup chopped
   watercress

Mix dressing ingredients together and chill thoroughly. Delicious on top of sliced pears or avocado.

Mrs. Donald J. Ross

ORION ROOM DRESSING

Makes 2 cups

Delightful on a mixed green salad.

1 cup mayonnaise
1 cup sour cream
1-1/2 T. Maggi liquid
  seasoning
2 T. lemon juice
2 T. red wine vinegar
2 T. chopped parsley
1/2 onion, chopped
1-1/2 tsp. black pepper
1 tsp. Knorr Swiss
  Aromat
1/2 tsp. salt
1/2 tsp. minced garlic

Mix all ingredients together. Store in refrigerator.

Mrs. Donald J. Ross

SWEET-SOUR DRESSING

Makes 1-1/2 cups

A tasty delight for individual fruit, lettuce or vegetable salads.

1/3 cup granulated sugar
1 tsp. salt
1 tsp. dry mustard
1 tsp. grated onion
1/3 cup vinegar
1 cup salad oil

Place sugar, salt, mustard, onion and vinegar in blender or food processor and mix quickly. Add oil in thin stream, until the mixture is blended and creamy. Store in the refrigerator in a tightly covered container; shake before using.

Mrs. William A. Brown, Jr.

Vegetables

BROCCOLI CASSEROLE

Serves 4

Light soufflé-like texture...

1 10-oz. pkg. frozen
  chopped broccoli
2/3 cup cream of
  mushroom soup
1 egg, beaten
1/2 cup grated sharp
  cheese
1/2 cup mayonnaise
1/2 small onion, diced
salt and pepper to taste
1/4 cup crushed Ritz
  crackers
1 T. butter

Cook and drain broccoli. Preheat oven to 350 degrees. Mix the soup, egg, cheese and mayonnaise together. Fold in broccoli and onion. Season with salt and pepper. Pour into a one-quart buttered casserole. Sprinkle crushed crackers on top. Dot with butter. Bake for 45 minutes.

NOTE: Can be doubled easily.

Mrs. John E. Vette

BROCCOLI-RICE CASSEROLE

Serves 8

Inexpensive— but rich in flavor!

1 cup raw rice
1 10-oz. pkg. frozen
  chopped broccoli
1 large onion, chopped
1 cup chopped celery
1/4 cup boiling water
1 10-3/4-oz. can cream
  of celery soup
1 cup cubed cheese
1/2 cup water
1/4 cup margarine

Preheat oven to 350 degrees. Cook rice. Combine broccoli, onion and celery; cook 5 minutes in water. Combine cooked rice and broccoli mixture. Add soup, cheese, water and margarine to hot mixture and stir carefully to mix. Bake for 30 minutes.

Kenilworth Union Church

BROCCOLI STUFFING CASEROLE

Serves 12 to 15

An attractive, hearty vegetable dish that's guaranteed to disappear!

3 10-oz. pkgs. frozen
 chopped broccoli
1 8-oz. pkg. stuffing mix
1/2 cup margarine or
 butter, melted
1 cup hot water

SAUCE
3 T. butter
1 medium onion,
 chopped
1/4 cup flour
2 cups milk
1/4 tsp. pepper
1/4 tsp. salt
3/4 to 1 lb. cubed
 Velveeta cheese

Preheat oven to 350 degrees. Cook and drain broccoli. Mix stuffing with butter and water. To prepare sauce, melt butter in fry pan. Sauté onion until golden. Stir in flour and cook for one minute. Add milk gradually, stirring vigorously. Season with salt and pepper. Cook while stirring until sauce boils. Add cubes of cheese and heat while stirring until cheese melts. If too thick, add more milk—up to 1/4 cup. Butter a 2-1/2-quart casserole. Arrange a layer of broccoli, then a layer of stuffing and pour on one-third cheese sauce. Repeat twice more, saving some stuffing for topping. Bake for 30 minutes.

NOTE: Can be made up to a day ahead, covered and refrigerated, so it's ready to bake just before serving.

Mrs. Arthur W. Bergman, Jr.

NORTHWOODS CARROTS

Serves 3 to 4

Madeira adds zip...

1 T. oil
1 small onion, chopped
1 clove garlic, crushed
2 cups sliced fresh
 carrots, cooked and
 drained
1/4 cup beef bouillon
1/4 cup Madeira wine
pepper
chopped parsley

Sauté onion and garlic in oil until tender. Add carrots, bouillon and wine. Cook over high heat until most of liquid evaporates. Season to taste with pepper and garnish with parsley, if desired. Very good with beef.

Mrs. Harry DuPrey

CARROT SOUFFLE

Serves 4 to 6

Colorful and carroty...

1/4 cup butter
1/4 cup flour
1/2 tsp. salt
dash white pepper
1 cup milk
2-1/2 cups carrots,
    peeled and cut in
    1/2-inch pieces
4 eggs, separated

Preheat oven to 350 degrees. In heavy pan, melt butter; blend in flour, salt and pepper. Gradually add milk while stirring. Cook and stir over medium heat until mixture thickens and bubbles. Remove from heat. Cook carrots in small amount of water until just tender. Place in food processor or blender and chop finely. In small bowl, beat egg yolks until thick and lemon colored. Add the slightly cooled white sauce to egg yolks, stirring constantly. Fold in carrots; cool 5 minutes. Using clean beaters and large mixing bowl, beat egg whites until stiff. Gradually fold carrot mixture into egg whites. Pour into ungreased 2-quart soufflé dish or casserole with straight sides. Place casserole in pan of hot water and bake for one hour or until a knife inserted in center comes out clean. Serve immediately.

Mrs. William A. Brown, Jr.

BOURBON CARROTS

Serves 4 to 6

Men ask for seconds.

2 T. butter
2 T. brown sugar
1/8 tsp. salt
8 medium carrots, cut
    diagonally
2 T. bourbon

Melt butter in a heavy fry pan. Add sugar, salt and carrots. Cover and cook slowly 10 to 15 minutes or until just tender. Add bourbon and cook over low heat, uncovered, for one minute.

NOTE: Do not add water.

Mrs. Stanton R. Cook

COLD COPPER CARROTS

Serves 12

Tangy year round vegetable dish...

2 lbs. carrots
1 small green pepper
1 medium onion
1 10-3/4-oz. can tomato
  soup, undiluted
1 T. Worcestershire sauce
1/2 cup granulated sugar
3/4 cup cider vinegar
1 tsp. dry mustard
salt and pepper to taste

Peel and slice carrots and boil covered until just fork tender (12 to 15 minutes). Cool. Slice green pepper and onion into thin rings. In serving dish, alternate layers of carrots, pepper and onion. To prepare marinade, blend soup, Worcestershire sauce, sugar, vinegar, mustard, salt and pepper well. Pour over vegetables and refrigerate overnight. Serve cold.

NOTE: Carrots may be cut in julienne strips, if preferred, and onion and green pepper may be chopped or julienne cut.

Mrs. Lyman Missimer

CHILIE-CORN CASSEROLE

Serves 8

Zippy flavor, delicate texture...

3 ears fresh or frozen
  raw corn
1 cup yellow cornmeal
2 tsp. salt
1 T. baking powder
1 cup sour cream
3/4 cup melted butter
2 well beaten eggs
1/4 lb. Monterey Jack
  cheese, finely diced
1 4-oz. can peeled
  green chilies,
  finely chopped
1/2 cup melted butter,
  reserved

Preheat oven to 350 degrees. Scrape kernels from corn; combine all ingredients and mix well. Pour into a well-buttered 9-inch Pyrex baking dish or a 2-1/2-quart soufflé dish. Bake for 50 to 60 minutes. Drizzle each serving with reserved melted butter. Delicious with roast beef or broiled chicken.

NOTE: One more egg may be added for a lighter texture.

VARIATIONS: Add one or more of the following: 2 T. chopped pimiento, 3 chopped green onions sautéed briefly in 1 T. melted butter, 2 T. chopped fresh parsley, 2 slices crisp crumbled bacon.

Mrs. John H. Fyfe

CURRIED CORN PUDDING

Serves 6 to 8

Yummy company casserole...

3 T. butter
1/2 cup minced onion
1/2 cup minced green
  pepper
1 T. curry powder or to
  taste
2 cups cooked corn
2 cups half and half,
  at room temperature
3 eggs, lightly beaten,
  at room temperature
1 tsp. salt
1/2 tsp. granulated sugar
parsley

Preheat oven to 350 degrees. Sauté onion and green pepper in butter until soft. Add curry powder, mix and sauté briefly. Transfer to a bowl; add corn, cream, eggs, salt and sugar. Pour into a well buttered one-quart soufflé dish. Bake for 45 minutes or until golden brown. Garnish with parsley.

Mrs. Donald J. Ross

COMPANY CAULIFLOWER

Serves 4

Rich and delicious!

1 medium head
  cauliflower
salt and pepper to taste
1 cup sour cream
1 cup grated
  sharp cheese
toasted sesame seeds

Preheat oven to 350 degrees. Rinse cauliflower and break into flowerets. Cook covered in a small amount of boiling salted water (or steam) for 10 to 15 minutes or until tender. Drain. Place half the cauliflower in a 1-quart casserole. Season with salt and pepper. Spread with 1/2 cup sour cream and 1/2 cup grated cheese. Top with sesame seeds. Repeat layers. Bake 10 minutes or until heated through and cheese is melted.

NOTE: A tablespoon or two of milk can be added to sour cream so it spreads more easily.

Mrs. Lyman Missimer

BRUSSELS SPROUTS WITH CELERY

Serves 6 to 8

Bona fide goodness...

2 10-oz. pkgs. frozen
   Brussel sprouts
2 cups sliced celery
6 T. butter
1 cup sour cream
1/2 tsp. salt
1/4 cup bread crumbs
1/4 cup slivered almonds
1 T. melted butter

Cook and drain sprouts. Preheat oven to 350 degrees. Sauté celery in butter for 3 minutes. Add sprouts, sour cream and salt. Transfer to buttered 1-1/2-quart casserole. Mix bread crumbs, almonds and butter. Top sprout mixture with crumb mixture. Bake 15 to 20 minutes to brown crumbs.

Mrs. Arthur W. Bergman, Jr.

SCALLOPED CABBAGE

Serves 4 to 5

Colorful accompaniment for sausage or pork...

4 cups shredded cabbage
1 T. chopped onion
1 cup diced fresh or
   canned tomatoes
salt and pepper to taste
1 cup fresh bread crumbs
1 cup grated sharp
   Cheddar cheese
1/2 tsp. basil
   (optional)
2 T. melted butter

Preheat oven to 350 degrees. Cook cabbage and onion in small amount of boiling water, uncovered, about 5 minutes or until tender. Drain. Butter a 1-1/2-quart casserole. Add 1/2 cabbage and 1/2 tomato; sprinkle with salt and pepper. Add 1/2 bread crumbs and 1/2 cheese. Repeat the layers. Sprinkle with basil, if desired, and drizzle melted butter over all. Place casserole in a pan of hot water and bake for 45 minutes.

NOTE: Ingredients can also be layered in the top of a double boiler, then cooked for 30 to 40 minutes over simmering water. Recipe can be doubled.

Mrs. Gordon R. Scott

HOT CABBAGE SLAW

Serves 6 to 8

Tangy year-round treat...

2 T. butter or margarine
2 eggs, slightly beaten
1/4 cup white vinegar
1/2 cup milk
1-1/4 to 2 T. granulated
   sugar
1/2 tsp. salt
1/4 tsp. dry mustard
1/8 tsp. paprika
dash of freshly ground
   pepper
1/4 tsp. celery seed
   or 1/4 tsp. caraway
   seed, if desired
5 cups shredded raw
   cabbage

Combine all ingredients, except cabbage, in a large skillet or deep saucepan. Cook over *very low* heat until slightly thickened, stirring constantly. Add cabbage; heat until wilted, but do not cook. Serve immediately.

Mrs. Edwin B. Bosler

CREAMY CUCUMBERS

Serves 6 to 8

A dilly of a dish!

6 medium cucumbers
2 tsp. salt
1/2 cup chopped onion
2 T. butter or margarine
2 T. flour
2 cups milk
1 T. chopped fresh
   parsley
1 T. chopped fresh dill
2 T. sour cream

Peel cucumbers, remove seeds, cut into 1-inch pieces. Place in bowl with salt for one hour. Toss 2 to 3 times during the hour. Drain. Sauté onion in butter; stir in flour and cook for one minute. Add milk, stirring until smooth and creamy. Add cucumbers and cook 15 minutes. Before serving, stir in parsley, dill and sour cream.

Mrs. Ellwood G. Peterson

GREEN BEANS THE SWISS WAY

Serves 6 to 8

An appealing way to serve beans for that special occasion.

2 T. butter
2 T. flour
1 tsp. salt
1/4 tsp. pepper
1 tsp. granulated sugar
1 tsp. grated onion
1 cup sour half and half
4 cups cooked green beans
1/2 lb. grated Swiss cheese
2 cups corn flakes
2 T. melted butter

Preheat oven to 400 degrees. Melt butter; stir in flour, salt, pepper, sugar and grated onion. Add sour half and half gradually while stirring constantly. Fold in beans. Pour into a 2-quart oblong casserole. Sprinkle grated cheese over beans. Crush corn flakes, add to melted butter and place on top of casserole. Bake for about 20 minutes.

Mrs. Arthur W. Bergman, Jr.

GREEN BEANS SUPREME

Serves 8 to 12

A delicious, rich vegetable...

2/3 cup minced onion
4 T. butter
4 T. flour
2 tsp. salt
1/2 tsp. pepper
1 pint sour cream
4 10-oz pkgs. frozen French style green beans, cooked and drained
1 cup grated sharp Cheddar cheese

Preheat oven to 350 degrees. Sauté onion in butter. Add flour, salt and pepper and mix well. Add sour cream and heat through. Blend with beans and pour into a 3-quart rectangular Pyrex baking dish. Top with grated cheese and bake for 30 minutes, or until heated through.

Mrs. Arthur A. Frank, Jr.

STRING BEANS IN CURRY SAUCE

Serves 6 to 8

Good flavor...

2 10-oz. pkgs. frozen
  French style green
  beans
3 T. butter
1/2 cup mayonnaise
1/4 tsp. paprika
1 tsp. curry powder
salt to taste

Cook beans according to package directions. Drain. To prepare sauce, melt butter in saucepan. Stir in mayonnaise, paprika, and curry powder. Salt to taste. Simmer for 2 minutes Toss beans and sauce together.

Mrs. Philip A. VanVlack III

PATIO BEANS

Serves 6

Great with hamburgers for a cookout. Men love it!

1/4 lb. bacon, chopped
1 medium onion,
  chopped
1 1-lb. can baked beans
  in tomato sauce
1 1-lb. can kidney beans,
  drained
1 1-lb. can lima beans,
  drained
1/4 lb. grated sharp
  cheese
1/2 cup brown sugar
1/3 cup catsup
1 T. Worcestershire sauce
Parmesan cheese

Preheat oven to 350 degrees. Fry bacon until crisp. Remove bacon and set aside. Drain off half of the bacon drippings. Sauté onion in remaining drippings. Combine beans, cheese, brown sugar, catsup and Worcestershire sauce. Stir in onion and bacon. Transfer to a 2-1/2-quart casserole. Sprinkle with Parmesan. Bake until until bubbly, about 45 minutes.

Mrs. Geoffrey C. Murphy

TRYON BAKED LIMA BEANS

Serves 10 to 12

Rich and sweet...

1 lb. dry baby lima beans
1 clove garlic, finely
chopped
1 tsp. salt
1 lb. brown sugar
1 lb. bacon, diced

Rinse beans, cover with water and soak overnight. Boil beans, garlic and salt until tender enough to pierce with a fork. Preheat oven to 325 degrees. Place beans in a casserole with some of the cooking water (save the rest of liquid). Add brown sugar and bacon. Bake 5 to 8 hours. Check frequently to be sure they do not dry out. Add reserved cooking water as necessary.

Ruth Palmer

DRIED LIMA BEAN CASSEROLE

Serves 8 to 10

A different vegetable with adult appeal.

1 lb. dry lima beans
4 tsp. brown sugar
1 T. butter
1/2 tsp. finely chopped
garlic
1/2 tsp. salt
1/4 cup chopped parsley
3 strips bacon

Soak beans overnight; cook until tender in salted water to cover but do not drain. Preheat oven to 250 degrees. Add sugar, butter, garlic, salt and parsley to beans. Turn into casserole and cover with strips of bacon. Bake for 2 hours.

Mrs. William R. Hodgson

GERMAN MUSHROOMS WITH SOUR CREAM

Serves 4 to 6

Always popular with guests...

1 lb. fresh mushrooms,
  stems removed
3 T. butter
1 tsp. onion salt
1/2 tsp. salt
1/8 tsp. pepper
2 T. white wine
2 T. sherry
3/4 cup sour cream
1 T. minced chives
3 T. chopped cucumber

Clean mushroom caps. Sauté in butter for four minutes. Add salts, pepper, white wine and sherry. Sauté one minute. Stir in sour cream, chives and cucumber. Heat through and serve immediately.

Mrs. Edwin B. Bosler

MADEIRA MUSHROOMS

Serves 4

Complements any meat entrée.

12 oz. sliced fresh
  mushrooms
1/4 cup margarine
1 T. onion soup mix
1/3 cup Madeira wine
pepper to taste (optional)

Sauté mushrooms in margarine. Sprinkle in soup mix and wine; stir and cook on medium high heat until liquid evaporates.

Mrs. Harry DuPrey

MUSHROOM-SPINACH CASSEROLE

Serves 4 to 6

Easy and delicious for buffet dining.

2 10-oz. pkgs. frozen
　chopped spinach,
　cooked and drained
1 tsp. salt
1 or 2 T. chopped onion
2 T. melted butter
1 lb. fresh mushrooms,
　sliced
2 T. butter
garlic salt
1 cup evaporated milk
1 cup grated American
　cheese

Preheat oven to 350 degrees. Line 9 x 9-inch shallow baking dish with cooked spinach which has been seasoned with salt, chopped onion and melted butter. Wash and dry mushrooms. Slice and sauté in butter. Arrange mushrooms over spinach, sprinkle with a little garlic salt. Prepare sauce by mixing milk and cheese in a saucepan. Bring to a simmer and allow to cook 2 or 3 minutes. Spoon sauce over mushrooms. Bake about 20 minutes, then place under broiler for several minutes until the top is golden brown.

Mrs. Barnard A. Savage, Jr.

STUFFED MUSHROOMS

Serves 8

Company casserole with an appealing zing!!!

1 lb. very large fresh
　mushrooms
1/3 cup butter
1 medium onion, finely
　chopped
3 slices soft bread
1/2 tsp. salt
1/4 tsp. pepper
1 T. catsup
1 T. lemon juice
4 slices bacon
1/2 cup half and half
fresh parsley

Preheat oven to 400 degrees. Wash mushrooms and dry well; remove stems and coarsely chop. Melt butter and cook onions and mushroom stems. Tear enough bread into small pieces to equal 2-1/4 cups. Add bread to onion mixture and cook 2 minutes. Remove from heat and add salt, pepper, catsup and lemon juice. Stuff mushroom caps with mixture and place in a 1-1/2-quart casserole. Garnish each cap with 2 narrow strips of bacon placed to form a cross. Pour cream around mushrooms. Bake for 20 minutes. Serve in baking dish, garnished with parsley.

Mrs. H. W. Jordan

148

ONIONS PARMESAN

Serves 6 to 8

Consommé adds color and flavor...

3 T. butter
3 T. flour
1 cup canned consommé
1/4 cup dry or medium
   sherry (or dry
   vermouth)
1/4 cup freshly grated
   Parmesan cheese
2 T. chopped fresh
   parsley
salt and pepper to taste
2 1-lb. jars small whole
   onions, drained
1/4 cup fine dry bread
   crumbs
2 T. melted butter

Preheat oven to 375 degrees. Melt butter and stir in flour. When mixture bubbles, add consommé, sherry, cheese, parsley, salt and pepper. Combine sauce with onions. Turn into greased 1-1/2-quart casserole. Mix crumbs and melted butter; sprinkle over onions. Bake for 25 minutes.

Mrs. James E. Sullivan

SCALLOPED PINEAPPLE BAKE

Serves 16

Serve this dish as an accompaniment to ham.

1/2 cup butter
1 cup granulated sugar
2 eggs
2 16-oz. cans pineapple
   chunks, drained
2 cups milk
4 cups cubed bread
   (Vienna style is best)

Cream butter and sugar. Add eggs and beat well. Add pineapple, milk and bread; mix together gently. It may have a curdled appearance. Pour into a buttered 12 x 8-inch pan. Refrigerate overnight. Preheat oven to 350 degrees. Bake for 1-1/2 to 2 hours, uncovered.

Mrs. Thomas Johnson

PEAS A LA ROBERT

Serves 6 to 8

Delicate blend of flavors...

1/2 lb. fresh mushrooms
1 T. butter
2 10-oz. pkgs. frozen
   LeSeur peas
6 finely chopped scallions
2 cups shredded lettuce
1 T. granulated sugar
3 T. whipping cream
1 tsp. chopped fresh
   parsley
salt and pepper to taste

Slice mushrooms and sauté until tender in melted butter in large pan. Cook peas until just tender; drain well. Add peas and all other ingredients except lettuce to mushrooms. Heat through; add lettuce and serve as soon as lettuce is warm.

Mrs. Donald J. Ross

PEAS AND CELERY

Serves 8

A nice change.

2 10-oz. pkgs. frozen
   peas
4 stalks celery, thinly
   sliced
1-1/2 chicken bouillion
   cubes
2 T. butter
1 tsp. or more basil
1/2 cup sherry
2-oz. slivered almonds

Put all ingredients into a saucepan of boiling water and steam for 7 to 8 minutes, covered. KEEP COVERED! Remove from heat and let stand 15 minutes, covered, before serving.

Mrs. Donald J. Ross

SPINACH SOUFFLE

Serves 6 to 8

A cheesy version of a luncheon classic.

1 16-oz. carton small
   curd cottage cheese
2 T. minced onion
2 T. chopped parsley
1/4 tsp. salt
1/8 tsp. pepper
1 tsp. Worcestershire
   sauce
1/2 tsp. freshly grated
   nutmeg
1/2 tsp. thyme
3 eggs, well beaten
1/4 cup flour
1 10-oz. pkg. frozen
   chopped spinach,
   thawed and well
   drained
2 cups grated Swiss
   cheese

Preheat oven to 350 degrees. Mix cottage cheese with spices, eggs and flour. Blend well. Add spinach and Swiss cheese; mix well. Pour into greased 11 x 7-inch baking pan. Bake for 45 minutes.

Mrs. Marvin R. East

SPINACH AU GRATIN

Serves 4

A great topping for baked potatoes, too!

4 slices bacon
1/4 to 1/2 cup spinach
   liquid
2 cups chopped cooked
   spinach
1/3 cup grated American
   cheese

Preheat oven to 350 degrees. Fry bacon until crisp. Remove from pan. Discard all but 2 T. bacon grease. Mix spinach liquid and drained spinach with bacon grease. Pour into a greased one-quart casserole. Top with cheese and crumbled bacon. Bake for 20 minutes.

Kathleen Mollison

SPINACH STUFFED ZUCCHINI

Serves 6

Colorful company vegetable...

3 medium zucchini
1 10-oz. pkg. frozen
   chopped spinach,
   thawed and drained
2 T. flour
1/2 cup milk
salt to taste
1/3 cup shredded
   Cheddar cheese
4 slices crisp bacon,
   cooked and crumbled

Preheat oven to 350 degrees. Bring 2 quarts water to a boil in large saucepan. Trim ends of zucchini and cook whole in boiling water for 10 to 12 minutes. Drain well and cut in half lengthwise. Scoop out centers and chop. Mix chopped zucchini and spinach. In saucepan, blend flour and milk; add spinach mixture. Cook and stir until thick. Place zucchini halves in a 9 x 9-inch baking dish; sprinkle with salt. Spoon spinach mixture into shells; top with cheese and bacon. Bake for 15 to 20 minutes.

Mrs. Geoffrey C. Murphy

SAVVY SPINACH

Serves 6

Spirited...

2 10-oz. pkgs. frozen
   chopped spinach,
   cooked and
   thoroughly drained
6 oz. cream cheese,
   cubed
1 cup sour cream
6 strips bacon, cooked
   and crumbled
1/2 cup chopped green
   onions
1-1/2 tsp. horseradish
   (optional)
dash salt
dash pepper

Preheat oven to 350 degrees. Blend spinach and cream cheese. Add rest of ingredients and mix thoroughly. Spoon into 1-1/2-quart casserole. Bake for 30 minutes.

NOTE: Sautéed mushrooms are a nice addition.

Mrs. John N. Fix

ZUCCHINI AND TOMATOES BEARNAISE

Serves 8 to 10

Delectable!

VEGETABLE MIXTURE
**8 medium zucchini, cut
  in 1/2 inch slices
3 T. butter
8 tomatoes, quartered
1/2 cup sliced onions
1 tsp. seasoned salt
1 clove garlic, crushed
1/2 tsp. pepper
2 T. lime juice
1/8 tsp. Tabasco**

Sauté zucchini in melted butter in very large skillet for 6 minutes, turning occasionally. Add tomatoes and onions and cook for 2 additional minutes, stirring. Add salt, garlic, pepper, lime juice and Tabasco and sauté 2 minutes longer. Place in 9 x 12-inch baking dish.

BEARNAISE SAUCE
**1 T. tarragon vinegar
3 T. white wine
1 tsp. tarragon
1 T. minced onion
1/8 tsp. pepper
3 egg yolks
1 T. lime juice
dash Tabasco
6 T. butter
1/2 cup buttered crumbs**

Combine vinegar, wine, tarragon, onion and pepper in saucepan; boil until reduced by half. Pour into blender and cool. Add egg yolks, lime juice and Tabasco; blend. Heat butter until it foams, but do not brown. Turn on blender and gradually add butter; blend until thick. Cover vegetables with Bearnaise Sauce; sprinkle with buttered crumbs. Place under broiler until golden brown.

Mrs. Howard R. Hayes

STUFFED ZUCCHINI

Serves 10 to 12

Flavorful combination!

6 medium zucchini
1 large onion, chopped
2 cloves garlic, minced
  (optional)
1 T. butter
1 T. minced parsley
1 10-oz. pkg. frozen
  chopped spinach,
  cooked, drained
1/4 cup dry
  bread crumbs
1/2 tsp. salt
1/2 tsp. pepper
3 eggs, beaten
1/2 cup grated
  American cheese

Boil whole zucchini until tender, but not soft. Cut in half lengthwise, remove and discard centers. Arrange in shallow buttered baking dish. Preheat oven to 350 degrees. Sauté onion and garlic. Add parsley, spinach, bread crumbs and seasonings. Stir in beaten eggs. Spoon stuffing into zucchini. Bake 15 minutes. Top with grated cheese and bake until cheese is bubbly.

Mrs. Alfred F. Buckman

COURGETTES FARCIS EN BATEAU

Serves 4

This makes a nice luncheon or supper dish.

2 medium zucchini
1 T. butter
2 T. chopped onion
2 fresh tomatoes,
  cored and chopped
1 clove minced garlic
salt and pepper to taste
1/2 cup fresh
  bread crumbs
1/2 cup grated
  Swiss cheese

Preheat oven to 350 degrees. Wash zucchini and cut lengthwise. Scoop out all the pulp, leaving only the shell—like a boat. Chop the pulp, removing seeds. Melt butter in a saucepan, add the onion and sauté for 3 minutes, but do not brown. Add the chopped tomatoes, zucchini pulp, garlic, salt and pepper to taste. Cook over high heat for about 5 minutes. Stuff the zucchini with this mixture. Sprinkle with mixture of bread crumbs and cheese. Place in a lightly oiled 11 x 7-inch shallow baking dish and bake for 40 minutes or until zucchini is tender when pierced with the point of a knife.

Mrs. James R. McClamroch

ZUCCHINI OR SUMMER SQUASH CASSEROLE

Serves 6 to 8

The pièce de résistance for a summer dinner!

3 generous cups squash
2 cups herb seasoned
stuffing, crumbled
1/3 cup melted butter
2 carrots, shredded
1 small onion, grated
1 2-oz. jar pimientos
1 cup cream of chicken
soup, undiluted
1/2 cup sour cream

Preheat oven to 350 degrees. Cut unpared squash into bite-size pieces. Lightly cook and drain. Mix stuffing with butter. Mix squash, carrots, onion, pimiento, soup and sour cream with 1/2 of the stuffing mixture. Put in greased 2-quart casserole and top with balance of stuffing. Bake 25 minutes or until brown and bubbly.

Mrs. John W. Puth

PEPPERS AND ZUCCHINI SAUTE *Serves 4 to 6*

Colorful change of pace...

3 slices bacon, cut in
1-inch pieces
1/2 cup sliced onions
1 green pepper, cut into
strips
2 red peppers, cut into
strips
1 medium zucchini, cut
into 1/2-inch slices
(1/2 lb.)
1/2 tsp. salt
1/4 tsp. thyme
leaves
dash pepper

In large skillet, sauté bacon until crisp. Remove bacon bits and set aside. Sauté onions until tender, about 5 minutes. Add peppers and zucchini. Sprinkle with salt, thyme and pepper. Cook over medium heat, covered, 15 minutes or just until vegetables are tender. Turn into serving dish and sprinkle with bacon.

Mrs. G. Preston Kendall

ZUCCHINI A LA SUISSE

Serves 5 to 6

Golden brown cheese tops this great vegetable dish...

3 cups thinly sliced
  zucchini
1 large Bermuda onion,
  sliced
2 T. butter
2 eggs, beaten
1/4 cup milk
1 tsp. salt
1/2 tsp. dry mustard
white pepper to taste
1 cup grated Swiss
  cheese

Preheat oven to 375 degrees. Sauté zucchini and onions in butter until squash is tender; place in 1-1/2-quart baking dish. Mix eggs, milk, salt, dry mustard, white pepper and 1/2 cup Swiss cheese. Pour mixture over zucchini; top with remaining 1/2 cup cheese. Bake until firm—about 20 minutes.

Mrs. G. Preston Kendall

CHEESY ZUCCHINI

Serves 8

Distinctive flavor.

4 medium zucchini,
  sliced thick
1 medium onion,
  chopped
2 T. butter
2 T. flour
1/2 cup white wine
1 cup cream of
  mushroom soup
1 cup grated Cheddar
  cheese

Preheat oven to 350 degrees. Parboil zucchini in salted water. Drain thoroughly. Place single layer in a buttered 9 x 13-inch Pyrex baking dish. Brown onion in butter. Add flour, wine and soup. Mix well and pour over zucchini. Sprinkle cheese evenly on top. Bake for 30 minutes.

Mrs. Samuel H. Ellis

YELLOW SQUASH SOUFFLE
Serves 6

A good hearty dish.

**2 lbs. yellow squash,
  sliced
1/2 lb. grated sharp
  cheese
4 slices white bread,
  crumbled
2 eggs, slightly beaten
salt and pepper to taste
1/4 cup butter, softened
green peas (optional)**

Preheat oven to 350 degrees. Grease 1-1/2-quart casserole. Cook squash in small amount of water approximately 10 minutes. Drain and mash squash; blend in cheese. Stir in crumbled bread, eggs, seasonings and butter. Pour into casserole. Bake 30 minutes. If desired, sprinkle cooked tiny peas over the top as a garnish.

Mrs. Wilfred H. Heitmann

CREAMY BAKED ACORN SQUASH
Serves 6 to 8

A delicious twice-baked squash.

**2 large or 3 small acorn
  squash
1 medium onion, finely
  chopped
1 cup sour cream
1/2 tsp. salt
1/2 tsp. dill
chopped parsley**

Preheat oven to 350 degrees. Cut squash into halves or quarters. Place cut side down in a 9 x 13-inch Pyrex pan with 1/2 inch water. Bake squash for 30 minutes, or until soft. Remove from oven. Drain. Scoop out squash and mix with remaining ingredients. Place seasoned squash back in shells and heat in oven until hot. Garnish with parsley and serve.

Mrs. Samuel H. Ellis

CHEESE SOUFFLE TOMATOES

Serves 8

Colorful vegetable-rice combination...

8 large firm tomatoes
1/4 cup butter
1/4 cup flour
1-1/4 tsp.salt
1/8 tsp. pepper
dash nutmeg
1/8 tsp. seasoned salt
1 cup milk
1/4 cup whipping cream
1-1/2 cups grated
  Swiss cheese
1-1/2 cups cooked rice
1/4 cup snipped parsley
4 egg yolks

Preheat oven to 350 degrees. Wash tomatoes; cut off tops and scoop out pulp. Drain, upside down. Melt butter; stir in flour, salt, pepper, nutmeg and seasoned salt. Slowly add milk and cream. Cook until smooth and thick. Reserve 2 T. cheese and add remaining cheese to sauce. Remove from heat. Stir in rice, parsley and egg yolks, one at a time. Cut foil collars to fit around each tomato, extending 1 inch above top of tomato. Fill tomatoes with cheese mixture and place in shallow 9 x 13-inch baking dish. Sprinkle with reserved cheese. Bake for 30 minutes. Remove foil before serving.

Mrs. Thomas M. Ritchie, Jr.

GREENBACK TOMATOES

Serves 8 to 12

Yummy partyfare...

12 *thick* **tomato slices**
2 10-oz. pkgs. frozen
  chopped spinach
2 cups fresh bread
  crumbs
6 chopped scallions
6 eggs, slightly beaten
3/4 cup melted butter
1/4 cup grated fresh
  Parmesan cheese
1/4 tsp. Worcestershire
  sauce
1/4 tsp. Tabasco sauce
1 tsp. salt
1 tsp. thyme
1/4 to 1/2 tsp. pepper

Preheat oven to 350 degrees. Arrange tomato slices in single layer in 9 x 13-inch baking dish. Cook spinach; drain well. Combine spinach with remaining ingredients; spread over tomatoes. Bake for 15 minutes.

Mrs. David M. Stone

EGGPLANT ITALIANO

Serves 6

Great company vegetable!

3 medium eggplants,
  peeled and cubed
1 green pepper, chopped
2 small onions, chopped
4 T. butter or margarine
1 tsp. salt
dash pepper
1/2 tsp. thyme, oregano
  or basil
1 egg, slightly beaten
3 tomatoes, peeled and
  sliced
1/2 cup seasoned bread
  crumbs

Preheat oven to 350 degrees. Cook eggplant in salted water until tender. Drain. Brown green pepper and onions in 2 T. butter. Mix carefully with eggplant, seasonings and egg. Place half of eggplant mixture in ungreased 2-quart casserole. Arrange half of tomato slices on top of eggplant. Repeat. Mix 2 T. melted butter with seasoned crumbs. Sprinkle crumb mixture on top. Bake for 45 minutes.

NOTE: May be doubled and made a day ahead.

Mrs. Arthur A. Frank, Jr.

CORN FLAKE POTATO CASSEROLE

Serves 8 to 12

Easy company side dish with a golden, crunchy topping.

2 10-oz. pkgs. hash
  brown potatoes,
  defrosted
1/2 cup melted butter
  or margarine
1 tsp. salt
1/2 tsp. pepper
1/2 cup chopped onion
1 10-3/4-oz. can cream
  of chicken soup
1 pint sour cream
2 cups grated sharp
  Cheddar cheese
1 cup chopped ham
  (optional)
2 tsp. chopped pimiento
2 cups crushed corn
  flakes
1/4 cup melted butter

Preheat oven to 350 degrees. Mix all ingredients together except corn flakes and 1/4 cup melted butter. Place potato mixture in a buttered 2-1/2-quart casserole. Mix corn flakes with melted butter and put on potato mixture. Bake for 45 minutes.

NOTE: May be made earlier in the day and refrigerated; do not add corn flakes until ready to bake.

Mrs. Lyman Missimer

TASTY POTATO STRIPS

Serves 4 to 6

Great with hamburgers!

4 large baking potatoes
1/2 cup butter or
** margarine, melted**
3/4 to 1 cup seasoned
** bread crumbs**
1/4 to 1/2 tsp. nutmeg

Preheat oven to 400 degrees. Butter a 9 x 13-inch Pyrex pan. Peel potatoes and cut lengthwise into 1/8-inch strips and place in pan. Mix seasoned crumbs and nutmeg. Sprinkle half of crumbs over potatoes. Gently spoon half of melted butter on potatoes. Bake for 20 minutes. Carefully flip potatoes over. Sprinkle remaining crumbs and melted butter over potatoes. Bake another 20 to 25 minutes. Serve immediately.

VARIATIONS: To each cup of regular bread crumbs add 1/2 tsp. bon appétit and 1/2 tsp. seasoned salt. Fresh Parmesan cheese (1/4 cup) can be added to each 3/4 cup regular crumbs with 1/2 tsp. garlic salt.

Mrs. Harry DuPrey

CHEESY POTATOES

Serves 10 to 12

Au gratin potatoes the easy way...

6 medium potatoes
1 cup sour cream
2 cups creamed cottage
** cheese**
1/4 cup grated onion
2 tsp. salt or to taste
3/4 cup grated sharp
** Cheddar cheese**

Cook potatoes; peel and cube. Combine with sour cream, cottage cheese, onion and salt. Place in a buttered 9 x 13-inch casserole. Top with cheese. Bake at 350 degrees for 20 to 30 minutes.

Mrs. Robert W. Htggins

POTATO CASSEROLE

Serves 8 to 12

Tender and creamy...

7 large potatoes
2 tsp. salt
2 10-3/4-oz. cans cream
of chicken soup
2/3 cup milk
1-1/4 cups grated sharp
Cheddar cheese
1 medium onion, grated
pepper, if desired

Peel and cube potatoes; parboil for 5 minutes in just enough water to cover, adding salt. Drain potatoes. Mix soup and milk in saucepan and heat. Add one cup cheese, onion and pepper, if desired. Stir until cheese melts. Alternate layers of potatoes and soup mixture in a 1-1/2-quart casserole. Top with remaining cheese. Bake at 350 degrees for 30 to 40 minutes.

Mrs. Gerald North

WILD RICE CASSEROLE

Serves 8

Do ahead for your dinner party!

1 cup wild rice
1/2 cup salad oil
1/2 cup chopped onions
1 cup canned tomatoes,
chopped
1 cup liquid from
tomatoes
1 cup chopped ripe olives
1 cup coarsely chopped
fresh mushrooms
salt and pepper
1 cup grated American
cheese

Rinse rice thoroughly 3 or 4 times. Cover with water and soak overnight. Drain rice. Preheat oven to 350 degrees. Place 2 T. of oil in skillet and cook onions slightly. Add tomato liquid and heat to boiling. Remove from heat and mix in tomatoes, olives, mushrooms, seasonings, rice, rest of oil and cheese. Place in a greased 2-quart casserole. Bake for one hour.

Mrs. John Vratimos

BAKED NOODLE DISH

Moist and creamy...make-ahead too!

1 8-oz. pkg. thin noodles
1 3-oz. pkg. cream cheese
1 cup sour cream
1 cup cottage cheese
1/4 cup finely chopped
  onions
2 T. Worcestershire sauce
1/2 tsp. salt
1/4 tsp. pepper
1 T. poppy seeds

Preheat oven to 325 degrees. Cook noodles. Drain thoroughly. Cut cream cheese in small pieces and blend thoroughly with sour cream, cottage cheese, onions and seasonings. Add cooked noodles and mix. Pour into a greased 1-1/2-quart casserole. Bake 30 to 40 minutes, or until warmed through.

NOTE: Add 1 T. of oil when cooking noodles to prevent boil-over.

Mrs. A. W. Phelps

NOODLES PARMESAN

Serves 6 to 8

A good company side dish.

1 large onion, chopped
2 T. butter
3/4 cup cottage cheese
1-1/2 cups sour cream
1-1/2 tsp.
  Worcestershire sauce
1/8 tsp. Tabasco sauce
1 tsp. Accent
1/4 tsp. pepper
1 tsp. salt
8 oz. medium egg
  noodles, cooked
1/4 cup Parmesan
  cheese
paprika
chopped parsley
  (optional)

Preheat oven to 350 degrees. Sauté onions in butter. Add cottage cheese, sour cream and seasonings; mix. Blend sauce and noodles together. Place in a 2-quart buttered casserole. Sprinkle with cheese. Cover and bake for 30 minutes; uncover and bake 10 minutes more. Sprinkle with paprika and parsley.

Mrs. Franklin A. Urbahns

NOODLES ALFREDO

Serves 6 to 8

Parmesan noodles— nice change from macaroni and cheese.

1 lb. noodles
1/2 cup butter
2/3 cup whipping cream
1-1/4 cups grated fresh
　Parmesan cheese
1/4 tsp. salt
dash white pepper
chopped parsley

Cook and drain noodles. Heat butter and cream in medium saucepan until butter is melted. Remove from heat. Add 1 cup Parmesan cheese, salt and pepper and stir until sauce is blended and fairly smooth. Add to noodles, tossing until well coated. Sprinkle with remaining Parmesan cheese and chopped parsley.

Mrs. Carroll G. Wells

PESTO GENOVESE

Serves 6 to 8

Prime pasta!

3 cups fresh basil
1 clove garlic, peeled
1/4 cup pignoli
　(pine nuts)
1/4 cup butter, softened
1/4 cup olive oil
1/2 cup freshly grated
　Parmesan cheese
salt to taste
2 lbs. spaghetti

Wash basil and pat it dry. Pull off the leaves, using part of the leaf stem if the herb is young and tender. Put the basil leaves, garlic, pignoli, butter, oil, Parmesan cheese and salt in a food processor and blend until puréed. The pesto will have the consistency of a thick purée. Cook the spaghetti according to package directions or to the desired degree of doneness. Drain it quickly in a colander and empty it immediately into a hot serving dish. Add the pesto and toss quickly. Serve with additional Parmesan cheese.

NOTE: Fresh basil can be purchased at a garden or specialty store.

Kenilworth Union Church

SPAGHETTI SPINACH BAKE

Serves 6

A hearty vegetarian entrée.

1/2 lb. fresh mushrooms,
  sliced
4 green onions, sliced
5 T. butter or margarine
2 T. flour
2 cups milk
1/2 tsp. salt
1/2 tsp. basil
1/8 tsp. pepper
dash nutmeg
8 oz. cooked spaghetti
2 cups shredded
  Mozzarella cheese
2 cups chopped fresh
  spinach

Preheat oven to 350 degrees. Stir fry mushrooms and onions in 3 T. butter for one minute. Set aside. Melt 2 T. butter in medium saucepan. Stir in flour, milk and seasonings until smooth. Cook and stir constantly until thickened. Place half the spaghetti in bottom of a 2-1/2 quart casserole. Put 1 cup of Mozzarella on top and then half of the mushroom mixture. Add all the spinach and then repeat layers. Pour cream sauce evenly over top. Bake for 20 to 30 minutes or until bubbly. Let stand 5 minutes before serving.

Paula Nordhem

SPAGHETTI CARBONARA

Serves 8

A dashing side dish...

1 lb. thin spaghetti
  or linguini
8 slices bacon, finely
  chopped
2 T. olive oil
1/3 cup dry white wine
4 eggs, at room
  temperature
1 cup grated Parmesan
  or Romano cheese
1/3 cup chopped fresh
  parsley
freshly ground black
  pepper

Place 2-1/2-quart casserole in a warm oven to heat. Cook pasta in 4 quarts of boiling salted water for 8 to 10 minutes or until *al dente.* Meanwhile, fry bacon until crisp and drain. Pour oil in a clean skillet, add bacon pieces and stir in wine. Cook over medium heat until wine has evaporated. Remove from heat. Beat eggs well; stir in cheese and parsley. As soon as pasta is cooked and drained, transfer into heated casserole dish. Add the egg/cheese mixture; toss until well combined. Add the bacon/wine mixture and toss again. Serve *immediately* with plenty of freshly ground black pepper.

Paula Nordhem

PASTA PRIMAVERA

Serves 6 to 8

Colorful combination of vegetables and spaghetti.

1 lb. spaghetti
2 T. butter or oil
1-1/2 cups coarsely
  chopped broccoli
1-1/2 cups snow peas
1 cup sliced zucchini
1 cup fresh or frozen
  baby peas
1 T. olive oil
2 medium tomatoes,
  chopped
1 T. minced garlic
1/4 cup chopped fresh
  parsley
salt and freshly ground
  pepper to taste
1/4 cup olive oil
1/3 cup pine nuts
  (pignoli)
10 sliced mushrooms
1 cup whipping cream
1/2 cup Parmesan cheese
1/3 cup butter
4 to 5 tsp. basil

Cook spaghetti with oil until barely tender; drain and set aside. Blanch broccoli, snow peas, zucchini and baby peas in boiling water for 3 to 4 minutes. Drain, rinse in cold water and set aside. In a medium skillet, heat 1 T. olive oil. Add tomatoes, 1 tsp. garlic, parsley, salt and pepper. Sauté 2 to 3 minutes. Set aside and keep warm. Heat small amount of butter or olive oil in large skillet and brown pine nuts. Add remaining oil and garlic, mushrooms and blanched vegetables. Simmer a few minutes. Add spaghetti, cream, Parmesan cheese, butter and basil. Mix gently with a fork. Top with sautéed tomatoes and serve immediately.

NOTE: Several grated carrots may be added at the last minute for color.

Mrs. Donald J. Ross

CHEESE GRITS SOUFFLE

Serves 8

Not unlike spoonbread...

6 cups water
1 tsp. salt
1-1/2 cups grits
3/4 cup butter
  or margarine
1 lb. Velveeta cheese,
  cubed
4 eggs

Preheat oven to 325 degrees. Boil grits in salted water for 10 minutes or until done. Add butter and cheese. Beat eggs and fold in. Cook about 2 minutes. Put in buttered 3-quart casserole and bake 45 minutes.

NOTE: Cheddar or garlic cheese will perk up the flavor.

Mrs. E. C. Blomeyer

BERT'S SPOON BREAD

Serves 6

Splendid side dish.

2 cups milk
1/4 cup yellow cornmeal
1/4 cup grits
1-1/2 tsp. butter
3/4 tsp. salt
4 eggs, separated

Preheat oven to 350 degrees. Heat milk to boiling; stir in cornmeal and grits. Cook 10 minutes, until a smooth mush. Remove from heat, add butter and salt. When cool, add unbeaten egg yolks. Mix well. Beat egg whites until stiff; fold gently into cornmeal mixture. Pour into a well-greased 2-quart baking dish. Bake for one hour or until golden. *Serve at once.* Top with melted butter or mushroom sauce.

Mrs. Julien H. Collins

Eggs and Cheese

ANYTIME CASSEROLE

Serves 4 to 5

Perfect for breakfast, brunch or a light supper!

8 slices bacon
2 cups bread pieces
1-3/4 cups milk
8 eggs
salt and pepper to taste
4 T. butter or margarine
4 oz. Swiss cheese,
   grated
Lawry's seasoned salt
2 T. melted butter
1/2 cup bread crumbs

Preheat oven to 450 degrees. Pan fry bacon until crisp; crumble. Set aside. Soak bread pieces in milk. Drain milk and save. Beat eggs slightly. Add salt, pepper and drained milk. Melt 4 T. butter in fry pan. Cook eggs slightly (until barely held together). Add bread mix. Place egg mixture in a greased 1-quart casserole. Cover with grated cheese. Sprinkle with seasoned salt and bacon. Mix 2 T. melted butter and bread crumbs together. Top with buttered bread crumbs. Bake for 15 to 20 minutes.

NOTE: Can be frozen before cooking, but more cooking time will be needed. Recipe may be doubled and baked in an 8 x 13-inch Pyrex pan.

Mrs. J. Wendell Crain

SWISS EGGS

Serves 8

An attractive entrée for Sunday breakfast or brunch.

12 slices Canadian bacon
12 slices Swiss cheese
12 eggs
1/2 pint half and half
Parmesan cheese, grated

Preheat oven to 450 degrees. Line a 9 x 13-inch casserole with Canadian bacon. Add layer of Swiss cheese. Carefully break the eggs over the casserole without breaking yolks. Drizzle with cream until the yolks peek through. Bake for 10 minutes. Remove from oven and sprinkle generously with Parmesan cheese. Bake for 8 to 10 more minutes. Cut into squares and serve immediately.

Mrs. Lyman Missimer

EGGS HUSSARDE

Serves 1

Superb for a small elegant brunch.

2 large thin ham slices,
  grilled
2 Holland Rusks
1/4 cup Marchand de Vin
  sauce
2 slices tomato, grilled
2 soft poached eggs
1/4 cup Hollandaise
  sauce
paprika

Lay a slice of ham across each Holland Rusk; cover with Marchand de Vin sauce. Lay slices of tomato on the sauce; place poached egg on tomato slices. Top with Hollandaise sauce; garnish with a sprinkling of paprika.

MARCHAND DE VIN SAUCE

3/4 cup butter
1/3 cup finely chopped
  mushrooms
1/2 cup minced ham
1/3 cup finely chopped
  shallots
1/2 cup finely chopped
  onion
2 T. minced garlic
2 T. flour
1/2 tsp. salt
1/8 tsp. pepper
dash cayenne
3/4 cup beef stock
1/2 cup red wine

Melt butter and lightly sauté mushrooms, ham, shallots, onion and garlic. When onion is golden brown, add flour and seasonings. Brown well, about 7 to 10 minutes. Blend in stock and wine and simmer over low heat 35 to 45 minutes. Excels on broiled steaks. Makes 2 cups.

HOLLANDAISE SAUCE

4 egg yolks
2 T. fresh lemon juice
1 cup butter
1/4 tsp. salt
salt and pepper

Beat egg yolks and stir in lemon juice. Cook very slowly in top of double boiler, never allowing the water in the bottom to come to a boil. Melt butter and add *very slowly* while stirring constantly with a wooden spoon. Add salt, further season to taste, and continue cooking slowly until thickened. Makes 1 cup.

Mrs. Reid Engelmann

LAYERED EGG BRUNCH

Serves 12

May be fixed ahead, refrigerated and baked just before serving.

SAUCE
4 slices bacon
1/4 cup butter
**1/2 lb. sliced fresh
    mushrooms**
**1/2 lb. coarsely shredded
    chipped beef**
1/2 cup flour
pepper to taste
1 quart milk

Sauté bacon and remove from fry pan. Add butter to bacon fat and melt. Sauté mushrooms in fat. Add chipped beef. Sprinkle flour and pepper over mushroom/beef mixture. Gradually stir in milk. Cook sauce until thickened and smooth, stirring constantly. Crumble bacon into sauce. Set aside.

Preheat oven to 275 degrees. For scrambled eggs, melt butter in a clean, large skillet. Combine eggs, evaporated milk and salt and scramble in butter. In a 13 x 9-inch Pyrex pan, alternate 4 layers, 2 of eggs and 2 of sauce, ending with sauce. Cover and bake for one hour. Garnish with parsley.

SCRAMBLED EGGS
1/4 cup butter
18 eggs
1 cup evaporated milk
1/4 tsp. salt

Mrs. Edward R. James

CHEESE BAKE

Serves 4 to 6

Super strata...so easy and so good!

8 slices bread
soft butter
2 cups ground ham
**2 T. prepared mustard
    or to taste**
2 cups grated cheese
2 eggs
2 cups milk

Butter bread on one side and cut each slice into quarters. Put half of bread, buttered side down, in a 12 x 8-inch casserole. Top with ham and dot with mustard. Cover with cheese. Cover with rest of bread, buttered side up. Beat eggs into milk. Pour over casserole. Let stand 30 minutes before baking in a 350 degree oven for 50 to 60 minutes.

NOTE: Super with mushroom sauce, too.

Mrs. Fred L. Stone

NAN'S EGG CASSEROLE

Serves 10 to 12

Tasty combination...

18 hard cooked eggs, thinly sliced
1/2 lb. bacon, fried and crumbled

SAUCE
1/4 cup butter
1 clove garlic, minced
1/2 cup flour
1 cup whipping cream, at room temperature
1 cup milk, at room temperature
1 lb. Cheddar cheese, grated
1/4 tsp. thyme
1/4 tsp. marjoram
1/4 tsp. basil
1/4 cup snipped fresh parsley

To prepare sauce, sauté garlic briefly in melted butter. Add flour, stirring constantly, until mixture bubbles. Gradually add cream and milk while continuing to stir. When mixture thickens, add cheese and seasonings and stir until cheese melts. Spoon 1/3 of sauce into a 9 x 12-inch baking dish. Top with half of eggs and half of bacon. Spoon 1/3 more of sauce on top and repeat egg and bacon layers. Top with rest of sauce. Casserole is best if made one or two days in advance and refrigerated. Bring casserole to room temperature before baking at 350 degrees for 25 to 30 minutes or until bubbly.

Mrs. Dane F. Hahn

SYRIAN THETCHOUKA VAN ELK

Serves 6 to 8

Interesting vegetarian combo...

4 large onions, sliced
4 T. vegetable oil
2 green peppers, cut in strips
1-1/2 lbs. peas (fresh, canned or frozen)
6 large tomatoes, cut in eighths
salt and pepper to taste
6 to 8 eggs
2 cups grated Cheddar cheese

Preheat oven to 375 degrees. Sauté onions in oil until golden. Add green pepper and cook for 3 minutes. Add peas; cook until tender. Add tomatoes. Continue cooking and turning vegetables until all are tender but not mushy. Season to taste. Transfer vegetables to a buttered 9 x 13-inch casserole (not metal). Make 6 to 8 hollows in the mixture and carefully drop an egg into each one. Sprinkle with cheese. Bake for 10 minutes—until eggs are set. Serve with rice pilaf.

Mrs. Jaak van Elk

SOUFFLE AU FROMAGE

Mellow yellow...

3 T. butter
3 T. flour
1 cup boiling milk
1/2 tsp. salt
1/8 tsp. freshly ground
pepper
pinch cayenne
pinch nutmeg
4 egg yolks
6 egg whites
pinch salt
3/4 to 1-1/2 cups grated
Gruyère

Preheat oven to 400 degrees. Prepare 6-cup soufflé dish by coating the inside with a little butter and a sprinkling of cheese. Melt butter in a small saucepan. Stir in flour and cook a minute or two without browning. Off heat, whisk in hot milk, stirring until the mixture is smooth. Add seasoning, return pan to heat and cook for one minute, stirring until the mixture is thick and smooth. Remove from heat. Let cool before beating in the egg yolks, one by one. Sauce may rest at this point; dot with butter to prevent a skin from forming and reheat to tepid before continuing. Whisk or beat egg whites with a pinch of salt until peaks are firmly formed. Stir one quarter of the egg whites into the sauce with the cheese. Gently fold in the remaining egg whites. Fill mold three-quarters full, tap dish lightly and smooth top. To make the traditional cap, make a one-inch groove in the mixture one inch from the edge of the dish. Set dish in the middle of the oven and lower the heat to 375 degrees. Leave undisturbed for 25 minutes, until the soufflé is puffed and golden. Sprinkle the top with a little grated cheese and cook a few minutes more until the desired inner texture is reached. Test with a skewer or thin knife.

Mrs. David D. Schafer

CHEESE-CRUSTED MUSHROOM SOUFFLE

Serves 2 to 4

Light and flavorful!

5 T. butter or margarine
1/2 lb. fresh mushrooms, finely chopped
1 T. chopped green onion
1/2 tsp. salt
1/4 tsp. white pepper
dash nutmeg
3 T. flour
1 cup milk
2 T. dry sherry
5 eggs, separated
1-1/4 cups shredded Swiss cheese

Preheat oven to 350 degrees. In a large skillet melt butter, add mushrooms and onion. Cook until all liquid evaporates (about 5 minutes). Add salt, pepper, nutmeg and flour; stir until blended. Gradually stir in milk and sherry; cook, stirring, until mixture boils and thickens. Remove from heat and blend in egg yolks one at a time. Beat egg whites until stiff, moist peaks form. Fold into mushroom mixture, one-third at a time until just blended. Then fold in *one cup* Swiss cheese. Spoon into a 1-1/2-quart, buttered soufflé dish. Sprinkle top with remaining cheese. Bake for 35 to 40 minutes or until puffed and golden. Serve immediately.

Mrs. Donald J. Ross

TOMATO QUICHE

Serves 6 to 8

Good and pretty!

1 9-inch deep unbaked pie crust
3 T. butter
3 large tomatoes, peeled, seeded, cored, chopped
1 medium onion, chopped
1 tsp. salt
1/4 tsp. thyme
1/4 tsp. basil
1/2 tsp. granulated sugar
1/2 lb. Swiss cheese, grated
3 eggs, beaten
1 cup half and half

Preheat oven to 400 degrees. Bake pie crust 10 minutes. Melt butter in large fry pan. Add tomatoes, onion, seasonings and sugar. Cook over medium heat until liquid is almost gone. Place cheese on crust; pour tomato mixture over cheese. Mix eggs and cream; pour over tomato mixture. Bake 10 minutes at 425 degrees, then 35 minutes at 375 degrees or until set. Let rest for a few minutes before cutting.

Mrs. Dane F. Hahn

WHOLE WHEAT QUICHE

Serves 6

Luscious and nutritious...

CRUST
1 cup whole wheat flour
1/2 tsp. salt
4 T. cold butter
  or margarine
4 T. cold water

FILLING
4 oz. Swiss cheese,
  grated
1 cup cooked vegetables
  (mushrooms and
  asparagus are good)
3 eggs
2 cups milk
1 tsp. salt
pepper (optional)
2 T. butter

Mix flour and salt together. With a pastry blender or 2 knives, cut butter into flour mixture until mixture resembles coarse cornmeal. Sprinkle cold water, one table-spoon at a time, over pastry mixture and mix with a fork. Shape pastry into a ball and *refrigerate overnight.* Roll the crust as thin as possible between 2 sheets of waxed paper. Carefully transfer pastry to 9-inch pie pan. Trim edges even with pan. Chill again.

Preheat oven to 350 degrees. Spread grated cheese on crust. Arrange vegetables on top of cheese. Mix eggs, milk and seasonings. Pour on top of vegetables. Dot butter on top. Bake for 1-1/4 to 1-1/2 hours. Let set a few minutes before serving.

Mrs. Len Young Smith

SALMON QUICHE

Serves 6 to 8

Delicate flavor, but not bland!

1 15-1/2 oz. can salmon
  (or substitute fresh
  poached salmon)
3/4 cup mayonnaise
3/4 cup milk
3 eggs
1-1/2 T. cornstarch
1/3 cup finely chopped
  onions
2-1/2 cups grated
  Cheddar cheese
unbaked 9-inch or 10-
  inch deep dish pie shell

Preheat oven to 350 degrees. Flake salmon, removing bones and skin, and set aside. Mix mayonnaise, milk, eggs and cornstarch well with mixer. Add onions and cheese; stir in salmon. Pour into pie shell. Bake for one hour or until knife inserted comes out clean. Chilled leftovers are tasty, too.

Mrs. Samuel H. Ellis

CHEESE DELIGHT

Serves 8 to 12

Golden brown brunch treat...

BATTER
1 cup butter
1/2 cup granulated sugar
4 eggs
1-1/2 cups milk
2-1/2 cups flour
2 tsp. baking powder
1 tsp. salt

FILLING
2 lbs. ricotta cheese
4 T. melted butter
2 eggs
2 T. granulated sugar
pinch salt

sour cream
jelly

To prepare batter, cream butter and sugar. Add eggs, one at a time, alternating with milk. Mix flour with baking powder and salt; add to mixture. Mix filling ingredients together thoroughly. Spread half of batter in a greased 9 x 12-inch baking dish. Carefully spread filling on batter; top with rest of batter. Refrigerate overnight. Bake at 350 degrees for 45 minutes or until golden. Serve in squares with sour cream and jelly. Also delicious with maple syrup.

NOTE: Recipe may be halved and baked in a 9 x 9-inch baking dish.

Mrs. Gerard Moons

ZUCCHINI CRESCENT PIE

Serves 6

This attractive quiche may be served as a luncheon entrée or a dinner vegetable.

1 8-oz. can crescent
    dinner rolls
3/4 cup cashew nuts
    (optional)
3 medium zucchini
3 T. butter
1/2 clove garlic, crushed
1/4 tsp. salt
1/4 tsp. dill weed
1/8 tsp. pepper
2 eggs, beaten
1 cup cubed Monterey
    Jack cheese
2 tsp. chopped parsley

Preheat oven to 325 degrees. Separate crescent dough into 8 triangles. Place in ungreased 8 or 9-inch pie pan, pressing pieces together to form a crust. Seal well. Sprinkle with nuts if desired. Slice zucchini 1/8-inch thick. Sauté in butter. Add seasonings. Spoon into crust; pour on eggs. Top with cheese and parsley. Bake for 45 to 50 minutes or until edges are golden brown.

Mrs. Philip N. Jones

PIZZA QUICHE

Serves 6 to 8

Spicy and appealing.

1 unbaked 10-inch
  quiche pastry shell or
  2 9-inch regular
  frozen shells
5 strips bacon, chopped
1 large sweet onion,
  peeled and chopped
4 medium tomatoes,
  peeled, seeded and
  chopped
1/2 tsp. granulated sugar
1 tsp. minced fresh basil
1 tsp. fresh thyme leaves
1/2 tsp. salt
pinch pepper
4 eggs
pinch cayenne
pinch nutmeg
2 cups hot milk
1 cup grated Mozzarella
  or Cheddar cheese

Preheat oven to 450 degrees. Line the unpricked pastry shell or shells with foil; fill with dried beans. Bake for 5 minutes. Carefully remove the beans and foil. Bake 5 to 7 minutes longer or until pastry is almost done. Reduce oven temperature to 375 degrees. In a skillet, fry bacon until crisp. Remove bacon from pan and set aside. Sauté onion in 3 T. bacon drippings for 3 minutes, add tomatoes and continue to sauté until *all* the liquid evaporates. Add sugar, basil and thyme and set aside. Beat eggs with salt, pepper, cayenne and nutmeg. Add hot milk a little at a time, beating continously. Continue to beat until the custard thickens slightly. Stir in 3/4 cup grated cheese. Spoon vegetables into pastry shell or shells; top with bacon; pour cheese custard over bacon and vegetables. Sprinkle remaining cheese on top. Bake until top is set, approximately 30 minutes.

Kathy Balderston

TOMATO PIE

Serves 4 to 5

Spicy, cheesey quiche...

1 9-inch baked deep dish
  pie shell
2 to 3 large tomatoes,
  sliced
2 T. snipped chives
3 to 4 scallions, minced
1/2 tsp. basil
2 cups shredded sharp
  Cheddar cheese
1/2 cup mayonnaise

Preheat oven to 375 degrees. Spread tomatoes over entire pie shell. Mix remaining ingredients and spread over tomatoes. Bake for 35 minutes or until brown. If desired, sausage or Canadian bacon may be added for a more filling main dish.

Mrs. Gordon R. Scott

ZUCCHINI AND MUSHROOM FRITTATA

Serves 6 to 8

Frankly fabulous...

1-1/2 cups minced
  zucchini
1-1/2 cups sliced
  mushrooms
3/4 cup chopped green
  pepper
3/4 cup chopped onion
1 clove garlic, minced
3 T. oil
6 eggs
1/4 cup half and half
1 lb. cream cheese, diced
2 cups stale white bread,
  cubed (crusts removed)
1-1/2 cups grated sharp
  Cheddar cheese
salt
pepper

Preheat oven to 350 degrees. Sauté zucchini, mushrooms, pepper, onion and garlic in oil for 5 minutes or until vegetables have softened. Remove and let cool. In bowl, beat eggs with cream. Then add cream cheese, bread, Cheddar cheese and vegetables. Salt and pepper to taste. Mix well. Pour into a well-buttered 9" or 10" spring form pan and bake 55 minutes or until set and browned. Let stand for 10 minutes. It may fall slightly in the middle. Remove sides of pan and transfer frittata, still on pan bottom, to heated serving plate. Cut into wedges with a very sharp knife and serve warm.

NOTE: A food processor or blender is almost a necessity for this recipe because the vegetables have to be chopped finely enough to blend with the eggs and cream. The frittata tastes good cold, too, and may be frozen.

Paula Nordhem

APPLE PANCAKE

Serves 4

A Father's Day special!

PANCAKE
3 large eggs
3/4 cup milk
3/4 cup flour
1/2 tsp. salt
1/2 cup thinly sliced
   apples
1-1/2 T. unsalted butter

Preheat oven to 450 degrees. Beat eggs, milk, flour and salt until smooth. Add thinly sliced apples. Melt butter in small cast-iron skillet (to be used for baking). Add batter to skillet, place in oven and bake 15 minutes at 450 degrees, then 10 minutes at 350 degrees. (If pancake puffs during baking, pierce with fork.) When pancake is brown and crisp, remove from oven. Place filling on top of pancake and serve.

FILLING
1/2 cup unsalted butter
1 lb. tart fresh apples,
   thinly sliced (approx. 5)
1 cup granulated sugar
cinnamon and nutmeg
   to taste

Prepare simultaneously with pancakes. In separate skillet, melt butter; add apples, sugar, cinnamon and nutmeg. Sauté approximately 5 minutes until apples are tender.

Mrs. James E. Sullivan

BIG DUTCH BABIES

Serves 2 or 3

Wonderfully puffy...

1/4 cup butter
3 eggs
3/4 cup milk
3/4 cup flour

Preheat oven to 425 degrees. Put butter in a 3-quart round Pyrex dish and place in oven. In blender, beat eggs on high speed one minute, gradually adding milk, then flour, continually whirling for 30 seconds. Remove bowl from oven and add the egg mixture. Do this quickly while the bowl is still hot. Bake in oven 20 to 25 minutes until well browned. Dust with confectioners sugar or lemon juice. Also good served with syrup or dusted with nutmeg. Must be served immediately.

Mrs. H. W. Jordan

COTTAGE CHEESE PANCAKES

Makes 12

The lightest fluffiest pancake ever—a cross between an omelette and a pancake.

4 eggs
1 cup creamed small curd
   cottage cheese
1/4 cup flour
1/2 tsp. salt

Separate eggs. Beat whites and keep in bowl. In another bowl, beat cottage cheese, yolks, flour and salt. Fold in whites. Cook on greased griddle. Need to be cooked long enough on first side so they hold together when flipped. Will stay puffy and warm in a 200 degree oven for a short time. Recipe can be doubled.

Mrs. Carl Fowler

MEXICAN QUICHE

Serves 6

Very colorful and appealing.

1 9-inch pie shell, baked

FILLING
6 thin slices ham, diced
1/2 onion, finely chopped
3 chilies, chopped
1 tomato, chopped
4-5 strips cooked bacon,
   crumbled
1/4 lb. Swiss cheese,
   grated
1/4 lb. sharp cheese,
   grated

CUSTARD
1 cup whipping cream
4 eggs, beaten
1 tsp. dry mustard

GARNISH
chopped parsley
nutmeg

Preheat oven to 450 degrees. Starting with ham and ending with cheese, layer one half of the filling ingredients in the pie shell. Repeat. Heat whipping cream slightly and add to eggs and mustard. Pour custard mixture over filling ingredients, jiggling pan to settle mixture. Sprinkle with parsley and nutmeg. Bake 35 to 45 minutes.

NOTE: If a hotter taste is preferred, use 1 to 3 jalapeños (hot chilies) instead of regular chilies.

Mrs. James Lynch

TOSTADA QUICHE

Terrific taste treat from South of the Border.

1 9-inch deep dish pastry shell
2 avocados, peeled and mashed
1 garlic clove, minced
3 T. lemon juice
1 tomato, peeled, seeded, chopped
1 4-oz. can whole green chilies, seeded, chopped (mild or hot depending on preference)
1/4 tsp. hot pepper sauce
8 oz. ground beef
1/4 cup chopped onion
1 to 2 T. taco seasoning mix
1-1/2 cups shredded Cheddar cheese
3 eggs, slightly beaten
1-1/2 cups half and half
1/2 tsp. salt
1/8 tsp. pepper
shredded lettuce
corn chips
chopped tomato

Preheat oven to 400 degrees. Do not prick the pastry shell. Bake 7 minutes. Remove from oven. Set aside. Reduce oven temperature to 375 degrees. In a small bowl, mix avocados, garlic and lemon juice. Stir in chopped tomato, 1 T. green chilies and hot pepper sauce. Cover and refrigerate. In a medium skillet, combine ground beef, onion, remaining green chilies and taco seasoning mix. Cook over medium high heat, stirring occasionally, until ground beef is browned and onion is tender. Drain ground beef mixture. Layer cheese and then ground beef mixture in the pastry shell. In a medium bowl, combine eggs, half and half, salt and pepper. Beat with fork or whisk until mixed well but not frothy. Pour egg mixture over ground beef mixture. Bake 45 minutes or until a knife inserted off-center comes out clean. Let stand 10 minutes before serving. Garnish with shredded lettuce, corn chips, additional chopped tomato and the avocado mixture.

Mrs. James Lynch

SOUR CREAM ENCHILADAS

Serves 6 to 8

For Mexican food fans...

2 cups sour cream
1 cup chopped green
  onions
1/4 tsp. cumin
4 cups shredded
  longhorn cheese
12 corn tortillas
salad oil
1 10-oz. can enchilada
  sauce

Preheat oven to 375 degrees. Blend 1-1/2 cups sour cream, 3/4 cup onions, cumin and cheese. Fry tortillas in hot oil (one at a time) until limp. Dip tortillas into hot enchilada sauce. Spread 2 to 3 tsp. sour cream filling down center of each tortilla. Fold each tortilla in half and roll up. Place side by side in 8 x 10-inch casserole dish. Bake uncovered for 20 minutes. Garnish with reserved sour cream and green onions.

Mrs. John G. Dorrer

AVOCADO ENCHILADAS

Makes 8 to 10

Attractive meatless dish to serve at a buffet brunch or supper.

8 to 10 corn tortillas
2 avocados, wedged or
  thinly sliced
3 chopped green onions,
  including tops
1/2 lb. Monterey Jack
  cheese, grated
1 8-oz. pkg. cream
  cheese, cut in spears
2 10-oz. cans green
  enchilada sauce
1 8-oz. carton sour cream

Preheat oven to 350 degrees. Heat corn tortillas in a greased skillet one at a time, until hot and pliable. Stack on top of one another in foil to keep warm until all are done. Into each tortilla, put some of the avocado, onion, grated cheese and cream cheese. Roll up and put seam down in a 13 x 8-inch Pyrex baking dish. Barely heat the enchilada sauce and stir in the sour cream. Pour over filled tortillas. Sprinkle with grated cheese. Bake for 10 minutes or until heated thoroughly. Garnish each enchilada with a wedge of avocado just before serving.

Mrs. James Lynch

CHILIE CHEESE CASSEROLE

Serves 6 to 8

Yummy brunch dish!

4 to 6 slices firm white
   bread
2 T. butter, softened
2 cups shredded sharp
   Cheddar cheese
2 cups shredded
   Monterey Jack cheese
1 4-oz. can green chilies
6 eggs
2 cups milk
2 tsp. paprika
1 tsp. salt
1/2 tsp. crushed oregano
1/2 tsp. black pepper
1/4 tsp. garlic powder
1/4 tsp. dry mustard

Trim crusts from bread and spread butter on one side of each slice. Arrange butter-side down in a 9 x 13-inch baking dish. Sprinkle cheeses over bread. Drain can of chilies. Remove seeds and finely mince chilies; distribute over cheeses. Beat together eggs, milk and spices; pour over cheeses. Cover and refrigerate overnight — or at least 6 hours. Bake uncovered at 325 degrees for 50 minutes or until top is lightly browned. Let stand for 10 minutes before serving.

Mrs. George W. Stamm

SAUSAGE CASSEROLE

Serves 9

Best made a day ahead and refrigerated overnight.

1 to 1-1/2 lbs. bulk pork
   sausage
9 eggs, slightly beaten
3 cups milk
1-1/2 tsp. dry mustard
1 tsp. salt
3 slices white bread, cut
   in small cubes
1-1/2 cups grated
   Cheddar cheese

Brown crumbled sausage and drain on paper towels. Cool. Mix eggs, milk, mustard and salt. Add sausage, bread and cheese. Pour entire mixture into greased deep 9 x 9-inch pan. Refrigerate. Preheat oven to 350 degrees. Bake uncovered 50 to 60 minutes.

Mrs. William A. Cox, Jr.

SPINACH AND CHEESE STRUDEL   *Serves 6*

Marvelous as a luncheon dish with fresh fruit salad.

1 16-oz. pkg. frozen
  filo sheets
2 lbs. fresh spinach
1/4 cup water
1/2 cup minced green
  onions
4 T. butter
4 eggs
6 oz. feta cheese,
  shredded
2 T. dill weed
1/2 cup minced fresh
  parsley
salt and pepper to taste
1/2 cup melted butter
1/2 cup fresh bread
  crumbs (very fine)

Thaw filo sheets according to package instructions. Wash spinach. Discard stems. Cook in 1/4 cup water in a large uncovered pot just until spinach wilts. Drain, pat dry with paper towels. Sauté onions in butter until soft. Purée the onions, spinach and eggs in food processor until well mixed. Mix cheese and dill together. Add spinach mixture to cheese mixture; mix in parsley and seasonings. Taste and correct seasonings.

Preheat oven to 375 degrees. Butter a baking sheet. Place filo sheet on a damp towel. Brush sheet with melted butter; sprinkle lightly with bread crumbs. Repeat 3 more times. Place 1/3 of spinach mixture 1/4 inch from long edge which should be placed nearest you. Roll in jelly roll fashion with a towel, if necessary. Tuck in ends. Place on baking sheet. Brush top with melted butter. Repeat 2 more times to make 3 strudel rolls. Bake in preheated oven for 30-35 minutes or until browned.

NOTE: Recipe may be prepared earlier in the day and covered with plastic wrap until baking time. May be frozen before baking.

Mrs. James R. McClamroch

Poultry

CHICKEN EN CROUTE GRECQUE

Serves 8 to 12

Make ahead, freeze, bake day of luncheon.

1 3-lb. chicken
4 T. butter
2 T. olive oil
3 minced shallots
2 cloves garlic, minced
3/4 lb. mushrooms, diced
2 10-oz. pkgs. frozen chopped spinach, thawed and drained
4 eggs
1/2 lb. Swiss cheese, shredded
1/2 to 1 cup grated fresh Parmesan cheese
1/4 tsp. pepper
1/8 tsp. nutmeg
1-1/4 tsp. salt
1 16-oz. pkg. phyllo dough
1/4 to 1/2 lb. butter

Simmer, bone and dice chicken. In a dutch oven, cook shallots and garlic in butter/oil for a few minutes, then add mushrooms and cook until transparent. Remove from heat, stir in diced chicken and spinach; then eggs, cheeses, pepper, nutmeg and salt. Melt 1/4 pound butter. Thoroughly dampen and wring out a cotton dish towel as dry as possible. Preheat oven to 375 degrees. Remove roll of phyllo leaves from packaging. Lay out flat on the counter to the right of the damp towel. Working quickly, remove one leaf at a time from the stack, baste it with melted butter and stack 3 to 5 buttered leaves on the towel. Place some chicken mixture at one end of the basted stack of leaves; roll and tuck under the chicken in the phyllo until you have a roll. Place on lightly greased baking sheet and baste with more melted butter. With a sharp knife slash the roll diagonally several times. Bake for 30 to 40 minutes until crust is golden brown and juices are sizzling.

NOTE: Rolls can be frozen uncooked. Brush frozen rolls with melted butter and bake until brown.

Paula Nordhem

YORKSHIRE CHICKEN

Serves 4 to 6

An elegant party dish.

3 whole chicken breasts,
  boned
1/2 cup flour
1 tsp. chicken stock base
paprika, salt and pepper
2 T. cooking oil
3 eggs
1-1/2 cups milk
1/4 cup melted butter
  or margarine
1 cup flour
1 tsp. baking powder
1 tsp. salt

Preheat oven to 350 degrees. Shake chicken pieces in combination of 1/2 cup flour, chicken stock base and seasonings in a small bag. Fry coated chicken in cooking oil to a golden brown. Place in a greased 10 x 16-inch pan. In a bowl, beat eggs, add milk and butter. Stir in flour, baking powder and salt that have been mixed together. Pour batter over chicken. Bake for one hour.

VARIATION: A 3-lb. chicken cut into 8 serving pieces can be substituted for the chicken breasts.

Mrs. Edwin B. Bosler

CHICKEN LASAGNA

Serves 6

For family or casual entertaining, it's terrific...

1 3-lb. chicken, cooked
  and cut into bite-size
  pieces
1 10-3/4 oz. can cream
  of celery soup
1/4 tsp. oregano
1 tsp. salt
1/2 cup milk or chicken
  broth
dash of pepper
1/2 lb. lasagna noodles,
  cooked and drained
6 oz. sliced Mozzarella
  cheese, cut in strips
10 oz. Velveeta cheese,
  cut in slices
1/3 cup freshly grated
  Parmesan cheese

Preheat oven to 350 degrees. Mix chicken pieces, celery soup, oregano and salt together. Add milk and pepper and blend. In a buttered 12 x 8-inch baking dish, arrange alternate layers of cooked noodles, chicken mixture and cheeses. Make 2 layers, ending with Parmesan cheese on top. Bake uncovered for 20 to 30 minutes.

NOTE: You may prepare this a day ahead and refrigerate or you may cover and freeze. If casserole is cold when put in the oven, allow 10 to 15 minutes more cooking time.

Patsy Vanatta

CHICKEN BUFFET DISH

Serves 6

This party dish can be made early in the day and refrigerated.

3 T. butter
1 T. cooking oil
3 chicken breasts,
  boned, skinned
  and split
8 oz. fresh mushrooms,
  sliced
1 T. flour
1 10-3/4 oz. can cream
  of chicken soup,
  undiluted
1 cup white wine
  (sauterne or chablis)
1 cup water
1/2 pint whipping cream
1 tsp. salt
1/2 tsp. tarragon
1/4 tsp. pepper
1 15-oz. can artichoke
  hearts, drained
6 green onions, chopped,
  including green part
2 T. chopped parsley

Heat butter and oil over medium heat in frypan. Add chicken and cook, turning, about 8 to 10 minutes or until brown on all sides. Remove chicken and place in 2-qt. casserole. In same frypan, sauté mushrooms until tender. Stir in flour. Add soup, wine and water. Simmer, stirring, about 10 minutes or until sauce thickens. Stir in cream, salt, tarragon and pepper. Pour sauce over chicken and bake, uncovered, at 350 degrees, for one hour. Mix in artichoke hearts; onions, and parsley. Bake about 5 more minutes.

NOTE: Flour may be increased to 2 T. if a thicker sauce is desired.

Mrs. James R. McClamroch

BAKED CHICKEN SUPREME

Serves 6

Tangy, fix-ahead dish...

3 or 4 chicken breasts,
  halved, boned and
  skinned
1 cup sour cream
2 T. fresh lemon juice
2 tsp. Worcestershire
  sauce
2 tsp. celery salt
1 tsp. paprika
1 tsp. salt
1/4 tsp. pepper
1 cup dry bread crumbs
1/2 cup butter

Combine sour cream and seasonings; coat chicken breasts. Refrigerate overnight. Roll chicken in crumbs. Arrange chicken in single layer in a 9 x 13-inch baking dish. Melt butter; spoon over chicken. Bake at 350 degrees for 45 to 60 minutes, basting occasionally with butter.

Mrs. Julien H. Collins, Jr.

MEXICAN CHICKEN CASSEROLE

Serves 8 to 10

A favorite of spicy food lovers...

4 whole chicken breasts
2 10-3/4 oz. cans cream
of mushroom soup
2 10-3/4 oz. cans cream
of chicken soup
1 large onion,
finely chopped
10 oz. grated extra sharp
Cheddar cheese
12 corn tortillas
2 3-1/2 oz. cans
green chili peppers

Bake chicken breasts, covered, at 400 degrees for one hour. Cool. Skin and bone chicken and cut into large, not bite-size, pieces. Mix soups, onion and half of cheese. Cut tortillas into one-inch pieces. Drain and seed chilies; cut into large strips. Layer ingredients in a buttered 9 x 13-inch casserole as follows: soup mixture, tortillas, chicken, chili peppers, remaining cheese. Refrigerate casserole for 24 hours before baking or freeze for future use. Preheat oven to 300 degrees. Bake covered for 1-1/2 hours.

NOTE: If a milder flavor is preferred, use only one can of chili peppers.

VARIATION: 2 cups sour cream may be substituted for 2 cans of soup.

Mrs. Paul S. Wise

QUICK COMPANY CHICKEN BREASTS

Serves 4

Can be doubled or tripled for easy gourmet fare.

4 chicken breasts,
skinned and boned
4 slices Swiss cheese
1 10-3/4 oz. can cream
of chicken soup
1/2 cup sherry
2 cups seasoned
stuffing mix
1/2 cup butter

Preheat oven to 350 degrees. In the bottom of a 9 x 13-inch shallow baking dish, place chicken breasts and cover each with a slice of cheese. Pour soup mixed with sherry over the top. Sprinkle stuffing over the top and drizzle with melted butter. Bake in preheated oven until tender, about one hour.

Mrs. Donald J. Ross

JOAN'S CHICKEN AND HAM

Serves 8

Attractive and tasty...

8 ham slices
4 whole chicken breasts,
　boned and skinned
1 10-3/4 oz. can
　mushroom soup
1 cup sour cream
milk
shredded Cheddar
　cheese
corn flakes

Preheat oven to 350 degrees. Place ham slices in a greased 8 x 12-inch Pyrex pan. Place one chicken breast on each slice of ham. Mix soup and sour cream together —thin with a little milk so it will spread easily. Pour sauce over meat. Cover lightly with Cheddar cheese. Sprinkle with corn flakes. Bake 1-1/2 hours.

Mrs. Donald Warfield

JADE CHICKEN

Serves 4 to 6

Colorful, quick entrée...

4 to 6 half chicken
　breasts, skinned and
　boned
1 T. oil
1/2 tsp. salt
1/2 tsp. MSG (optional)
2 T. dry sherry
1 T. soy sauce
3/4 cup chicken broth
　or water
3 cups fresh broccoli
　flowers (not stems)
6 green onions, sliced,
　including some
　green tops
1/3 lb. mushrooms,
　sliced
2 large stalks celery,
　sliced
1 8-oz. can water
　chestnuts, drained
　and sliced
1-1/2 T. cornstarch

Cut each chicken breast in crosswise strips. Heat oil in skillet over medium high heat; add chicken. Sprinkle chicken with salt and MSG and stir fry until chicken turns white. Mix sherry and soy sauce with broth; pour over chicken. Add broccoli and cook covered for 4 minutes. Add remaining vegetables and cook 3 minutes. Mix cornstarch and small amount of water. Add to skillet and stir until sauce thickens. Serve at once with rice. If desired, top with canned chow mein noodles. Warm noodles in 250 degree oven for 15 minutes between paper towels on a cookie sheet.

Mrs. Julien H. Collins, Jr.

BAKED PINEAPPLE CHICKEN   *Serves 6 to 8*

Attractive, different and delicious!

8 chicken pieces
2 T. butter, melted
salt and pepper to taste
2 T. cornstarch
3/4 cup pineapple juice
1/2 cup chicken broth
2 T. soy sauce
3 T. lemon juice
1 20-oz. can crushed
  pineapple, drained
1/3 cup sliced
  green onions
1 6-oz. pkg. frozen
  Chinese pea pods

Preheat oven to 400 degrees. Place chicken in an 11-3/4 x 7-1/2-inch Pyrex baking dish. Brush chicken with melted butter, sprinkle with salt and pepper. Bake for 30 minutes. Meanwhile, combine cornstarch and pineapple juice together in a sauce pan. Stir in broth, soy sauce and lemon juice. Cook, stirring constantly, until sauce thickens. Pour over chicken. Reduce heat to 350 degrees and bake for 25 minutes. Add crushed pineapple, green onions and pea pods. Baste with pan juices and bake uncovered for an additional 10 minutes. Serve with rice.

Mrs. Julien H. Collins, Jr.

TURKEY CLUB CASSEROLE   *Serves 6*

A great way to use leftover turkey or chicken.

2 cups diced cooked
  turkey or chicken
1 10-3/4 oz. can cream
  of mushroom soup,
  undiluted
1 T. mayonnaise
1/4 tsp. garlic salt
1/8 tsp. rosemary
dash of white pepper
1 cup small curd
  cottage cheese
1 10-oz. pkg. frozen
  chopped spinach,
  cooked and drained
2 cups cooked noodles
3/4 cup shredded
  Mozzarella cheese
paprika

Preheat oven to 350 degrees. Mix turkey, soup, seasonings and mayonnaise. Mix together cottage cheese and spinach. In a buttered 2-qt. casserole alternately layer half the noodles, turkey mixture and spinach mixture. Sprinkle with half the Mozzarella. Repeat. Bake for 40 minutes or until top is bubbling and lightly browned. Sprinkle with paprika. Let stand 10 minutes for easier serving. Can be prepared in advance, refrigerated and baked at serving time. Add 15 minutes baking time if refrigerated.

Mrs. Wilfred H. Heitmann

CHEESY CHICKEN

Serves 4 to 6

Finger-licking good!

1 3-lb. chicken, cut up
1/2 cup flour
1/2 cup freshly grated
  Parmesan cheese
1 tsp. garlic salt
2 eggs
1/2 cup melted butter

Preheat oven to 350 degrees. Mix flour, cheese and garlic salt in a bowl. Beat eggs in another bowl. Use tongs to dip chicken pieces into eggs, then into flour mixture, coating well on all sides. Place pieces in a single layer in a 9 x 13-inch buttered baking dish. Drizzle with melted butter. Bake uncovered for about one hour or until golden brown.

Mrs. Robert C. Becherer

CHICKEN KIEV

Serves 4 to 8

A chicken that's tops!

8 boned chicken breasts
8 T. butter
1 T. chopped chives
1 T. chopped fresh
  tarragon
flour
salt and pepper
2 beaten eggs
2 cups bread crumbs
oil

Pound breasts between sheets of waxed paper. Be careful not to break the flesh. The flattened piece should be rather fan-shaped. Make eight small, tapered "fingers" of butter. Roll the butter in chives and tarragon and chill in freezer for 15 minutes. Roll breasts around butter, tucking in the ends of meat to make a neat package. Roll in flour seasoned to taste with salt and pepper. Dip in beaten egg and roll in bread crumbs. Cook in 360-degree oil to cover until golden brown. Drain on absorbent paper.

VARIATIONS:
Niçoise: Mix chopped garlic, black olives, and sweet basil with the butter before chilling instead of chives and tarragon.
Alsacienne: Spread chicken with foie gras before rolling around the butter.

Mrs. David D. Schafer

CHICKEN CHAUDFROID

Serves 8

An elegant luncheon entrée

4 chicken breasts,
   boned and split
2 10-3/4 oz. cans
   chicken broth
3-oz. cream cheese
4 T. mayonnaise
2 T. lemon juice
1/2 tsp. grated
   lemon peel
1/4 tsp. salt
2 T. fresh snipped dill
   or 1 T. dried dill weed
Romaine lettuce leaves
8 thick, peeled tomato
   slices
Lawry's seasoned salt
toasted, slivered almonds
snipped dill
sliced avocado
French or Italian
   dressing

Simmer chicken breasts and broth in covered saucepan for 30 minutes or until fork tender. Refrigerate in broth until 30 minutes before serving. Drain broth and remove chicken skin. Make a paste of cream cheese, mayonnaise, lemon juice, lemon peel, salt and dill. Coat the rounded side of each breast.

To assemble: Place a tomato slice on a bed of Romaine; sprinkle with seasoned salt. Place chicken over tomato; sprinkle with almonds and dill. Garnish long edges of breast with avocado. Serve with French or Italian dressing.

Mrs. James R. McClamroch

COQ AU VIN BLANC

Serves 4

Elegant for company!

1 2-1/2 to 3-lb. fryer,
   cut up
1/4 cup butter
   or margarine
1/2 lb. small
   white onions
2 medium carrots,
   cut into 1/4 inch
   thick slices
1/2 lb. small mushrooms
1/4 cup flour
1/2 tsp. salt
1/4-1/2 tsp. pepper
1 envelope chicken
   flavor bouillon
1-1/2 cups white wine

Brown chicken on all sides in hot butter. Remove from pan; place in bowl. Cook onion, carrots and mushrooms in drippings until lightly browned. Put in bowl with chicken. Skim all but 2 tablespoons fat from skillet; stir in flour, salt, pepper and bouillon until blended. Gradually stir in white wine and cook until smooth, stirring constantly. Put chicken, onions, carrots and mushrooms back into pan; bring to boil. Reduce heat to low; cover and simmer 40 minutes or until chicken and onions are fork tender, basting occasionally with sauce.

Mrs. James E. Sullivan

CHICKEN ALMOND CASSEROLE · *Serves 6*

Crunchy and creamy...

SHERRY SAUCE
1/4 cup butter
1/4 cup flour
1/2 tsp. salt
1/4 tsp. pepper
1-1/2 cups chicken broth
1/2 cup milk
2 T. sherry or to taste

CHICKEN MIXTURE
6 oz. fresh mushrooms,
  sliced
1 T. butter
3 to 4 cups cubed,
  cooked chicken
1 5-oz. can water
  chestnuts, drained and
  sliced
1/2 cup slivered almonds
1/2 cup sliced
  green onions
paprika

To prepare sherry sauce, melt butter over low heat. Add flour, salt and pepper. Stir until mixture bubbles; add milk and broth. Heat to boiling, stirring constantly. Remove from stove when thickened and add sherry. Preheat oven to 350 degrees. Sauté mushrooms in butter and set aside. Spread one half of chicken in an 11 x 7-inch baking dish. Sprinkle with mushrooms, water chestnuts, almonds and onions. Top with remaining chicken. Cover with sherry sauce and sprinkle with paprika. Bake for 45 minutes.

Mrs. Julien H. Collins, Jr.

CHINESE CHICKEN AND SHRIMP   *Serves 4*

Ah! So attractive and good!

2 whole chicken breasts,
  boned, skinned and cut
  in 2-inch pieces
2 T. oil
1/4 tsp. ginger
1/4 tsp. salt
1 onion, thinly sliced
1/4 cup thinly sliced
  celery
1/2 T. cornstarch
1 cup chicken broth
1 T. brown sugar or
  molasses
1 green pepper,
  cut in squares
1 T. sherry
1/2 lb. raw shrimp
2 T. soy sauce
2 T. slivered almonds
6 oz. fresh or frozen
  peapods
4 oz. fresh mushrooms,
  sliced

Using medium high heat, brown chicken in oil until crisp. Either a large frying pan or a wok may be used. Add ginger, salt, onion and celery and sauté until soft (3 minutes). Blend in cornstarch, broth and brown sugar and bring to a boil. Reduce heat to a simmer and add green pepper, sherry, shrimp and soy sauce. Cook for 5 to 7 minutes, until shrimp turns opaque and sauce is shiny. Raise heat and add almonds, peapods and mushrooms just before serving. More cornstarch may be used if a thicker sauce is desired.

Mrs. L. Steven Minkel

TERRI'S CHICKEN   *Serves 8 to 12*

Great for a crowd!

8 whole chicken breasts,
  boned and skinned
flour
1/2 cup lemon juice
1/4 cup soy sauce
1/2 cup melted butter
dash of pepper
1-1/2 lbs. fresh
  mushrooms, sliced
cornstarch

Preheat oven to 325 degrees. Flour the chicken and place in 4-qt. casserole. Mix together lemon juice, soy sauce and melted butter; pour over chicken. Sprinkle chicken lightly with pepper. Cover chicken with mushrooms. Bake covered in a 325-degree oven for 30 minutes; uncover and bake 30 minutes more. Easily doubled! If desired, sauce may be thickened with cornstarch at serving time—one T. cornstarch for one cup of liquid.

Mrs. Ronald Bess

TURKEY TETRAZZINI

Madeira gives it a wonderful touch.

8 T. butter, divided
1/4 lb. fresh mushrooms,
  thinly sliced
4 T. flour
1-1/2 cups turkey stock
1 egg yolk
1/2 cup whipping cream
salt and white pepper
  to taste
1 T. Madeira
3 cups cooked turkey,
  cut into 1-inch pieces
1/2 lb. vermicelli or
  other pasta, cooked
1/4 cup fresh Parmesan
  cheese
2 T. dry bread crumbs

Melt 3 T. butter in fry pan. Add mushrooms and cook, stirring constantly, until they have absorbed the butter and wilted but not browned. Remove immediately to a small bowl. Melt 3 more T. butter in fry pan and add flour. Make a roux and then add all of turkey stock at once. Bring to a boil, stirring constantly with a whisk. Cook until smooth and thick, then simmer another 5 minutes. Mix egg yolk and cream in a small bowl. Gradually beat a small amount of the sauce into the eggs, then a small amount of eggs into sauce. Keep repeating procedure until egg mixture is warmed and can be added to sauce in one step. Cook mixture a few seconds; remove from heat. Season quite highly with salt, white pepper and 1 T. Madeira. Fold in mushrooms and turkey. Preheat oven to 350 degrees. To serve *en casserole,* butter a 1-1/2-qt. dish; place half cooked pasta in bottom. Cover with half of turkey mixture, then spread with remaining pasta. Spread rest of turkey mixture atop and sprinkle with Parmesan cheese mixed with bread crumbs. Dot with bits of remaining butter. Bake at 350 degrees for 45 to 50 minutes.

NOTE: Cooked chicken and chicken stock may be substituted for turkey and stock.

Mrs. Geoffrey C. Murphy

ROCK CORNISH HENS WITH GRAPES

Serves 2 to 4

Tender entrée with heavenly sauce...

2 rock cornish
   game hens
salt and pepper
6 slices bacon
2 slices bread
2 T. butter

SAUCE
pan juices
1/2 cup cognac
1/2 cup whipping cream
1 T. butter
2 scallions, finely
   chopped
1 8-1/4 oz. can light
   seedless grapes,
   drained
1 cup port wine
salt and pepper
1 tsp. lemon juice

Preheat oven to 350 degrees. Wash cornish hens and pat dry; sprinkle with salt and pepper. Place in well buttered 9 x 14-inch roasting pan. Cover each hen with 3 slices bacon. Roast for 50 to 60 minutes, basting several times with pan juices. Meanwhile, sauté bread in hot butter until golden; drain on absorbent towels. When hens are tender, remove from oven and cut in half. Arrange on bread triangles and keep warm on a hot platter. To prepare sauce, place roasting pan over direct heat. Add cognac to liquid and cook until reduced by half. Add cream and boil until sauce is reduced to a creamy consistency. Heat butter in a small saucepan. Add scallions and sauté 2 minutes. Add grapes and port. Heat and ignite. Stir gently until flame burns out. Strain cream gravy from roasting pan into grape sauce. Correct seasonings with salt and pepper and add lemon juice. Pour sauce over hens and serve immediately.

NOTE: Hens may be prepared ahead and reheated in a warm oven. Prepare sauce just before serving with reserved pan juices.

VARIATIONS: Substitute boneless chicken breasts for hens.

Mrs. Edwin B. Bosler

CASSEROLE OF PHEASANT

Serves 6

An authentic Scottish recipe...

2 pheasants
2 T. butter or olive oil
1/2 lb. peeled fresh
  chestnuts
1/2 lb. peeled
  pearl onions
3 T. flour
grated rind and juice of
  1/2 orange
1 tsp. red wine vinegar
  or 1 oz. burgundy
2 cups good quality stock
1 tsp. red currant jelly
1 bouquet garni
salt and pepper to taste
chopped fresh parsley

Heat butter in an ovenproof pan. Brown pheasants slowly on all sides; remove from pan and set aside. Add chestnuts and onions to pan. Sauté over medium heat until they begin to change color, shaking the pan frequently. Remove from pan and set aside. Add flour to pan and mix well; add rest of ingredients except parsley and bring to a boil. Add pheasants, chestnuts and onions and cover tightly. Bake in a 325 degree oven for 1-1/2 to 2 hours, or until pheasants are tender. Joint the pheasants and place in a 2-quart casserole with chestnuts and onions. Remove the bouquet garni from liquid. Skim the fat and reduce if needed. Adjust seasonings and pour liquid over pheasants. Dust casserole with parsley.

NOTE: This dish reheats well and may be frozen. Four cornish hens may be substituted for pheasants; one 10-oz. can chestnuts for fresh chestnuts; one 16-oz. jar boiled small onions (drained) for pearl onions.

Mrs. James Pierpont

CREAMY CHICKEN NOODLE BAKE

Serves 16 to 20

Vegetables add color, water chestnuts add crunch...

9 whole chicken breasts,
  stewed
1 lb. fresh mushrooms,
  sliced
2 T. butter
3 15-oz. cans artichoke
  hearts, drained and
  quartered
6 oz. chopped pimiento,
  drained
3 6-oz. cans water
  chestnuts, drained
  and sliced
3 10-3/4 oz. cans cream
  of chicken soup
3 10-3/4 oz. cans cream
  of celery soup
12 oz. noodles,
  cooked and drained
salt and pepper to taste
12 oz. shredded Cheddar
  cheese
2 cups buttered
  bread crumbs

Remove skin and bones from chicken and cut into bite size pieces. Sauté mushrooms in butter. Combine chicken, mushrooms, artichokes, pimiento, water chestnuts, soups and noodles in large bowl. Season with salt and pepper. Place mixture in two 9 x 13-inch buttered casseroles. Top each with half the cheese and half the crumbs. Bake at 350 degrees for 45 minutes.

NOTE: Casseroles may be prepared and refrigerated the day before serving.

Mrs. Franklin A. Urbahns

Fish and Seafood

CLAIRE'S CURRY BROILED FILETS

Serves 4

Tender sole served with a gingery sauce...

CURRY COATING
2/3 cup mayonnaise
1 T. curry powder
1-1/4 lbs. fish filets,
 preferably sole
1-1/2 cups fresh
 bread crumbs

Preheat broiler to 450 degrees. Mix mayonnaise and curry powder; spread on both sides of filets. Coat with bread crumbs. Broil filets about 5 inches below heat for 5 to 6 minutes per side, until fish is flaky and crumbs are brown.

GINGER SAUCE
2 T. butter
2 T. ginger marmalade
2 T. fresh lime juice

Heat ingredients together until gelatinous part of marmalade dissolves. Spoon over cooked filets or serve in separate pitcher.

VARIATION: If preferred, fish may be coated on one side with half recipe of curry coating and bread crumbs. Bake at 350 degrees for 15 minutes without turning the fish.

Mrs. L. Steven Minkel

FISH IN CHEESE SAUCE

Serves 4

Tasty fish entrée.

1 lb. fish filets (4 pieces)
salt and pepper to taste
1/4 to 1/2 tsp. dill weed
1 cup grated Cheddar
 cheese
1/2 cup skim milk
1/2 cup cottage cheese

Preheat oven to 350 degrees. Arrange fish in a shallow 8 x 12-inch Pyrex pan or separate ramekins. Sprinkle with salt, pepper and dill weed. Blend cheeses and milk in blender until smooth. Cover fish with sauce and bake for 20 minutes.

Mrs. Adolph Pifko

WHITEFISH CAPER

Serves 4

Wonderful, easy fish entrée...

1 large slice whitefish or
  halibut (at least 1-inch
  thick)
salt and pepper
1/2 cup capers with a
  little vinegar
3 T. grated onion
2 cups sour cream
paprika

Preheat oven to 350 degrees. Place fish in oblong Pyrex baking dish. Season with salt and pepper. Add capers with vinegar and onion to sour cream and pour over fish. Sprinkle with paprika. Bake for 30 minutes. Delicious with parsley potatoes and green beans.

Mrs. Carl Fowler

WINE SAUCED FISH FILETS

Serves 6

Elegant!

2-1/2 lbs. fish filets
2 T. chopped green
  onions
salt and pepper
1-1/2 T. butter
1 cup white wine
1/2 cup water

Preheat oven to 350 degrees. Place fish in large frying pan. Sprinkle with onion, salt and pepper; dot with butter and barely cover with wine and water. Cover fish with waxed paper. Bring to simmer on stove, then place in oven for 8 to 12 minutes. Drain liquid from fish; reduce to one cup. Prepare sauce and spoon over fish. Sprinkle with cheese. Broil 2 to 3 minutes to brown cheese.

SAUCE
3/4 lb. mushrooms,
  sliced
5 T. butter
2-1/2 T. flour
1 cup reduced poaching
  liquid
1/2 cup whipping cream
  or more
salt and pepper to taste
lemon juice to taste

Sauté mushrooms quickly in 2 tablespoons butter. Add salt and pepper to taste. Combine remaining butter and flour and beat into the hot poaching liquid. Add cream and bring to a boil. Add as much additional cream as necessary to make sauce coat spoon. Add mushrooms, salt, pepper and lemon juice to taste.

Mrs. David M. Stone

TOPPING
1/4 cup grated Swiss
  cheese

BABY SNAPPER FILETS

Serves 4 to 6

Tomatoes make this special...

2 tomatoes, peeled and
  thinly sliced
3/4 cup seasoned
  bread crumbs
salt and pepper to taste
2 lbs. *small* snapper filets
1/2 cup white port wine
1/4 cup butter
1 tsp. lemon or lime juice
freshly grated Parmesan
  cheese
paprika to taste

Preheat oven to 500 degrees. In one 8 x 12-inch Pyrex baking pan, arrange a layer of sliced tomatoes. Sprinkle with seasoned bread crumbs and salt and pepper. Top with filets. In a saucepan, combine the port, butter and lemon juice and cook over low heat until the butter is melted. Increase the heat to moderate and boil the mixture for several minutes. Pour the sauce over the filets; sprinkle with Parmesan cheese and paprika to taste. Bake for 10 minutes.

NOTE: May be divided into serving size portions and baked in individual baking dishes.

Mrs. Robert W. Higgins

SWORDFISH A L'ESPAGNOLE

Serves 3

Spicy tomato topping...

1 lb. swordfish
salt and freshly ground
  pepper to taste
6 T. olive oil
1 medium onion,
  finely chopped
1 clove garlic, minced
1/4 cup chopped fresh
  parsley
1/2 tsp. thyme
1 large tomato,
  peeled and chopped
1 bay leaf
2 T. tomato paste
1/2 cup dry sherry
3 lemon slices

Preheat oven to 350 degrees. Sprinkle fish with salt and pepper and place in 9 x 13-inch dish with 2 T. oil. Sauté onion, garlic, parsley and thyme in remaining 4 T. oil until wilted. Add tomato and bay leaf; simmer until blended. Add tomato paste and sherry; simmer 5 minutes. Salt sauce to taste. Pour sauce over fish, top with lemon slices. Bake 30 minutes, basting occasionally.

Mrs. Geoffrey C. Murphy

FINNAN HADDIE A LA CREME   *Serves 4 to 6*

A springtime delicacy...

1-1/2 lbs. thick,
  boneless, smoked
  haddock (finnan
  haddie)
2 cups milk
1/2 tsp. thyme
1 bay leaf
1 small onion,
  thinly sliced
3 T. butter
4 T. flour
1/4 cup whipping cream
1/4 tsp. nutmeg
2 hard cooked eggs,
  sliced
6 slices fresh toast,
  cut into triangles
freshly ground pepper

Place fish in skillet; add next four ingredients. Let stand one hour, then simmer over low heat for 10 minutes or until fish flakes easily. Drain fish and reserve cooking liquid. Flake fish and set aside. Heat butter in pan; stir in flour. When roux bubbles, add cream and reserved fish liquid. Stir well with a wire whisk. When thickened and smooth, add nutmeg. Fold in flaked fish and eggs; season to taste with pepper. Serve on toast.

Mrs. Geoffrey C. Murphy

SAUCY TUNA STACK-UP   *Serves 4*

Make it today—serve it tomorrow.

1 6-1/2-oz. can water
  pack tuna, drained
1/4 cup chopped ripe
  olives
1 T. chopped green
  onions
1 6-oz. can mushroom
  pieces, chopped
2 T. chopped pimiento
  (optional)
1/4 cup mayonnaise
12 slices sandwich bread
1/2 pt. sour cream
1 10-3/4-oz. can cream
  of mushroom soup
paprika

Mix tuna with olives, onions, mushrooms, pimiento and mayonnaise. Cut crusts off bread. Spread tuna mixture on eight bread slices—stack to make four open sandwiches; top with remaining bread slices. Wrap each sandwich separately in foil and refrigerate overnight. Remove sandwiches from refrigerator one hour before baking. Preheat oven to 350 degrees. Bake wrapped sandwiches 20 minutes; unwrap and bake 10 minutes more or until lightly browned. Combine sour cream and soup in double boiler and heat. Serve sauce over hot sandwich. Sprinkle with paprika.

Mrs. Franklin A. Urbahns

SAUTEED SOLE GRENOBLOISE

Serves 6

Exquisite entrée for a very special dinner party.

SAUCE
1 cup white wine
1/2 cup water
1/4 cup fresh lemon juice
1 T. shallots, minced
2 tsp. cornstarch
1 T. water
3/4 cup butter, softened

Before sautéeing fish, prepare sauce and garnishes. Place white wine, water, lemon juice and shallots in saucepan; rapidly reduce volume in half. Mix cornstarch and water and blend with above ingredients. Cook, stirring constantly, until sauce is thickened and clear. Remove from heat and whisk in butter, a small amount at a time. Taste for seasonings. Keep warm but do not boil.

FISH
6 fresh filets (grey sole, flounder, etc.)
1/3 cup flour
1 tsp. salt
1/4 tsp. pepper
6 T. butter

Lightly flour fish on both sides; season with salt and pepper. Heat butter and cook fish until lightly browned, about 5 minutes total time. Place fish on platter. Sprinkle with garnishes and sauce. Serve at once.

Mrs. David M. Stone

GARNISH
2 lemons, peeled and diced
1/2 cup croutons, toasted in butter
minced fresh parsley
1/4 cup capers (optional)

SEA BASS A LA JULIENNE DE LEGUMES

Serves 4 to 6

Beautiful presentation...

1 carrot, cut in fine
  julienne strips
4 oz. fresh green beans,
  French cut
4 tsp. fresh tiny peas
1-3/4 lbs. sea bass filet
1 tomato, peeled, seeded
  and finely chopped
1 shallot, minced
salt and pepper to taste
6 T. dry Chablis wine
6 T. unsalted butter,
  softened

Steam carrots and green beans until partially cooked; add peas and steam until all vegetables are tender-crisp. Arrange tomato and shallot in bottom of sauté pan. Cut bass into serving-size pieces and place on top of tomato. Sprinkle with salt, pepper and wine. Bring to a boil, cover pan and remove from heat. Let sit until fish is opaque. Place fish on heated serving platter. Reduce pan liquid to about one teaspoon. Whisk in butter, one tablespoon at a time. Check for seasoning and add steamed vegetables. Bring to a boil and pour over fish.

NOTE: Grouper may be substituted for sea bass.

Mrs. Franklin A. Urbahns

SCALLOPED OYSTERS

Serves 4

Wonderful addition to a holiday dinner...

2 cups coarsely
  crumbled saltines
1/2 cup butter, melted
1 pint oysters
freshly ground pepper
1 cup whipping cream
1/4 tsp. Worcestershire
  sauce
1/2 tsp. salt

Preheat oven to 350 degrees. Pour butter over saltines and mix lightly with a fork. Drain oysters, reserving their liquor. Butter a one-quart casserole. Place 1/3 of the buttered crumbs on bottom; spread 1/2 of oysters on top. Sprinkle with pepper. Repeat cracker and oyster layers. Combine reserved oyster liquor with enough cream to make one cup; stir in Worcestershire sauce and salt. Pour over oysters and top with remaining crumbs. Bake for 40 minutes.

Mrs. Geoffrey C. Murphy

LEMON CREAM TUNA

Serves 4 to 6

Appealing luncheon entrée...

1/2 cup chopped fresh
  parsley
1/2 cup chopped
  scallions
1/4 cup diced celery
1 clove garlic, minced
1/4 cup melted butter
1-1/2 cups sliced
  fresh mushrooms
1 T. butter
1-1/2 T. flour
1/4 tsp. salt
1/8 tsp. nutmeg
1/2 cup half and half
1 egg yolk, beaten
1 T. lemon juice
2 7-oz. cans water-
  pack tuna, drained
  and flaked
1 cup finely shredded
  Swiss cheese

Sauté the first four ingredients in butter until wilted; add mushrooms and continue cooking until they are golden. For cream sauce, make a roux of the butter, flour, salt and nutmeg. Add half and half, stirring constantly until thickened. Remove from heat; stir a small amount of sauce into egg yolk. Add egg mixture to sauce, stirring briskly. Stir in lemon juice. Stir cream sauce into sautéed ingredients; gently fold in tuna. Spoon into individual baking shells or a shallow 1-1/2-quart baking dish. Top with cheese and broil just until cheese is browned.

Mrs. Geoffrey C. Murphy

SHRIMP FRIED RICE

Serves 6 to 8

Fix ingredients ahead; stir fry together just before serving with a green salad.

2 to 3 T. oil
1 medium onion,
  chopped
1 cup sliced celery
1 cup sliced fresh
  mushrooms
4 cups cooked rice
1-1/2 lbs. fresh shrimp,
  cooked and peeled
4 eggs, beaten
3 T. soy sauce
pepper to taste

Heat oil in Dutch oven or wok. Add vegetables and cook over medium heat for 5 minutes. Add rice and shrimp; cook until warm. Add eggs and stir until firm. Season with soy sauce and pepper.

Mrs. Julien H. Collins, Jr.

209

BOUNTY FROM THE SEA

Serves 10 to 12

Scrumptious casserole for a special luncheon...

CREAM SAUCE
1/2 cup butter
1/2 cup flour
1 tsp. salt
1 tsp. dry mustard
1 qt. milk
1 tsp. Worcestershire
 sauce
1 small onion, grated
4 T. dry sherry

To prepare white sauce, melt butter and add flour, salt and dry mustard. Cook, stirring, until the mixture bubbles. Add milk. Cook over medium heat, stirring, until the mixture thickens. Season with Worcestershire sauce, onion and sherry.

SEAFOOD MIXTURE
1/2 lb. fresh mushrooms,
 sliced
1 T. butter
1 lb. raw shrimp
1 1-1/2-lb. lobster tail
 (3 cups raw lobster
 chunks)
1 7-oz. can snow crab-
 meat, drained and
 flaked
6 hard cooked eggs,
 peeled and chopped
1-1/2 cups grated
 Cheddar cheese
2 cups fresh bread
 crumbs

Preheat oven to 350 degrees. Sauté mushrooms in butter and set aside. Mix cream sauce with mushrooms, seafood, eggs and 1/2 cup cheese. Sprinkle one cup bread crumbs in the bottom of a deep 9 x 13-inch casserole; spoon in seafood mixture. Top with remaining bread crumbs and cheese. Bake for one hour.

NOTE: Can be prepared in individual serving shells.

Mrs. Dane F. Hahn

COQUILLES
A LA MER

Makes 8 to 10 appetizer servings

Sensational sea fare...

SEAFOOD-MUSHROOM MIXTURE

1 lb. bay scallops, rinsed and drained
1/2 cup dry white wine
2 shallots, finely minced
4 T. butter
1 lb. small uncooked shrimp, fresh or thawed
2 T. butter
1/2 lb. fresh mushrooms, sliced
2 T. fresh lemon juice
1/2 tsp. salt
1/4 tsp. white pepper

WHITE SAUCE

4 T. butter
6 T. flour
1 cup milk
reserved scallop liquid
reserved mushroom juice
1/4 tsp. salt
1/8 tsp. white pepper
cayenne pepper to taste
3 T. grated Parmesan cheese
3 T. grated Gruyère cheese

TOPPING

1/4 cup grated Parmesan cheese
1/4 cup grated Gruyère cheese

Preheat oven to 400 degrees. Put scallops in saucepan; add wine, shallots and enough water to cover. Bring to a boil. Remove from heat and let scallops sit, covered, for 2 minutes. Remove scallops with slotted spoon to a bowl. Over high heat, reduce liquid to 1/4 cup; reserve. Melt 4 T. butter in skillet and sauté shrimp over medium heat until they turn pink. Do not overcook. Transfer shrimp with slotted spoon to bowl containing scallops. Add 2 T. butter, sliced mushrooms, lemon juice, salt and pepper to skillet. Sauté until mushrooms are tender but not brown. Transfer mushrooms with slotted spoon to seafood bowl; reserve pan juices.

To prepare white sauce, melt butter in heavy saucepan. Add flour and cook, stirring, for two to three minutes. Add milk and reserved scallop and mushroom juices. Stir mixture with a wire whisk until it boils. Season with salt, pepper and cayenne. Add cheeses and stir until sauce is smooth. Remove from heat; fold in shrimp, scallops and mushrooms. Divide mixture among 8 to 10 scallop shells. Mix together Parmesan and Gruyère cheeses and sprinkle over shells. Bake for ten minutes, then broil until brown.

NOTE: Serves 6 over rice as a luncheon entrée.

Mrs. Robert W. Higgins

211

NEPTUNE CASSEROLE

Serves 8 to 10

Delicious blend of flavors...

8 oz. fresh mushrooms,
  sliced
1/2 cup diced
  green pepper
1/2 cup diced celery
1/2 cup diced onion
2 T. butter
2 cups cooked rice
1 cup tomato juice
1 8-oz. pkg. frozen
  cooked shrimp
1 7-1/2 oz. can crabmeat
1 6-oz. can water
  chestnuts, sliced
1 cup mayonnaise
1/4 cup slivered almonds
1/2 cup Cheddar cheese,
  shredded

Preheat oven to 350 degrees. Sauté mushrooms, green pepper, celery and onion in butter until tender, about 10 minutes. Add rice, tomato juice, shrimp, crab, water chestnuts and mayonnaise; mix well. Place in greased 2-1/2-qt. casserole. Top with almonds and cheese. Bake 40 minutes.

The Kenilworth Union Church

LOBSTER SUPREME

Serves 6 to 8

Expensive but so delicious!

1/2 lb. fresh mushrooms,
  sliced
1/2 cup butter
1/3 cup flour
2 cups chicken broth
1 cup whipping cream
2 3-oz. pkgs. cream
  cheese, cubed
1/2 cup sherry
1/8 tsp. white pepper
salt to taste
1 T. chopped pimiento
4 cups cooked lobster
  or crab chunks

Sauté mushrooms in 2 tablespoons of butter. Set aside. Melt remaining butter, stir in flour. Add broth and cream. Cook until thick, stirring constantly. Add cheese and sherry. Stir over low heat until cheese melts. Season with pepper, salt and pimiento. Add lobster and buttered mushrooms. Heat thoroughly. Serve with hot rice.

Mrs. Samuel H. Ellis

SCRUMPTIOUS SEAFOOD CASSEROLE

Serves 6 to 8

Perfect for a special luncheon...

1/4 cup butter
1/2 lb. fresh mushrooms,
   sliced
1 cup chopped celery
1 medium onion,
   chopped fine
1 cup cooked
   wild and long grain
   rice mix or 1/2 cup
   wild rice, cooked
4 5-oz. lobster tails,
   cooked, or 1 lb. lump
   crabmeat
1-3/4 to 2 cups cooked
   shrimp
3 T. chopped pimiento
1/2 cup chopped
   green pepper
2 10-3/4 oz. cans
   condensed cream of
   mushroom soup
1/2 cup blanched,
   slivered almonds,
   toasted

Preheat oven to 350 degrees. Melt butter in a 2-quart saucepan. Sauté mushrooms, celery and onion for 5 minutes. Combine rice, cooked onion mixture, lobster or crab, shrimp, pimiento, green pepper and soup. Put in a greased 2-quart casserole. Sprinkle with almonds and bake for 35 minutes.

Mrs. Robert W. Higgins

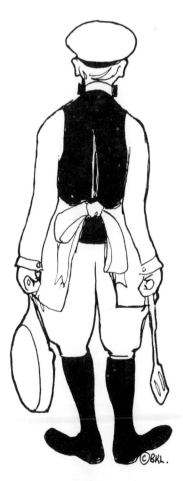

213

MRS. REARDY'S SHRIMP ARTICHOKE CASSEROLE

Serves 4 to 5

Mrs. Reardy was the housekeeper for Adlai Stevenson while he served as U.S. Ambassador to the UN. When this was served to President Kennedy, he requested the recipe.

6-1/2 T. butter
4-1/2 T. flour
3/4 cup whipping cream
3/4 cup milk
salt and freshly ground
  pepper to taste
1 20-oz. can artichoke
  hearts or 1 pkg. frozen
  artichoke hearts,
  cooked
1 lb. shelled and
  deveined shrimp,
  cooked
1/4 lb. fresh mushrooms
1/4 cup dry sherry
1 T. Worcestershire
  sauce
1/4 cup Parmesan
  cheese
paprika

Preheat oven to 375 degrees. Melt 4-1/2 T. of the butter and stir in the flour. Cook one minute. Add milk and cream, *stirring constantly.* When thick and smooth, season with salt and pepper. Set aside. Arrange artichokes in bottom of a buttered 2-qt. casserole. Scatter shrimp over artichokes. Cook mushrooms in rest of butter and arrange over shrimp. Add sherry and Worcestershire sauce to cream sauce and pour over casserole. Sprinkle with cheese and paprika. Bake for 20 minutes.

Mrs. Philip A. VanVlack III

CURRIED SHRIMP

Serves 4

There will be no leftovers!

1/2 medium onion,
  chopped
1 T. butter
1 10-3/4 oz. can cream
  of mushroom soup
1 lb. cooked, cleaned
  shrimp
1 tsp. curry powder
4 to 6 T. sour cream
1 T. lemon juice
cooked rice

Brown onion in butter. Add soup, shrimp and curry powder. Heat mixture in double boiler. When ready to serve, add sour cream and lemon juice. Serve with rice.

SUGGESTED GARNISHES: french fried onion, chutney, raisins, coconut, grated egg yolk, peanuts, chopped bananas, chopped green pepper.

Mrs. Carl Fowler

SHRIMP AND RICE WITH SAUTERNE

Serves 4 to 5

Perfect for an informal luncheon or multiplied to accommodate a buffet.

1-1/2 cups chicken
  broth
1/2 cup sauterne
1/2 tsp. salt
1 cup rice, uncooked
1 lb. cooked shrimp
1 8-oz. can sliced
  water chestnuts
3 chopped green onions
1/2 cup butter
2 T. soy sauce
1/2 cup chopped parsley

In 12-inch electric frying pan, or Dutch oven, combine broth, wine, butter and salt—heat to a slow boil. Stir in rice, cover and cook on low heat until moisture evaporates—about 1/2 hour. Add shrimp, water chestnuts and onions. Heat thoroughly and add butter and soy sauce. Just before serving, gently stir in the chopped parsley.

VARIATION: Cooked chicken would make a great substitute for shrimp.

Mrs. Douglas Moir

CRABMEAT REMICK

Serves 6

Divine...

2 cups flaked snow
  crabmeat
6 slices bacon, fried
  crisp, crumbled
1 tsp. dry mustard
1/2 tsp. paprika
1/2 tsp. celery salt
few drops Tabasco
1/2 cup chili sauce
1 tsp. tarragon vinegar
1-3/4 cups mayonnaise

Preheat oven to 350 degrees. Fill 6 buttered shells with crab. Heat in oven until warm. Top crab with crumbled bacon. Blend remaining ingredients; spread over warm crab. Set oven to broil. Brown under broiler.

NOTE: Delicious served on toasted English muffins for brunch.

Mrs. David M. Stone

CRABMEAT ON RUSKS

Serves 12

Great and quick!

1 8-oz. pkg. cream
   cheese, at room
   temperature
1 tsp. Worcestershire
   sauce
1 T. lemon juice
1 medium onion, grated
1/2 cup butter,
   at room temperature
1 tsp. prepared mustard
1 7-oz. can crabmeat,
   flaked
12 rusks (one 4-oz. pkg.)
3 tomatoes, cut into
   12 slices
8 oz. Velveeta cheese,
   cut into 12 slices
12 slices partially
   cooked bacon

Preheat oven to 350 degrees. Cream together the cream cheese, Worcestershire sauce, lemon juice, onion, butter and mustard; stir in crabmeat. Spread generously on rusks. Top each rusk with a slice of tomato, slice of cheese and slice of bacon. Place on 2 cookie sheets and bake until cheese melts, about 15 to 20 minutes.

Mrs. Ted Payseur

CRAB IMPERIAL

Serves 4

Fit for royalty...

3 T. butter
1-1/2 T. flour
1 cup half and half,
   scalded
1 egg, beaten
1/4 cup snipped chives
2 T. fresh lemon juice
2 tsp. Dijon mustard
1/2 tsp. salt
1/4 tsp. white pepper
dash nutmeg
1 lb. lump crabmeat
1/2 to 1 cup
   cracker crumbs
2 T. butter

Preheat oven to 350 degrees. Melt butter and add flour; cook 2 minutes over medium high heat. Whisk in half and half; cook until thick and boiling. Stir 1/4 cup sauce into egg. Whisk egg into sauce, stirring constantly. Add chives, lemon juice (slowly), mustard, salt, pepper and nutmeg. Fold in crab. Pour mixture into buttered one-quart casserole. Sprinkle with crumbs and dot with butter. Bake for 30 minutes.

NOTE: Three 6-oz. packages frozen lump crabmeat, thawed and well drained, may be substituted for fresh crab.

Casey Bohnstedt

CRAB AND ARTICHOKE CASSEROLE

Serves 12

A rewarding combination...

1/2 cup butter
3 T. minced onion
1/2 cup flour
1 qt. whipping cream,
heated to boiling point
1/2 cup Madeira wine
salt and pepper
2 T. lemon juice
4 cups crabmeat
3 9-oz. pkgs. frozen
artichokes, cooked
and drained
2-1/2 cups shell
macaroni, cooked
and drained
2 cups grated Swiss or
Gruyère cheese
paprika (optional)

Preheat oven to 350 degrees. Melt butter in large heavy pan. When butter sizzles, add onion and sauté until golden. Stir in flour, cooking over low heat until flour is pale yellow. Add cream, stirring vigorously. Return to moderate heat and stir until sauce boils. Reduce heat and add Madeira. Season with salt and pepper. Pour lemon juice over crabmeat and toss lightly. Combine crab, artichokes, macaroni and sauce in a 6-qt. buttered casserole. Sprinkle with cheese and dust with paprika. Bake 25 to 30 minutes or until heated through. Can be prepared a day before and refrigerated.

Mrs. David M. Stone

CRAB-SPINACH SOUFFLE

Serves 4 to 6

Terrific texture and taste...

3 eggs
1 12-oz. pkg. frozen
   spinach soufflé,
   defrosted
1 lb. small curd
   cottage cheese
3 T. flour
1/4 cup butter, diced
4 oz. Cheddar cheese,
   grated
1 7-1/2 oz. can crabmeat

Preheat oven to 350 degrees. Butter an 8 x 8-inch Pyrex pan. Beat eggs slightly. Mix in remaining ingredients. Pour in prepared pan. Bake 50 to 60 minutes or until set. Serve immediately.

Mrs. George W. Stamm

SEAFOOD LASAGNA

Serves 8 to 10

Perfect for your next buffet...

1/2 lb. lasagna noodles
1 cup chopped onion
1 T. butter
2 10-3/4 oz. cans cream
   of shrimp soup
3 6-oz. pkgs. frozen
   lump crabmeat,
   defrosted and
   thoroughly drained
2/3 cup beer, flattened
1 cup cottage cheese
1 8-oz. pkg. cream
   cheese, softened
1 egg, beaten
1/4 tsp. pepper
2 tsp. basil
1-3/4 oz. pkg. dry Italian
   salad dressing mix
2 oz. small raw shrimp
3/4 cup freshly grated
   Parmesan cheese

Cook and drain lasagna noodles according to package directions. Sauté onion in butter until transparent. Mix soup, crab and beer in large saucepan; heat until bubbly. Mix cottage cheese, cream cheese, egg, seasonings and onion; add to soup mixture. Add shrimp. Butter a 3-quart casserole. Place half of noodles in bottom of casserole, top with half of sauce. Repeat layers; top with cheese. Bake at 350 degrees for one hour.

VARIATION: 1/2 lb. cooked shrimp may be placed on top of casserole before serving.

Mrs. Samuel H. Ellis

COLD FILET OF BEEF, JAPONAIS

Serves 15 to 20

Cool extravaganza on a mid-summer night.

1 large filet of beef,
   trimmed of all fat
   (about 7 lbs.)
1 cup Japanese soy sauce
1 cup olive or peanut oil
1 cup sherry
6 garlic cloves, chopped
1 tsp. Tabasco
dash of freshly ground
   pepper

Marinate the filet in remaining ingredients for 24 hours, turning several times. Remove and dry. Rub with additional oil. Preheat oven to 475 degrees. Roast on a rack for 25 minutes for very rare; 28 to 30 minutes for rare. Baste with marinade 3 or 4 times during the roasting. Allow it to cool. If possible, do not refrigerate. Arrange on a platter with watercress and tiny cherry tomatoes.

NOTE: This is a good marinade for less expensive cuts of beef.

Mrs. David Schafer

BARBECUE BRISKET

Serves 8 to 16

Tender and spicy...

3 to 6 lbs. beef brisket
1-1/2 tsp. celery salt
1 tsp. onion salt
1/2 tsp. garlic salt
1/2 cup liquid smoke
1/2 cup Worcestershire
   sauce
1-1/2 cups barbecue
   sauce

Rub the three salts into the meat. Pour liquid smoke and Worcestershire sauce over meat. Marinate overnight in the refrigerator in a baking pan large enough to hold the meat. Bake uncovered at 350 degrees for 2 to 3 hours, turning the meat occasionally. Pour barbecue sauce over top of meat. Cover and cook one more hour. Slices best if taken from the oven 10 to 15 minutes before serving. Slice across grain of meat. Serve the sauce as gravy. Any leftovers may be reheated in sauce and served on buns.

Mrs. Harry M. Kelso III

CONTINENTAL FLANK STEAK

Serves 4

Excellent marinade. Can be cooked on the outdoor grill.

3 T. butter, softened
2 T. Dijon mustard
1 T. fresh lemon juice
1 tsp. soy sauce
1 tsp. Worcestershire
  sauce
1/2 tsp. curry powder
1/4 tsp. salt
1/4 tsp. pepper
1 2-lb. flank steak
1/2 cup dry sherry
1 lb. mushrooms, thinly
  sliced
2 T. butter
1 cup sour cream
1 to 2 T. brandy
fresh parsley, chopped

Mix softened butter, mustard, lemon juice, soy sauce, Worcestershire, curry, salt and pepper in a small bowl. Put steak in shallow dish. Spread with mustard mixture. Pour sherry over steak; marinate 8 hours or overnight. Let steak come to room temperature. Broil until rare. Thinly slice meat on diagonal; arrange slices on ovenproof serving platter; keep warm. Sauté mushrooms in butter 5 minutes; add pan juices from broiler pan. Stir in sour cream and brandy; do not boil. Pour over steak. Broil 1 minute. Garnish with parsley.

NOTE: Bourbon may be substituted for the brandy.

Mrs. James R. McClamroch

SWEET-SOUR BEEF AND VEGETABLES

Serves 6

This tasty meal cooks while you have a day away from the kitchen.

2 lbs. round or chuck
  steak
2 T. vegetable oil
6 medium carrots, pared
1 large green pepper
2 cups small white
  onions, peeled
1 15-1/2 oz. can tomato
  sauce
2 tsp. chili powder
2 tsp. paprika
1/4 cup granulated sugar
1 tsp. salt
1/4 cup vinegar
1/4 cup molasses

Cut steak in 1-inch cubes. Brown meat in hot oil in skillet. Transfer to crock pot. Cut carrots and green pepper in large pieces. Place in crock pot along with the rest of the ingredients. Mix well. Cook 10 to 12 hours on low or 5 to 6 hours on high. Serve with shell macaroni or rice sprinkled with fresh or freeze-dried chives.

Mrs. Arthur W. Bergman, Jr.

SLOW-COOKED BEEF IN BEER   *Serves 4 to 6*

Easy entrée for a busy day...

2 lbs. round or chuck
  steak
1/8 tsp. instant minced
  garlic
1/4 cup flour
1/4 cup oil
1-1/2 tsp. salt
1/8 tsp. pepper
1 onion, sliced
1 cup tomato sauce
1 cup beer, flattened

Cut steak into serving-size portions, removing fat and bones. Combine garlic and flour; dredge steak with mixture. Heat oil in skillet and brown steak on both sides. Season meat with salt and pepper and place in a crock pot. Sauté onions in skillet and pour over meat along with tomato sauce and beer. Cover and cook on low heat for 6 to 8 hours. Thicken gravy, if desired. Serve with noodles.

Mrs. Arthur W. Bergman, Jr.

STROGANOFF STEAK SANDWICH   *Serves 6*

Perfect for an informal buffet...

2/3 cup beer, flattened
1/3 cup oil
1 tsp. salt
1/4 tsp. garlic powder
  (optional)
1/4 tsp. freshly ground
  pepper
1 2-lb. flank steak
2 T. butter or margarine
1/2 tsp. paprika
dash of salt
4 cups sliced onions
1 cup sour cream,
  warmed slightly
1/2 tsp. horseradish
12 slices French bread

In a shallow dish, combine beer, oil, salt, garlic powder and pepper. Place flank steak in marinade; cover. Marinate overnight in refrigerator or 2 hours at room temperature. Turn meat a few times. Drain. Broil flank steak 3 inches from heat for 5 to 7 minutes on each side, until medium rare. In saucepan, melt butter; blend in paprika and salt. Add onions and cook until tender but not brown. Combine sour cream and horseradish in a serving bowl. To serve, thinly slice meat on the diagonal. For each serving, arrange meat slices over 2 slices French bread. Top with onions, then with sour cream. Sprinkle with paprika for color, if desired.

Mrs. Edwin B. Bosler

FAVORITE GREEN PEPPER STEAK

Serves 4

It'll become a favorite of yours...

1-1/2 lbs. flank steak
1/2 cup soy sauce
1 clove garlic, crushed
1 cup water
1/4 cup peanut or salad
  oil
2 medium green peppers,
  thinly sliced
1 medium onion, thinly
  sliced
5 stalks celery, thinly
  sliced diagonally
1 T. cornstarch
tomato wedges
hot steamed rice

With very sharp knife, cut steak into paper-thin slices diagonally, cutting across the grain of meat. Mix soy sauce, garlic and 1/2 cup water; marinate meat in this mixture for 15 minutes. Drain meat, reserving liquid. In an electric fry pan or large skillet, heat oil until very hot. Brown meat in oil quickly (about 2 minutes). Push meat to one side of pan and add green peppers, onion and celery. Cook 2 minutes more or until vegetables are crisp/tender. Mix the reserved liquid with cornstarch and remaining 1/2 cup water and stir into meat and vegetables. Cook until liquid is thickened. Arrange on hot steamed rice and garnish with tomato wedges.

Mrs. David P. O'Donnell

CRANBERRY BRISKET OF BEEF

Serves 8 to 10

A great dish for the family or informal company!

1 large brisket of beef,
  4 to 5 lbs.
suet or oil
1 15-oz. can tomato
  sauce
1 10-oz. can whole
  cranberry sauce
4 bay leaves
1/2 tsp. thyme
1/4 tsp. rosemary
1 pkg. dry onion soup mix

Preheat oven to 350 degrees. Brown beef in large skillet in as little fat as needed. When browned, remove meat from pan. Stir in remaining ingredients until smooth. Place brisket in 3-qt. baking dish. Pour on sauce. Cover. Bake for 1 hour per pound.

Mrs. Edward Ruegg

ENCHILADA CASSEROLE

Serves 10 to 12

Mild Mexican fare for a crowd...

SAUCE I
2 lbs. ground chuck
1 large onion, chopped
2 1-lb. cans tomatoes
1 10-oz. pkg. frozen
  chopped spinach
salt and pepper to taste

Brown chuck and drain excess fat. Add onion and sauté for several minutes. Drain tomatoes thoroughly and chop coarsely. Cook spinach briefly in boiling water and drain well. Add tomatoes and spinach to meat mixture and season to taste with salt and pepper.

SAUCE II
1 T. butter
1 clove garlic, minced
1 10-3/4-oz. can cream
  of mushroom soup
1 10-3/4-oz. can Golden
  Mushroom soup
1/2 cup milk
1 cup sour cream

Sauté garlic in butter for 3 minutes. Add soups and milk, stirring until well mixed. Add sour cream and continue cooking and stirring until heated through.

2 4-oz. cans chopped
  green chilies, drained
12 to 16 flour tortillas
8 oz. grated sharp
  Cheddar cheese

Dip half of the tortillas in Sauce II and arrange on the bottom and sides of a deep 9 x 13-inch casserole. Spoon Sauce I over tortillas. Sprinkle with chilies and half of the grated cheese. Cover with the remaining tortillas and Sauce II, spreading evenly. Top with the rest of the cheese. Refrigerate, covered, overnight. Bake for 35 to 45 minutes at 350 degrees.

Mrs. David B. Sterrett, Sr.

BEEF NEOPOLITAN

Serves 6 to 8

Hearty casserole...

2 lbs. sirloin tip, well
  trimmed, cut into
  1-inch cubes
2 T. olive oil
8 oz. sliced fresh
  mushrooms
1 tsp. salt
1/8 tsp. pepper
1/3 cup dry sherry
1 16-oz. can stewed
  tomatoes
1 10-oz. pkg. frozen
  chopped spinach,
  thawed
1 5-1/2-oz. box Noodles
  Romanoff mix
1/2 cup grated Cheddar
  cheese
1/4 cup freshly grated
  Parmesan cheese

Preheat oven to 350 degrees. Sauté meat in oil until lightly browned. Add mushrooms and sauté for a few minutes. Add salt, pepper, sherry and tomatoes; heat to boiling. Reduce heat and simmer, covered, for 10 minutes. Add spinach and un-cooked noodles with seasonings and cheese from mix. Blend well. Place in a greased two-quart casserole. Top with grated Cheddar cheese and bake for 30 minutes, or until noodles are tender. Sprinkle with Parmesan cheese and serve.

Mrs. Thomas M. Ritchie, Jr.

SHORT-CUT SAUERBRATEN

Serves 8

Spice up your chuck roast!

1 3 to 3-1/2-lb. boneless
  chuck roast
1/2 cup wine vinegar
1 bay leaf, crumbled
1 clove garlic, crushed
dash pepper
1 envelope onion soup
  mix
2 ginger snaps, crushed

Trim excess fat from roast. Arrange large sheet of heavy-duty foil in shallow baking pan. Place meat in center and add vinegar. Sprinkle with bay leaf, garlic and pepper. Bring foil up over meat and over-lap. Marinate at room temperature for 30 minutes or in refrigerator 2 to 3 hours. Sprinkle dry soup mix over meat, coating all sides. Close foil, sealing with double fold. Bake at 325 degrees for 3 hours, or until tender. Transfer meat to heated plat-ter. Strain drippings into pan; skim off fat. Add crushed ginger snaps and cook until thickened. Pour gravy over sliced meat.

Mrs. David H. Robertson

9/10/97

9:46AM

Pam

Barb Woodards
called. She is at work
and would just like to
holler at you before you
leave — If you have the
time.

Jim

CARBONNADE FLAMANDE

Serves 6 to 8

Beer's the secret of this stew's delicious flavor.

3 lbs. boneless beef chuck
  or rump, excess fat
  trimmed
2 T. unsalted butter
2 T. bacon fat
1-1/2 lbs. yellow onions,
  sliced into 1/2-inch
  rings
salt and pepper to taste
2 cloves minced garlic
12 oz. good quality beer,
  at room temperature
1 cup good quality beef
  stock
1 T. brown sugar
1 bay leaf
6 sprigs fresh parsley
1 tsp. thyme
2 T. cornstarch
2 T. vinegar

Preheat oven to 350 degrees. Cut beef into 1/2-inch slices; brown well in butter and bacon fat. Remove to platter. Reduce heat and brown onions with salt and pepper; add garlic. Layer beef and onions in a 2-qt. baking casserole. Mix beer, beef stock and brown sugar. Pour over beef. Tie parsley, bay leaf and thyme in cheesecloth to make a bouquet garni; place in casserole. Cover and bake for 2-1/2 hours. Discard bouquet. Pour off pan juices into a small saucepan. Mix vinegar and cornstarch. Add to juices and simmer until thickened.

Mrs. H. H. Hanlon

FANCY FLANKS

Serves 8

Good flavor!

1/2 cup chopped onion
1 clove garlic, crushed
  (optional)
2 T. oil
1 10-1/2-oz. can beef
  broth
1/2 cup catsup
1 T. brown sugar
1 T. Worcestershire sauce
2 tsp. prepared mustard
2 flank steaks

Sauté onion and garlic in oil until tender. Add broth, catsup, sugar, Worcestershire and mustard; simmer 15 minutes. Cool marinade and pour over flank steaks. Marinate at least 2 hours—up to 24 hours. Grill to desired doneness.

Mrs. David M. Stone

MEAT LOAF WELLINGTON

Serves 8

All dressed up...every place to go!

MEATLOAF
1-1/2 lbs. ground beef
2 cups chopped celery
1 cup drained tomatoes
1/2 cup liquid from
tomatoes
3 slices bread, crumbled
1 egg, beaten
2 tsp. salt
1 tsp. sage
1/4 tsp. pepper

CRUST AND FILLING
1 17-1/4-oz. pkg.
Pepperidge Farm
puff pastry (one
sheet pastry)
1 cup grated Cheddar
cheese
1/2 cup chopped
cooked mushrooms
1/4 cup minced green
onions
1 egg beaten with
2 T. water

Preheat oven to 375 degrees. Mix meat loaf ingredients together lightly. Turn into greased and foil-lined 8-1/4 x 4-1/4-inch loaf pan. Bake 1 hour and 15 minutes. Drain off grease. Cool, and remove from pan. Chill. Preheat oven to 400 degrees. Remove one pre-rolled sheet of pastry. Thaw enough to roll into a 13 x 20-inch rectangle. Place meat loaf in center. Combine cheese, mushrooms and onions. Spread filling on top of meat loaf. Bring sides of pastry up, overlap and seal. Place on greased baking sheet and brush with mixture of egg and water. Bake for 30 minutes. Cool 10 minutes. Slice and serve.

Mrs. Steven E. Lindblad

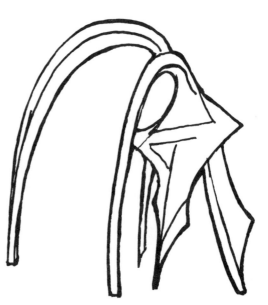

COMPROMISE MEATLOAF

Serves 6

A combination of several meatloaf recipes.

1-1/4 cups milk
1 cup stale bread crumbs
1-1/2 lbs. lean ground
   beef
1/3 cup chopped onion
1/3 cup chopped green
   pepper
1 beaten egg
1 T. catsup
1 T. prepared horseradish
1/2 tsp. baking powder
salt and pepper to taste

Preheat oven to 350 degrees. Combine milk and bread crumbs; let sit until thick. Combine all ingredients and mix well. Place in ungreased 9 x 5-inch loaf pan. Bake for 1-1/2 hours. Cool 10 minutes before serving.

Mrs. Julien H. Collins, Jr.

MY FAVORITE MEAT LOAF

Serves 4 to 6

Good cold for sandwiches, too.

1 medium onion,
   chopped
1/2 cup herbed stuffing
   mix
1/2 cup bouillon
1 lb. ground beef
4 sprigs parsley, chopped
3 T. grated Parmesan
   cheese
1 egg, slightly beaten
1 tsp. salt
1/4 tsp. pepper
butter
1 8-oz. can tomato sauce
1 tsp. oregano

Preheat oven to 375 degrees. Sauté onion in butter. In large bowl, mix stuffing mix, bouillon, onion, ground beef, chopped parsley, Parmesan cheese, egg, salt and pepper. Blend well. Form into loaf in loaf pan or flat pan. Dot with butter. Bake 30 minutes. Pour tomato sauce over top and sprinkle with oregano. Bake 20 minutes longer.

Mrs. Carroll G. Wells

SWEET-SOUR MEAT LOAF

Serves 8

A new flavor twist...

1 8-oz. can tomato sauce
1/4 cup brown sugar,
  packed
1/4 cup vinegar
1 tsp. mustard
2 lbs. ground chuck
1 medium onion, minced
1/2 cup crushed saltines
1 egg, slightly beaten
1-1/2 tsp. salt
1/4 tsp. pepper

Preheat oven to 350 degrees. Mix tomato sauce with brown sugar, vinegar and mustard. Stir until sugar is dissolved. Mix chuck, onions, crackers, egg, salt, pepper and 1/2 cup of tomato mixture. Place in a loaf pan and pour rest of tomato mixture over top. Bake one hour or until done. Baste with sauce.

Mrs. John N. Fix

CALIFORNIA ZUCCHINI BAKE

Serves 6

Family favorite...

1 lb. hamburger
3 medium zucchini,
  sliced
1/4 cup sliced green
  onions with tops
2 tsp. chili powder
2 tsp. salt
1/4 tsp. garlic powder
1 7-oz. can green chilies,
  chopped
3 cups cooked rice
1 cup sour cream
3 cups grated Monterey
  Jack cheese
1 large fresh tomato,
  sliced
salt and pepper

Preheat oven to 350 degrees. Sauté meat, zucchini, onions and spices until meat is brown. Add chilies, rice, sour cream, and 1 cup of cheese. Turn into shallow, buttered 2-quart casserole. Top with tomato slices. Season with salt and pepper. Top with remaining cheese. Bake for 20 to 25 minutes.

Mrs. Donald J. Ross

KÖTTBULLAR
(Swedish Meat Balls)

Serves 6

Fluffy and light...the secret is to beat, beat, beat.

3/4 lb. ground round
1/2 lb. ground veal
1/4 lb. ground pork
1-1/2 cups soft bread
   crumbs (about 3 slices)
1/4 cup milk
1/2 cup chopped onion
2 T. butter
1 cup half and half
1/4 cup finely chopped
   fresh parsley
1 tsp. salt
1 tsp. monosodium
   glutamate (optional)
1/4 tsp. ginger
dash pepper
dash nutmeg
2 T. butter
1 T. flour
3/4 cup half and half
1/2 to 1 tsp. instant
   coffee
1/2 tsp. concentrated
   meat extract (B.V.)
dash monosodium
   glutamate (optional)

Have meats *ground twice* by your butcher or grind again at home. Soak bread in milk for 5 minutes. Cook onion in butter until tender but not brown. Combine ground meats, bread crumbs, onion, 1 cup half and half, parsley and seasonings. Beat vigorously until fluffy, about 5 minutes at medium speed in electric mixer. (Mixture will be soft.) Form into 1-inch balls, wetting hands for easier shaping. Brown lightly in 2 T. butter, shaking skillet to keep balls round. Don't try to brown too many meatballs at one time! Remove meatballs. Stir flour into drippings in skillet; add 3/4 cup half and half, coffee, meat extract and MSG. Heat and stir until gravy thickens. Return meatballs to gravy and let simmer about 10 minutes or until done.

Mrs. Robert W. Higgins

231

SUPPER NACHOS

Serves 12

Just super!

1 lb. lean ground beef
1 large onion, chopped
salt to taste
liquid hot pepper
   seasoning, to taste
1 to 2 16-oz. cans
   refried beans
1 4-oz. can chopped
   green chilies
2 to 3 cups grated
   Monterey Jack or mild
   Cheddar cheese or
   combination of both
3/4 cup prepared taco
   sauce (green or red)
12 corn tortillas

GARNISH
1/4 cup green onions,
   chopped, including
   some tops
1 cup pitted ripe olives
1 cup avocados,
   coarsely chopped
1 cup sour cream
parsley sprigs (optional)
mild red pickled peppers
   (optional)

Preheat oven to 400 degrees. Crumble beef in a frying pan; add onion. Cook, stirring, until meat is lightly browned. Discard fat; season meat with salt and liquid pepper to suit your taste. Spread beans in a shallow 10 x 15-inch pan. Top evenly with meat. Sprinkle chilies over meat. Cover with cheese. Drizzle taco sauce over cheese. Bake, uncovered for 20 to 25 minutes, or until thoroughly heated. Cover and chill if making ahead. Heat tortillas in foil until hot and pliable. Spread or spoon meat mixture on each tortilla. Sprinkle green onion, ripe olives, avocado and a spoonful of sour cream on top. If you wish, add a fresh parsley sprig and mild pepper.

Mrs. James Lynch

HEAVENLY SPAGHETTI

Serves 5 to 6

Great for a teenage crowd.

11-oz. spaghetti
1 T. butter
1-1/2 lbs. ground beef
2 8-oz. cans tomato
  sauce
salt and pepper
1/2 lb. cottage cheese
1 8-oz. pkg. cream
  cheese
1/4 cup sour cream
1/3 cup chopped
  scallions
1 T. minced green pepper
2 T. melted butter

Preheat oven to 350 degrees. Cook spaghetti and drain. Sauté beef in butter until brown. Drain off fat. Add tomato sauce, salt and pepper. Remove from heat. Combine cottage cheese, cream cheese, sour cream, scallions and green pepper. In a 2-qt. casserole spread one half spaghetti and cover with cheese mixture. Add remaining spaghetti and pour melted butter over it. Spread tomato/meat sauce over top. Bake covered for 45 minutes.

NOTE: Can be made a day ahead. Freezes nicely.

Mrs. Kenneth T. Wright

PORTERHOUSE STEAK-CHICAGO STYLE

Serves 4 to 6

Succulent sauce!

1/4 cup chopped
  scallions
1/4 cup crumbled
  Roquefort cheese
2 garlic cloves, finely
  minced
4 T. butter, cut into
  small pieces
1 2-inch thick porter-
  house steak, room
  temperature

Preheat broiler. Prepare a loose mixture of first four ingredients. Broil steak almost to desired degree of doneness. Before removing steak from broiler, spread mixture over steak and return to broiler long enough to melt butter and cheese.

NOTE: This Roquefort sauce can be used over hamburgers, too!

Mrs. A. W. Phelps

TEXAS STYLE BEEF BRISKET

Serves 6 to 8

Extremely easy!

whole beef brisket,
   trimmed of most fat
1 12-oz. can beer
1 pkg. onion soup mix

Preheat oven to 300 degrees. Place brisket in large covered casserole or baking pan. Sprinkle with onion soup mix. Pour on the beer. Bake 3 hours or until tender. Slice thinly across the grain. Can be served on buns or noodles.

NOTE: 1 cup of red wine may be substituted for the beer.

Mrs. Edward R. James

MARINATED FLANK STEAK

Serves 4

Excellent, aromatic marinade...

1 large garlic clove,
   crushed
1-1/2 tsp. ginger
1/4 cup honey
2 T. vinegar
3/4 cup vegetable oil
1/4 cup soy sauce
1 flank steak

Mix all marinade ingredients. Marinate flank steak for 5 hours or overnight. Grill 4 minutes on each side. Slice across grain of meat.

Mrs. Franklin A. Urbahns

FAR EAST PORK CHOPS

Serves 4 to 6

Scrumptious Oriental fare...

6 large pork chops
1/4 tsp. freshly
  ground pepper
3/4 tsp. cumin seed
1 large green pepper,
  coarsely chopped
1-3/4 cups unsweetened
  pineapple juice
3 T. soy sauce
1 12-1/2-oz. jar
  preserved kumquats,
  undrained
1 11-oz. can mandarin
  oranges, drained
3/4 cup brown sugar,
  packed
1/2 cup white vinegar
3-1/2 T. cornstarch
1/4 cup water

Preheat oven to 350 degrees. Sprinkle chops with pepper. Place in 9 x 12-inch baking dish. Sprinkle cumin seed on top. Bake about 30 minutes or until browned; drain fat. As chops are baking, prepare the sauce. Simmer green pepper in pineapple juice for 10 minutes. Add all other ingredients except cornstarch and water. Stir cornstarch in water until well blended and add to sauce. Cook until thickened. Pour sauce over pork chops and bake for 30 minutes. Arrange fruit and some of the sauce on chops; serve remaining sauce over rice.

Mrs. L. Steven Minkel

QUICK SWEET AND SOUR PORK

Serves 4

An easy dish to fix after a busy day.

2 T. corn oil
1 lb. boneless pork,
  cut into 1-inch cubes
1 20-oz. can pineapple
  chunks in own juice
1/2 cup light or dark
  corn syrup
1/4 cup cider vinegar
2 T. catsup
2 T. soy sauce
1 clove garlic, crushed
1/2 cup green pepper,
  cut into 1-inch squares
2 T. cornstarch
2 T. water
salt to taste

In large skillet, heat oil over medium heat; add meat and brown well. Add next 6 ingredients and bring to a boil. Add green pepper. Mix cornstarch and water and stir into pork mixture. Stir constantly, bring to a boil and boil for one minute. Add salt. Serve with rice.

Mrs. Scott Lockridge

SUCCULENT MING PORK

As great as its name!

1-1/2 lbs. lean pork
1/4 cup water
1-1/2 tsp. ginger
2 tsp. Spice Islands Mei
  Yen seasoning powder
2 T. butter
2 cups sliced fresh
  mushrooms
1 13-1/2-oz. can
  pineapple chunks
  in own juice
1/2 cup red wine vinegar
2 tsp. chicken seasoned
  stock base
3 T. sugar
1 large green pepper,
  seeded, sliced
1 T. arrowroot powder
1 cup halved cherry
  tomatoes

Cut pork into 1-inch cubes, trimming off excess fat. Combine water, 1/2 tsp. ginger and 1 tsp. Mei Yen seasoning. Pour over pork in a large skillet. Cover and simmer pork 1/2 hour. Drain off all pan liquid. Add butter to skillet and brown pork slowly. Add mushrooms; sauté until lightly browned. Drain pineapple well, reserving 1/2 cup juice. Combine pineapple juice, vinegar, stock base, sugar, 1 tsp. ginger, 1 tsp. Mei Yen seasoning. Pour over pork. Recipe can be prepared in the morning to this point. Add green pepper slices and simmer 5 to 7 minutes, until pepper is just tender. Stir arrowroot into pan juices. Cook slowly, stirring constantly, until thickened and clear. Add drained pineapple and tomatoes. Cook 2 to 3 minutes longer. Serve over rice. Can be easily doubled or tripled.

Mrs. Edwin B. Bosler

MANDARIN GLAZED PORK CHOPS

Unusual sweet-sour sauce...

6 thick pork chops
3 T. brown sugar
1/2 tsp. cinnamon
3 whole cloves
1 tsp. salt
1 tsp. prepared mustard
1/4 cup catsup
1 T. vinegar
1 11-oz. can mandarin
  oranges, undrained

Preheat oven to 350 degrees. Put pork chops in a 9 x 13-inch casserole. Combine remaining ingredients and pour over chops. Bake for 1 hour or until chops are tender.

Mrs. James E. Sullivan

CHINESE PORK ROAST

Serves 6 to 8

An uptown pork roast with a sophisticated sauce.

3 to 4 lb. rolled pork roast
2/3 cup soy sauce
1/3 cup lemon juice
1/3 cup granulated sugar
1 onion, sliced
4 green onions, cut in
   1-inch lengths
1/2 tsp. ginger
1 garlic clove, crushed
1 10-1/2-oz. can
   condensed beef broth

Mix soy sauce, lemon juice and sugar. Rub into pork. Add onion slices, green onion, ginger and garlic. Add all but 1/2 cup of beef broth. Cover well and let stand 2 to 4 hours or refrigerate overnight. Turn often. Preheat oven to 325 degrees. Add remaining beef broth and roast uncovered for 2-1/2 to 3 hours or until well done. Remove pork from roasting pan and keep warm. Skim fat and thicken the remaining marinade with flour and water to make a gravy. Slice pork in 1/2-inch pieces and serve with gravy.

NOTE: Fresh crushed ginger root may be used in place of dried ginger.

Mrs. Arthur W. Bergman, Jr.

PORK TENDERLOIN DELUXE

Serves 1

An old favorite! Make as many as you need.

2 slices bacon (slightly
   precooked)
1 slice onion
1 slice tomato
1 pork tenderloin patty

Preheat oven to 350 degrees. Criss-cross two bacon slices, top with pork tenderloin, then onion slice, then tomato slice. Again cross the bacon strips over the top of the tomato and secure with toothpicks. Bake 45 to 50 minutes.

NOTE: Prepare two for men and one apiece for women. These can be prepared ahead of time, brought to room temperature and then put into the oven to bake.

Mrs. James R. Beall

GRILLED PORK TENDERLOINS

Serves 4

An interesting and attractive treat from the grill.

1 pkg. Adolf's meat marinade
1/3 cup orange juice
2 T. plus 2 tsp. lemon juice
2 T. plus 2 tsp. dry white wine or sherry
1 8-oz. jar apricot preserves
2 whole pork tenderloins, well trimmed

Mix all marinade ingredients together and pour over meat; marinate 1 to 2 hours. Drain marinade and pour into pan. Arrange hot coals in bottom of covered grill at cooking time for "indirect" method. Place tin foil pan in center for dripping. Cook meat 45 to 55 minutes, depending on size and heat of coals. Turn several times during cooking and baste with reserved marinade. Reheat remaining marinade. Slice in 1/2-inch slices, pour marinade over meat or pass separately.

NOTE: Recipe can be doubled or tripled easily. Leftovers are great cold.

Mrs. R. Scott Stratton

PORK SCHNITZEL

Serves 6

Sensational and so easy!

6 large pork loin cutlets (butterfly)
1/4 cup flour
1 tsp. seasoned salt
1/4 tsp. pepper
1 egg, beaten
2 T. milk
3/4 cup dry bread crumbs
2 tsp. paprika or to taste
3 T. shortening
3/4 cup chicken broth
1 T. flour
1/4 tsp. dill weed
  or to taste
1/2 cup sour cream

Pound pork to 1/4 to 1/8-inch thickness, slitting edges to prevent curling. Combine flour, seasoned salt and pepper. Combine egg and milk. Combine crumbs and paprika. Coat pork with flour mixture, then with egg mixture, lastly with crumb mixture. Cook cutlets in hot shortening, 2 to 3 minutes per side. Remove to platter and keep warm. Pour broth into skillet, scraping pan to loosen drippings. Blend flour and dill weed into sour cream; stir into broth. Cook until thick but do not boil.

Mrs. Dane F. Hahn

SWEET-SOUR PEPPER PORK

Serves 3 to 4

Ah! so good...

1 whole pork tenderloin
  (12 oz.)
2 medium green peppers
1 egg yolk
2 tsp. water
1 T. flour
1 T. cornstarch
salad oil
1 clove garlic
1 6-oz. pkg. frozen
  peapods
1-1/2 cups sliced celery
1 8-oz. can water
  chestnuts, drained
  and sliced
1/4 to 1/2 cup slivered
  almonds
hot cooked rice

SEASONING SAUCE
3/4 cup water
1 T. cornstarch
1 T. chili sauce
1 T. soy sauce
5 T. granulated sugar
3 T. wine vinegar
few drops hot pepper
  sauce

Remove fat from pork. Cut into 2-inch crosswise sections. Cut each of these into lengthwise strips 1/2-inch in diameter. Seed green peppers and cut into 1/4-inch wide strips. Beat egg yolk with water; blend in flour and cornstarch until smooth. Coat pork with this mixture. Pour salad oil into frying pan to 1/2-inch depth; set over medium high heat. When oil has reached 340 degrees, add all meat. Stirring occasionally, fry until the crust is golden brown, about 10 minutes. Be certain the meat is thoroughly cooked. Remove meat, drain and set aside. Heat 2 tsp. salad oil in a frypan over medium high heat. Add garlic clove and cook until golden brown; discard garlic. Add pepper strips and cook for one minute, stirring. Add fried pork, peapods, celery and water chestnuts and almonds. Add seasoning sauce to pan. Stir until it boils and thickens. Serve immediately with rice.

Mix cornstarch and water until smooth. Stir in remaining ingredients.

Mrs. L. Steven Minkel

239

GLAZED HAM LOAF RING WITH MUSTARD SAUCE

Serves 8

Guaranteed good!

MUSTARD SAUCE
1/2 cup dry mustard
  (Colman's)
1/2 cup vinegar
1 egg
1/3 cup granulated sugar
dash salt
1 cup mayonnaise,
  or to taste

Start to prepare *mustard sauce* a day ahead. In a jar, mix mustard and vinegar; cover and let stand overnight. In top of double boiler, beat egg, stir in sugar, salt and mustard mixture. Cook over hot (not boiling) water until mixture thickens slightly and coats spoon. Cool. To serve, add mayonnaise.

HAM LOAF
1-1/2 lbs. ground ham
1-1/4 lbs. ground pork
1-1/2 cups soft bread
  crumbs
1/2 cup chopped onion
2 beaten eggs
1/2 cup milk

Thoroughly combine meats, crumbs, onions, eggs and milk. Press into lightly oiled 6-1/2 cup ring mold; invert on shallow baking pan; remove mold. Preheat oven to 350 degrees. Bake ham loaf for 1-1/4 hours. At end of 45 minutes baking time, brush loaf with glaze. Continue baking loaf until done, basting 3 or 4 times. Serve with mustard sauce.

SWEET/SOUR GLAZE
1/2 cup dark brown sugar
1 T. prepared mustard
2 T. vinegar
1 T. water

Blend ingredients.

Kenilworth Union Church

HOT HAM SANDWICHES

Makes 8

A hit with the teenage— or tailgating— crowd!

1/2 cup margarine,
  softened
2-1/2 T. mustard
  with horseradish
2 T. minced onion
1 T. poppy seeds
8 hamburger buns
8 oz. ham (more for
  thicker sandwiches)
8 slices Swiss cheese

Mix together margarine, mustard, onion and poppy seeds. Spread on both sides of buns. Place shaved or very thin ham slices on each side of bun with a piece of Swiss cheese in center. Put buns together and wrap in foil. Can be refrigerated at this point. Bake on cookie sheet at 350 degrees for 20 minutes. Serve immediately.

NOTE: If making sandwiches for a crowd, use these proportions:
2 cups margarine, softened
1 9-oz. jar mustard with horseradish
1 cup minced onion
4 T. poppy seeds

Mrs. Franklin A. Urbahns

HUNGARIAN VEAL PAPRIKA

Serves 6

Heavenly...

1-1/2 lbs. veal, sliced
  3/8-inch thick
1/2 cup flour
1-1/2 tsp. salt
pepper
1/2 cup butter
3/4 T. paprika
1 medium onion,
  thinly sliced
1/2 cup hot water
1 8-oz. pkg.
  medium noodles
1/2 cup sliced almonds
1 T. poppy seeds
1 cup sour cream

Flatten veal slices. Blend flour, salt, and pepper and pound into meat. Cut meat into 2-inch squares and sauté in butter. Drain excess butter. Sprinkle paprika and onions over meat. Add water and simmer 30 minutes. Cook noodles and combine with poppy seeds and almonds. Beat the sour cream and add to meat mixture at the last minute. Heat gently until bubbly, but watch carefully so that sauce doesn't curdle. Serve immediately on noodles.

NOTE: Chicken breasts may be substituted for veal.

Mrs. G. Preston Kendall

VERNAL VEAL

A springtime favorite...

1-1/2 lbs. thinly sliced
  veal cutlet, well
  trimmed
2 T. butter
1 T. flour
1-1/2 cups consommé
dash cayenne pepper
2 T. tomato paste
1 small bay leaf
1 lb. fresh asparagus

Melt butter in large frypan; brown veal quickly on both sides over medium high heat. Remove from pan and set aside. Reduce heat and sprinkle flour in pan; stir until roux bubbles. Gradually add consommé, scraping any brown bits from the bottom of the pan. Add tomato paste, pepper and bay leaf. Bring sauce to a boil; add veal. Reduce heat to simmer. Cover pan and cook 10 minutes. Add asparagus and simmer for 20 additional minutes or until veal and asparagus are tender. Remove bay leaf and serve with rice.

Mrs. Julien H. Collins, Jr.

LAKE LUCERNE VEAL

Serves 4

Tantalizing...

2 T. olive or salad oil
2 T. butter
1-1/2 lbs. thin veal,
  cut into strips
2 green onions, chopped
1 clove garlic, minced
2 ripe tomatoes, peeled
  and chopped
1/4 tsp. pepper
1/2 tsp. salt
1/2 lb. fresh mushrooms,
  sliced into thirds
1/2 cup dry vermouth
  or white wine
1/2 tsp. dried basil or
  or rosemary, optional
1 lb. fresh peas or
  1 10-oz. pkg.
  frozen peas

Sauté veal, onion and garlic in hot butter and oil until the veal changes color—about 3 minutes. Stir veal constantly to brown all sides. Add tomatoes, pepper, salt, mushrooms and vermouth. Bring to a boil. Reduce heat, cover skillet and simmer for 15 to 20 minutes or until veal is tender. If desired, basil or rosemary may be added before simmering. Meanwhile, cook peas until tender and keep hot. Pour veal into serving dish, sprinkle peas over top. Serve with rice.

Mrs. Wilfred H. Heitmann

OSSO BUCO

Splendid version of a classic...

VEAL
8 lbs. veal hind shanks, cut into 2-inch thick rounds (16 pieces)
1/2 cup flour
2-1/2 tsp. salt
1 tsp. basil
1/2 tsp. thyme
1/2 tsp. freshly ground black pepper
3 T. butter
3 T. oil
1 large garlic clove, minced
1 cup minced onion
1-1/2 cups dry white wine
2 28-oz. cans Italian tomatoes, drained
1/4 tsp. granulated sugar
1-1/2 cups beef broth
1 bay leaf
salt and pepper to taste
lemon slices

Coat veal with flour, salt, basil, thyme and pepper. Heat butter and oil and brown veal on all sides. Set aside. Save pan drippings and sauté onion and garlic until soft. Add white wine and reduce to approximately one cup. Preheat oven to 350 degrees. Place veal shanks in a single layer in a 3-quart casserole. Set shanks upright so the marrow won't fall out during cooking. Pour contents of skillet over veal. Add coarsely chopped tomatoes, sugar, one cup beef broth, bay leaf, salt and pepper. Bake covered for 2 to 3 hours or until meat is fork-tender. Turn meat twice during cooking but be certain shanks remain upright. Add balance of beef broth, if necessary. Adjust seasoning. May be prepared to this point 3 days in advance or may be frozen. At serving time, sprinkle half of gremolata over veal. Turn carefully and sprinkle other side with remaining gremolata. Heat gently for 2 minutes to blend flavors. Transfer to a serving dish and garnish with lemon slices.

GREMOLATA
1 clove garlic
zest of 1 lemon
zest of 1 orange
1 cup fresh parsley leaves

Chop garlic and add zests and parsley. Chop finely by hand or in food processor. Set aside.

NOTE: For a milder flavor, use half quantity of gremolata.

Mrs. Donald J. Ross

VEAL ALMONDINE

Serves 6

Elegant fix-ahead party dish...

6 (4 to 6 oz.) veal scallops
salt and pepper to taste
2-1/2 cups stale bread
  crumbs
1-1/2 cups sliced,
  blanched almonds,
  lightly toasted
1/3 cup fresh minced
  parsley
3 T. grated lemon rind
3 egg whites
3/4 cup clarified butter
  or margarine
2 lemons, sliced

Flatten veal scallops between wax paper until they are 1/4-inch thick; season with salt and pepper. In a shallow bowl, combine bread crumbs, almonds, parsley and lemon rind. In another shallow bowl, beat egg whites lightly. Dip the scallops into egg whites and then into the crumb mixture, pressing the mixture onto them. Chill scallops on a baking sheet for at least 30 minutes. In a large skillet, sauté the scallops in butter for 1 to 2 minutes per side, until golden and just cooked. Transfer to a heated platter and garnish with lemon slices. Squeeze additional lemon juice over scallops, if desired. You may freeze the scallops after cooking and reheat in a 350-degree oven until warmed through, about 20 to 30 minutes.

Mrs. Robert M. Levy

OVEN LAMB CURRY

Serves 8

Easy company entrée...no need to brown the meat!

4 lbs. lean, boneless lamb
1 10-3/4-oz. can cream of
  celery soup
1 small onion, finely
  chopped
1/2 cup dry sherry
1 T. curry powder
2 T. tapioca
2 T. soy sauce
chutney
toasted coconut

Combine all ingredients and place in a two-quart casserole. Bake, covered, for 3 to 3-1/2 hours, at 350 degrees. Turn meat occasionally. Correct seasoning before serving. Serve with side dishes of chutney and toasted coconut. Good over wild or white rice.

NOTE: For best results, buy a whole leg of lamb (6 to 7 lbs.) and have butcher cut meat into 1-1/2-inch cubes.

Mrs. A. W. Phelps

SAVORY LAMB CHOPS

Serves 4

Golden honey glaze tops these tender chops...

**4 large shoulder lamb
chops or lamb steaks
2 T. oil
1 cup honey
1 cup dry white wine
2 T. Worcestershire sauce
1 large clove garlic,
crushed
1/2 tsp. ginger**

Brown chops slowly on both sides in oil. Combine remaining ingredients, mix well and pour over chops. Simmer over low heat for 45 minutes to one hour. Serve chops and sauce over hot buttered noodles sprinkled with poppy seeds.

Mrs. Dane F. Hahn

BASIL BROILED LAMB CHOPS

Serves 4

Deliciously different flavor twist.

**8 1-inch thick lamb
chops
1 tsp. salt
1/3 cup minced onion
1/4 cup honey
1 T. basil
3 T. oil
1-1/2 T. soy sauce
1 to 1-1/2 T. minced
garlic
1 tsp. fresh pepper**

Arrange chops in a 9 x 13-inch Pyrex baking pan; sprinkle with salt. Mix remaining ingredients and pour over chops. Marinate covered for 2 hours, turning chops once. Reserve marinade and broil chops about 4 inches from heat. Meanwhile, reduce marinade over high heat by half and serve over chops.

Casey Bohnstedt

POT ROASTED LAMB IN WHITE WINE

Serves 6

Intriguingly different...

2 T. oil
2 T. butter
2-1/2 lbs. lamb roast or
   boneless shoulder
1/2 tsp. rosemary
3 cloves crushed garlic
1 tsp. salt
1/4 tsp. pepper
2/3 cup dry white wine

Heat oil and butter in large Dutch oven over medium heat. Add meat, rosemary and garlic. Brown 8 to 10 minutes. Sprinkle meat with salt and pepper. Add wine; bring to boil. Stir often. Cook one minute, then reduce heat to low; cover and cook until tender, about 2 to 2-1/2 hours, turning every 20 minutes. Skim fat off broth and serve with lamb.

NOTE: Can substitute lamb cubes or shoulder lamb chops and simmer for one hour. Skimmed sauce may be thickened with 2 tsp. cornstarch.

Casey Bohnstedt

EASTERN LAMB SHANKS

Serves 4 to 6

Exotic sauce, tender meat...

1 16-oz. can purple
   plums with extra heavy
   syrup
4 to 6 lamb shanks
1 tsp. garlic salt
2 T. red wine vinegar
2 T. lemon juice
2 T. honey
1/2 tsp. cinnamon
1/4 tsp. each allspice,
   ginger, rosemary
2 tsp. cornstarch
2 T. cold water

Drain plums, reserving syrup. Brown lamb shanks in heavy kettle or Dutch oven. Drain excess fat. Combine plum syrup with garlic salt, vinegar, lemon juice, honey and spices; pour over lamb. Cover and simmer slowly one hour or until meat is tender. (If preferred, lamb may be baked in 350 degree oven for 1-1/2 to 2 hours.) Baste lamb with sauce occasionally. Combine cornstarch and water; pour into sauce, stirring until thickened. Pit and halve the plums and add to sauce just before serving.

Mrs. Victor J. Voorhies

LUAU LAMB-KEBABS

Serves 6

Luscious...

MARINADE
reserved pineapple juice
1/4 cup vinegar
1/4 cup honey
3 T. melted butter
1 clove garlic, minced
1 tsp. Worcestershire
  sauce
1 tsp. salt
1/8 tsp. pepper
1/4 tsp. ginger

KEBABS
3 large green peppers
1-1/2 to 2 lbs. leg of lamb,
  cut into 1-1/2-inch
  cubes
1 pint cherry tomatoes
1/2 lb. large mushrooms
1 1-lb. 4-1/2-oz. can
  pineapple chunks,
  drained, reserve liquid

Combine marinade ingredients thoroughly in a large bowl. Seed green peppers and cut into squares; parboil for one minute. Add green peppers and lamb to marinade; marinate for several hours. Have charcoal grill hot or preheat broiler. Arrange 2 or 3 cubes each of lamb, tomato, green pepper, mushroom and pineapple on long skewers. Brush kebabs with marinade. Broil 3 or 4 inches from source of heat for 15 to 20 minutes, or until done. Serve with rice.

Mrs. Edwin B. Bosler

247

ITALIAN SAUSAGE LASAGNA
Serves 18 to 24

Lots of cheese makes it special!

1 lb. mild Italian sausage
1-1/2 lbs. lean
  ground beef
2 medium onions,
  chopped
2 cloves garlic,
  minced
1 28-oz. can Italian
  tomatoes, undrained
1 15-oz. can tomato
  sauce
2 beef bouillon cubes,
  crushed
1/4 cup chopped fresh
  parsley
1 T. granulated sugar
2-1/2 tsp. salt
1 tsp. crushed basil
1 bay leaf
1 T. tapioca (or 1 T.
  cornstarch)
1 6-oz. can tomato paste
  (optional)
1/4 cup Burgundy wine
  (optional)
1-1/2 lbs. ricotta cheese
2 eggs, beaten
1 cup Parmesan cheese
1-1/2 tsp. oregano
1/8 to 1/4 tsp. pepper
1-1/2 lbs. Mozzarella
  cheese, grated
1 lb. lasagna noodles,
  cooked and drained

Remove casing from sausage. Brown sausage and beef. Drain fat off meat, reserving 2 T. for sautéeing the onions and garlic. Put *well drained* crumbled meat, cooked onions and garlic, cut up tomatoes and juice, tomato sauce, bouillon cubes, parsley, sugar, salt, basil, bay leaf and tapioca in a 2-1/2-quart crock pot. Cook on low for 8 to 10 hours. After cooking add tomato paste and/or the wine. Preheat oven to 350 degrees. Mix ricotta cheese, eggs, 1/2 cup Parmesan cheese, oregano and pepper. Assemble in 2 13 x 9-inch Pyrex pans. Pour a thin layer of sauce on bottom. Layer half cooked noodles, spread 1/2 ricotta cheese on the noodles, sprinkle 1/2 mozzarella cheese over and top with 1/2 of the remaining sauce. Repeat. Sprinkle each pan with 1/4 cup grated Parmesan cheese. Bake for 45 minutes.

NOTE: Sauce may be made 2 days in advance. Lasagna may be put together a day in advance. This lasagna freezes well.

Mrs. Arthur W. Bergman, Jr.

Cookie's and Candie's

ALMOND CRISPS

Makes 50 cookies

Delicate and delicious.

1-1/2 cups granulated
  sugar
1/2 cup brown sugar
1 cup butter or margarine
1 egg
1 tsp. vanilla
1/2 tsp. salt
1 tsp. baking soda
1 tsp. cream of tartar
2 cups flour
small bowls of water and
  granulated sugar
sliced almonds

Preheat oven to 425 degrees. Cream sugars and butter. Add egg and vanilla. Add dry ingredients. Roll into balls. Dip top half of each cookie into water and then into granulated sugar. Place on greased cookie sheet, sugar side up, and press down in center with finger. Sprinkle with almonds. Bake for 8 to 10 minutes or until just golden. Watch closely as they may need less baking time or a cooler oven.

Mrs. John S. Stiles

CARROT BARS

Makes 48 bars

Spicy, frosted treats for family and friends.

1-1/4 cups flour
1 tsp. baking soda
1 tsp. cinnamon
1/2 tsp. salt
2 eggs
1 cup granulated sugar
3/4 cup vegetable oil
2 4-1/2-oz. jars baby food
  carrots
1 tsp. vanilla
1/2 cup chopped nuts

Preheat oven to 350 degrees. Sift together dry ingredients. Beat eggs, add sugar, add oil and beat well for three minutes. Add carrots, vanilla and nuts. Add dry ingredients and mix well — about three more minutes. Pour into greased and floured 9x13-inch pan. Bake for 30 minutes. Cool. Top with frosting.

FROSTING
1-1/2 cups confectioners
  sugar
3 oz. cream cheese
1/4 cup butter or margarine
1 tsp. vanilla

Beat frosting ingredients together until smooth.

Mrs. Bruce Gooden

DEVIL'S FOOD COOKIES

Makes 3-1/2 dozen

Special children's cookie.

1/2 cup butter
1-1/2 squares unsweetened
   chocolate
1-2/3 cups flour
1 tsp. baking powder
1/4 tsp. baking soda
1/8 tsp. salt
1 egg
1 cup brown sugar
1/3 cup milk
1/2 tsp. vanilla

Preheat oven to 350 degrees. Melt butter and chocolate in double boiler over hot water. Sift flour, baking powder, soda and salt together and set aside. Beat egg in mixing bowl. Add sugar and continue beating until well blended. Mix melted butter and chocolate mixture into eggs and sugar. Add flour mixture alternately with milk and vanilla. Stir until blended. Drop by teaspoonfuls on lightly greased cookie sheet. Bake about 8 minutes. Cool and frost or sprinkle with confectioners sugar.

FROSTING
1 T. cocoa
1/4 cup boiling water
1/2 T. butter or margarine
1 cup confectioners sugar
1/2 tsp. vanilla

Make paste of cocoa and boiling water. Add butter, sugar and vanilla and stir.

Mrs. Walter Hallsteen

PECAN CRISPIES

Makes 6 dozen

Quick and easy and so delicious!

2 cups butter, softened
2-1/2 cups packed light
   brown sugar
2 well-beaten eggs
2-1/2 cups flour
1/4 tsp. salt
1/2 tsp. baking soda
1 cup chopped pecans

Preheat oven to 350 degrees. Cream butter (do not substitute margarine) and sugar. Beat in eggs one at a time. Add dry ingredients and stir. Mix in nuts. Drop by teaspoonfuls 2 inches apart on greased cookie sheet. Bake 12 to 15 minutes.

Mrs. Steven E. Lindblad

COLETTE'S YUMMY SQUARES

Makes 6 dozen

Coconutty!

COOKIE CRUST
3 cups flour
2 tsp. baking powder
1 cup butter
2 cups granulated sugar
1 egg and 4 egg yolks
2 tsp. vanilla

Preheat oven to 350 degrees. Sift flour and baking powder together. Cream butter and sugar. Beat in egg and egg yolks one at a time. Add vanilla. Stir in flour-baking powder mixture. Spread on 11-1/2 x 17-3/8-inch jelly roll pan. Bake for 15 to 20 minutes. Cool.

MERINGUE TOPPING
4 egg whites
2 cups brown sugar
1 cup chopped walnuts
1 3-1/2 oz. can coconut

Whip egg whites until soft peaks form when beater is raised. Add brown sugar 2 T. at a time, beating well after each addition. Fold in walnuts and coconut. Spread on baked cookie crust and bake for 15 to 20 minutes. Cut into squares while warm and sprinkle with confectioners sugar.

Kenilworth Union Church

CHOCOLATE NUT COOKIES

Makes 6 dozen

Rich nutty flavor...

1-1/4 cups butter
3/4 cup granulated
  sugar
1/2 cup unsweetened
  cocoa (Droste
  preferred)
2 cups flour
1 tsp. vanilla
2 cups chopped pecans
confectioners sugar

Cream butter and sugar until fluffy. Mix cocoa and flour and add to butter mixture. Add vanilla and nuts. Chill for 2 hours. Preheat oven to 350 degrees. Roll dough into balls. Bake about 20 minutes. While warm, coat with confectioners sugar.

Mrs. Bert R. Prall

OATMEAL REFRIGERATOR COOKIES

Makes 80 cookies

Gene's favorites!

1 cup margarine or butter
1 cup granulated sugar
1 cup brown sugar
2 eggs, beaten
1-1/2 cups flour
1 tsp. salt
1 tsp. baking soda
1 tsp. vanilla
3 cups quick oats

Cream butter and sugars. Add beaten eggs. Sift flour, salt and soda together. Add sifted dry ingredients to butter/sugar mixture and blend together. Add vanilla and oats, stirring until well mixed. Shape into 4 logs or rods. Chill until firm. Each log makes 20 cookies to fit on a lightly greased cookie sheet. Slice thin and bake for 10 to 12 minutes in 375 degree oven.

Mrs. Arthur W. Bergman, Jr.

OLD-FASHIONED RAISIN BARS

Makes 48 bars

A tasty bar cookie—easy to make and not too sweet.

1 cup raisins
1 cup water
1/2 cup shortening
1 cup granulated sugar
1 slightly beaten egg
1-3/4 cups sifted flour
1/4 tsp. salt
1 tsp. soda
1 tsp. cinnamon
1/2 tsp. nutmeg
1/2 tsp. allspice
1/4 tsp. cloves
1/2 cup chopped walnuts

Preheat oven to 375 degrees. Combine raisins and water in a saucepan. Bring to a boil. Remove from heat and stir in shortening. Cool to lukewarm. Stir in sugar and egg. Sift together dry ingredients; beat into raisin mixture. Stir in nuts. Pour into a greased 15 x 10-inch baking pan. Bake for 12 minutes or until done. When cool, cut into bars. Dust with confectioners sugar.

Kenilworth Union Church

CHEESE-RIBBON BROWNIES *Makes 9 to 12 bars*

A rich, layered version of brownies guaranteed to please both adults and children.

1 8-oz. pkg. cream cheese
1/3 cup granulated sugar
1 egg
1/2 tsp. vanilla
2 squares unsweetened
  chocolate
1/2 cup butter
2 lightly beaten eggs
1 cup granulated sugar
3/4 cup flour
1/2 tsp. baking powder
1/2 tsp. salt

Preheat oven to 350 degrees. Soften cream cheese; thoroughly blend with sugar, egg and vanilla. Set aside. In a medium saucepan, melt chocolate with butter over low to medium heat. Cool slightly, then stir in eggs, sugar and dry ingredients. Spread half of the chocolate batter into a greased 8-inch square pan. Spoon cream cheese mixture over chocolate layer, using a spatula to spread evenly. Pour remaining chocolate batter on top and spread carefully so as not to blend with cheese layer. Bake for 45 minutes. Remove from oven and cool in pan on wire rack.

EASY CHOCOLATE FROSTING

1/4 cup butter
2 cups confectioners sugar
1/2 cup cocoa
1 tsp. vanilla
half and half

Cream butter. Blend in sugar, cocoa, vanilla and enough half and half to make a frosting of spreading consistency. Top cooled brownies with frosting and cut into 1-1/2-inch squares.

Margaret Jones

SHORT WHITE COOKIES

Makes 36 cookies

A guaranteed hit!

1 cup butter
1 cup granulated sugar
1 cup confectioners sugar
2 eggs
1 tsp. vanilla
4 cups flour
1 tsp. salt
1 tsp. baking soda
1 tsp. cream of tartar
1 cup vegetable oil

Cream butter and sugars. Add eggs 1 at a time. Add vanilla. Mix flour, salt, soda and cream of tartar together. Add flour mixture alternately with oil. Refrigerate tightly wrapped for a few hours or overnight. Preheat oven to 350 degrees. Form dough into walnut-sized pieces, roll in granulated sugar and flatten each piece with the bottom of a glass. Bake on greased cookie sheet for 10 minutes.

Mrs. Donald J. Ross

MELTING MOMENTS

Makes 42 cookies

A delicate bite-size cookie that really melts in your mouth.

1 cup softened butter
1/3 cup confectioners sugar
3/4 cup cornstarch
1 cup sifted flour

Beat butter and gradually add sugar and cornstarch. Add sifted flour. Mix well and chill for an hour or overnight. Preheat oven to 350 degrees. Drop by rounded teaspoonfuls onto an ungreased cookie sheet. Bake for 15 minutes or until slightly browned. Cool and frost.

FROSTING
2 T. butter
1 cup confectioners sugar
1 tsp. lemon juice
food coloring (optional)

Mix all ingredients together.

Mrs. G. Preston Kendall

CAMM'S FAVORITE BARS

Makes 48 bars

Sinfully calorific but worth it! Favorite of children and sweet toothers.

36 Brach's wrapped
  caramels
3 T. cream or evaporated
  milk
3 T. butter
3/4 cup melted butter
1 cup flour
3/4 cup brown sugar
1 cup oatmeal
3/4 tsp. salt
1 cup chocolate chips
1/2 cup chopped nuts

Preheat oven to 350 degrees. Melt caramels with cream and butter (3 T.) in double boiler. In a bowl, mix 3/4 cup melted butter, flour, brown sugar, oatmeal and salt. Pat 3/4 of oatmeal mixture in a 9 x 13-inch pan. Bake 10 minutes. Pour caramel sauce over baked crust. Sprinkle with chocolate chips, and chopped nuts. Sprinkle remaining crumb mixture over top. Bake for 12 minutes. Cool and cut into bars.

Kenilworth Union Church

COWBOY COOKIES

Makes 7 dozen cookies

Chocolate chip cookies with a difference!

2 cups sifted flour
1 tsp. baking soda
1/2 tsp. salt
1/2 tsp. baking powder
1 cup margarine
1 cup granulated sugar
1 cup brown sugar
2 eggs
2 cups quick oats
1 tsp. vanilla
6 oz. pkg. chocolate chips
6 oz. pkg. butterscotch
  chips

Preheat oven to 350 degrees. Sift dry ingredients together. Cream margarine and sugars together. Add eggs one at a time. Beat until light and fluffy. Add flour mixture to sugar and margarine mixture. Mix well. Add oats, vanilla and chips. Drop by teaspoonfuls on greased cookie sheet. Bake 12 to 15 minutes. Cool on rack. These cookies keep very well in the freezer for several months.

Mrs. Arthur W. Bergman, Jr.

CHOCOLATE DREAM BARS

Makes 36 bars

Heavenly treat to satisfy your sweet tooth!

FIRST LAYER
1/2 cup butter or
   margarine
1/4 cup granulated sugar
1/3 cup cocoa
1 T. vanilla
1 egg
1-1/2 cups graham
   cracker crumbs
3-1/2 oz. coconut
1/2 cup chopped nuts

Stir butter, sugar, cocoa and vanilla together in top of double boiler; add egg. Cook for 5 minutes, stirring constantly. Add crumbs, coconut and nuts. Press mixture firmly into 9 x 13-inch pan. Refrigerate 5 minutes.

SECOND LAYER
1/2 cup butter or
   margarine, softened
2 T. vanilla
   pudding mix
3 T. milk
2 cups confectioners
   sugar

Cream butter until fluffy. Mix pudding with milk and add to butter, mixing well. Gradually add confectioners sugar. Spread over first layer and refrigerate 30 minutes.

THIRD LAYER
6 oz. chocolate chips
4 T. butter

Melt chips and butter, stirring well. Cool and spread on top of bars.

Mrs. Eric Wagner

LEMON CHEESE CAKE BARS

Makes 24 bars

Perfect dessert for your next luncheon.

CRUMB MIXTURE
1 cup all purpose flour
1/3 cup softened butter
1/2 cup firmly packed dark
  brown sugar

Preheat oven to 350 degrees. Combine flour, butter and brown sugar. Blend with mixer at low speed for 2 to 3 minutes, until in fine particles. Reserve 1 cup of mixture for topping; pat remainder in ungreased 8-inch square pan. Bake near center of oven for 8 to 10 minutes, until lightly browned. Beat filling ingredients until smooth; spread over partially baked crust. Sprinkle with reserved crumb mixture. Return to oven for 23 to 30 minutes or until golden brown. Cool. Cut into bars. Store in refrigerator.

FILLING
8 oz. cream cheese,
  softened
1/4 cup granulated sugar
1 egg
2 T. milk
2 T. lemon juice
grated rind of one lemon
1/2 tsp. vanilla

Beat ingredients until smooth.

Mrs. Joen Johnson

CHOCOLATE CARAMEL LAYER SQUARES

Makes 24 to 30 bars

These tasty bars can be frozen.

1 14-oz. pkg. caramels
2/3 cup evaporated milk
1 18-oz. pkg. German
  chocolate cake mix
3/4 cup butter or
  margarine, softened
1 cup chopped nuts
1 6-oz. pkg. semi-sweet
  chocolate pieces

Preheat oven to 350 degrees. Combine caramels and 1/3 cup evaporated milk in top of double boiler. Stir until caramels are completely melted. Remove from heat. Combine cake mix, remaining 1/3 cup milk and butter with electric mixer until dough holds together. Stir in nuts. Press half of cake into greased 9 x 13-inch baking pan. Bake for 6 minutes. Sprinkle chocolate morsels over cake. Pour caramel mixture over top. Crumble remaining cake mixture on top. Bake 15 to 18 minutes. Chill for 30 minutes. Cut into squares.

Mrs. Howard R. Hayes

PECAN BARS

Makes 36 bars

This is a rich, chewy pecan bar—easy to make.

1 18-1/2 oz. pkg. butter or
  yellow cake mix, divided
1/2 cup margarine, melted
4 eggs
1-1/2 cups dark corn syrup
1/2 cup brown sugar,
  packed
1 tsp. vanilla
1 cup chopped pecans

Preheat oven to 350 degrees. Reserve 2/3 cup dry cake mix for filling. Combine remaining dry cake mix, margarine and 1 egg in large bowl. Mix until crumbly. Press into a greased 13 x 9-inch baking pan. Bake 15 to 20 minutes until light golden brown. Combine reserved cake mix, corn syrup, sugar, 3 eggs and vanilla. Beat at medium speed 1 to 2 minutes. Pour over crust. Sprinkle with pecans. Continue baking 30 to 35 minutes until filling is set. Cool. Cut into squares.

Mrs. G. Preston Kendall

HANNAH'S TOFFEE COOKIES

Makes 5 to 6 dozen

This recipe came from the Swedish housekeeper my family had when I was a child.

1 cup butter
1 cup dark brown sugar
1 unbeaten egg yolk
2 cups flour
1/2 tsp. salt
1-1/2 tsp. cinnamon
1 egg white, slightly beaten
1/3 to 1/2 cup chopped
   pecans

Preheat oven to 350 degrees. Cream butter, sugar and egg yolk. Sift dry ingredients and add to butter mixture. Pat very thin on ungreased 11 x 14-inch jelly roll pan. Brush with egg white. Sprinkle nuts on top. Bake for 25 minutes. Cut into small diamonds while warm. Delicious with sherbet or ice cream.

Mrs. Edwin B. Bosler

BUCKEYES

Makes 3 to 4 dozen

Candy-like cookies. Attention peanut butter lovers!

1/2 cup softened butter
1 lb. confectioners sugar
1 tsp. vanilla
1-1/2 cups peanut butter

CHOCOLATE COATING
12 oz. chocolate chips
1 oz. paraffin

Mix butter, sugar, vanilla and peanut butter together until sticky. Form into balls. Chill at least 2 hours. Melt chocolate chips and paraffin in double boiler. Using a toothpick, dip each ball into warm chocolate, leaving small area bare. Put on waxed paper and refrigerate.

Mrs. Stanton R. Cook

FLORENTINE COOKIES

Makes 48 single cookies

A classic favorite...

1/2 cup whipping cream
1/2 cup granulated sugar
1/4 tsp. salt
1-1/4 cups blanched
  almonds
1/4 cup candied
  orange peel
1/4 cup flour

CHOCOLATE GLAZE
8 oz. semisweet chocolate,
  melted
3 T. butter
1 T. Grand Marnier

Preheat oven to 325 degrees. Heat cream, sugar and salt together. In food processor, coarsely chop nuts and candied orange peel. Add flour and process with quick on and off turns. Stir flour mixture into cream mixture and cook until the mixture thickens (about 2 minutes). Drop batter by teaspoons, 2 inches apart, on a well-greased cookie sheet. Bake until brown around the edges (about 12 minutes). Cool slightly on cookie sheet. Remove and let cool until crisp. Mix glaze ingredients together. Spread the flat side of one cookie with glaze and top with a second cookie, or top single cookie with glaze. Decorate with candied cherry, if desired.

Mrs. James R. McClamroch

LACE COOKIES

Makes 36 cookies

A pretty cookie that's easy to make.

1/2 cup butter, melted
1 cup granulated sugar
1 egg
1 cup old fashioned oats
3 T. flour
1/4 tsp. baking powder
1/4 tsp. salt

Preheat oven to 375 degrees. Mix butter and sugar together. Stir in the egg. Mix oats, flour, baking powder and salt together. Stir oat mixture into butter mixture. Take a scant tsp. of batter and place on foil-lined cookie sheet—place far apart as the batter does spread. Bake for 10 minutes or until the cookies are nicely browned. After baking, slide the foil off the cookie sheet. Let the cookies cool and they will remove easily.

Mrs. Emmett L. Kearney

PEANUT BUTTER YUMMIES

Makes 48 balls

Tastes like crunchy peanut butter cups.

1/2 cup margarine,
  softened
2 cups crunchy peanut
  butter
1 lb. confectioners sugar
3-1/2 cups Rice Krispies

Combine margarine, peanut butter, sugar, and Rice Krispies. Mix well with mixer. Roll small round balls (hickory nut size) and refrigerate several hours or overnight. Melt chocolate and paraffin. Dip balls individually in chocolate coating. Place on wax paper in 9 x 13-inch pan to cool. Store in covered container. Will keep for weeks.

CHOCOLATE
COATING
6 oz. chocolate chips
  (semi-sweet chocolate
  bits or milk chocolate
  bits; may substitute
  butterscotch bits)
8 oz. Hershey's
  chocolate candy bar
1 oz. paraffin

NOTE:
Keep chocolate coating warm while dipping or you may run short.

Mrs. Bruce Gooden

PEANUT CLUSTERS

Makes 48

Great tasting candy.

1 2-lb. pkg. almond bark
1 12-oz. pkg. chocolate
  chips
1 square unsweetened
  chocolate
2 12-oz. cans cocktail
  peanuts

Put everything but nuts in a crock pot on high heat until melted. Stir occasionally. Add nuts. Stir mixture until nuts are well coated. Drop by teaspoonfuls onto cookie sheet lined with waxed paper. When cool, store in tin.

Mrs. Thomas Leith

GOOD SUGAR COOKIES

Makes 48 cookies

Christmas couldn't come to our house without these cut out cookies.

1 cup sugar (granulated or
   part light brown)
1/2 cup butter or margarine
2 eggs
1 tsp. vanilla
1/2 tsp. lemon extract
2-1/2 cups flour
1/2 tsp. nutmeg
2 tsp. baking powder
1/2 tsp. salt

Cream butter and sugar. Add flavorings and eggs one at a time. Add sifted dry ingredients. Place dough in refrigerator for several hours. Preheat oven to 425 degrees. Roll *thin* on pastry cloth. Cut as desired. Sprinkle with colored sugar before baking or pipe with icing after baking. Bake on ungreased cookie sheet for 5 to 8 minutes.

ICING
1-1/2 cups sifted
   confectioners sugar
1/8 tsp. cream of tartar
1 egg white
1/4 tsp. vanilla
red and green food coloring

Combine sugar and cream of tartar in a small mixing bowl. Add egg white and vanilla. Beat on high speed of mixer until frosting holds its shape. Divide frosting in half. Add red food color to one half and green food color to the other half. Cover with damp cloth until ready to use. Pipe through a pastry tube fitted with a small rosette tip. Outline cookies.

Mrs. Arthur W. Bergman, Jr.

CASSEROLE COOKIES

Makes 30 cookies

These crunchy treats are baked before shaping into rolls or logs.

2 eggs
1 cup granulated sugar
pinch of salt
1 cup chopped dates
1 cup canned Angel Flake
  coconut
1 cup chopped pecans
  or walnuts
1 tsp. vanilla
1/4 tsp. almond extract
confectioners sugar

Preheat oven to 350 degrees. Beat eggs and sugar well. Add other ingredients and mix well. Bake in an ungreased 2-quart casserole for 30 minutes. Beat while hot with a *wooden* spoon. Cool. Roll into balls or small logs. Dough is very sticky. Roll in confectioners sugar.

Mrs. Wayne Aden

SPICED PECANS

Makes 2 cups

Cinnamon makes these nuts special.

1 egg white
1 T. water
1 lb. unsalted pecans
1 cup granulated sugar
1 tsp. cinnamon
1/2 tsp. salt
3 T. butter

Preheat oven to 275 degrees. Beat egg white and water until stiff but not dry. Add pecans and stir. Mix sugar, cinnamon and salt. Blend sugar mixture into nuts. Melt butter and spread on a large cookie sheet or jelly roll pan. Pour nut mixture onto sheet. Bake for 45 minutes, stirring every 15 minutes.

Mrs. Bruce J. Gooden

CREME DE MENTHE BON BONS   *Makes 72*

Lovely to look at...

**8 tsp. crème de menthe
(either white or green)
1/4 lb. butter, softened
1 1-lb. box confectioners
sugar
12 oz. chocolate chips
1 oz. paraffin**

Mix crème de menthe, butter and confectioners sugar. Knead and roll into small balls about the size of a cherry. Use two cookie sheets and place balls in refrigerator, chilling at least an hour. Melt chocolate bits and paraffin in a double boiler. Remove one cookie sheet at a time. With a toothpick, dip balls into the chocolate and paraffin mixture. Let dry on wax paper. Refrigerate.

Mrs. John M. Mitchell

AUNT SALLY'S TOFFEE   *Makes 50 pieces*

A great gift or a nice holiday treat!

**1/2 lb. butter, do not
substitute margarine
1 cup granulated sugar
5 T. water
1/4 tsp. salt
4 oz. milk or semi-sweet
chocolate
1/2 cup finely chopped
pecans**

Combine butter, sugar, water and salt in saucepan. Cook over a medium high heat, stirring continually. Heat to 300 degrees —hard crack stage—use a candy thermometer. Pour onto greased cookie sheet, and let cool. Melt chocolate in a double boiler, pour over the cooled toffee, sprinkle pecans on top. Break into bite-sized pieces, and store in a covered tin.

Mrs. Mark T. Hogan

Cakes and Pies

SCRIPTURE CAKE

This is truly divine!

1/2 cup Judges 5:25
2 cups Jeremiah 6:20
2 T. I Kings 14:3
6 Jeremiah 17:11 (yolks)
1-1/2 cups I Kings 4:22
2 tsp. Amos 4:5
II Chronicles 9:9 to taste
pinch Leviticus 2:13
1/2 cup Judges 4:19
2 cups Nahum 3:12
2 cups Numbers 17:8
6 Jeremiah 17:11 (whites)

Preheat oven to 300 degrees. Cream Judges 5 with Jeremiah 6; add I Kings 14. Beat the 6 Jeremiah yolks and add. Then add I Kings 4, Amos, Chronicles and the pinch of Leviticus alternately with 1/2 cup Judges 4. Add Nahum and Numbers, then fold in the 6 stiffly beaten Jeremiah whites. Bake 2 hours in a greased tube pan.

TRANSLATION
1/2 cup butter
2 cups granulated sugar
2 T. honey
6 beaten egg yolks
1-1/2 cups sifted flour
2 tsp. baking powder
2 tsp. cinnamon
1/2 tsp. ginger
1 tsp. nutmeg
1/2 tsp. cloves
pinch salt
1/2 cup milk
2 cups chopped figs
   (14 oz.)
2 cups chopped almonds
6 stiffly beaten egg whites

Preheat oven to 300 degrees. Cream butter and sugar; add honey. Add 6 well beaten egg yolks. Sift flour with baking powder, cinnamon, ginger, nutmeg, cloves and salt. Add alternately with milk. Stir in chopped figs and chopped almonds. Fold in stiffly beaten egg whites. Bake 2 hours in a greased tube pan.

Mrs. William Sethness

GRAMMA WILSON'S FABULOUS ANGEL FOOD CAKE

Serves 10 to 12

You'll never go to a box cake again!

1-1/4 cups sifted cake flour
1/2 cup sifted granulated sugar
1-1/2 cups egg whites (about 12)
1/4 tsp. salt
1-1/4 tsp. cream of tartar
1 tsp. vanilla
1-1/3 cups sifted granulated sugar

Preheat oven to 375 degrees. Sift flour once, measure, add 1/2 cup sugar and sift 4 more times. Combine egg whites, salt, cream of tartar and vanilla in large bowl. Beat with whisk until whites form soft peaks, but are still moist and glossy. Add rest of sugar slowly by sprinkling about 5 tablespoons at a time over whites and beating until sugar is blended — about 25 beating strokes each time. Add flour and sugar mixture in 4 additions, sifting it over the egg whites slowly. Fold in each time with wire whisk, turning bowl gradually. Be sure flour is entirely blended without breaking down egg whites. Pour batter into a tube pan. Bake for 35 to 40 minutes. When done, invert pan and let stand one hour or until cake is cool.

Mrs. David M. Stone

SOUR CREAM CHOCOLATE FROSTING

Makes 2 cups

Makes ample frosting for a large layer cake.

1 6-oz. pkg. semi-sweet chocolate pieces
4 T. butter or margarine
1/2 cup sour cream
1 tsp. vanilla
1/4 tsp. salt
2-1/2 to 2-3/4 cups sifted confectioners sugar

Melt chocolate pieces and butter in a double boiler. Remove from heat. Stir chocolate mixture into sour cream, vanilla, and salt. Add confectioners sugar and mix until of spreading consistency. Beat well. Spread on cake.

Mrs. Edward Ruegg

LEMON BLOSSOM CAKE

Serves 10

Much of the work can be done ahead — looks spectacular.

CAKE
1 17-oz. pkg. pound cake
   mix
3/4 cup milk
2 eggs, separated
1 T. grated orange rind

FILLING
3 egg yolks
1/2 cup granulated sugar
1/4 cup fresh lemon juice
2 T. butter
1 T. grated lemon rind

MERINGUE
3 egg whites
1/8 tsp. cream of tartar
1/2 cup granulated sugar

Preheat oven to 325 degrees. Blend cake mix and 1/2 cup milk until dry ingredients are moistened. Beat two minutes. Blend in 2 egg yolks and orange rind; beat one minute. Add remaining 1/4 cup milk; beat one minute. In small bowl, beat 2 egg whites until they form moist peaks. Gently fold into batter. Pour into greased 9-inch spring form pan. Bake for 50 to 60 minutes, until top springs back when lightly touched. Cool in pan on wire rack 10 minutes. Remove side of pan. Cool completely. Cake may be prepared a day ahead.

TO PREPARE FILLING: Beat 3 egg yolks in top of double boiler. Stir in sugar, lemon juice, butter and lemon rind. Cook, stirring occasionally, until mixture is thick and smooth. Remove from heat, cover and cool completely. May be made a day ahead.

TO PREPARE MERINGUE: Beat 3 egg whites and cream of tartar until foamy; then beat in 1/2 cup sugar a tablespoon at a time. Beat until meringue is stiff and glossy.

Split cooled cake into two layers. Spread bottom layer with half of lemon filling. Replace top. Place on cookie sheet. Spoon meringue in a 1-inch band around top of cake. Spread remaining meringue around side. Bake in preheated 325 degree oven for 15 minutes. Remove to serving platter. Cool one hour. Spread remaining filling on top.

Mrs. Julien H. Collins, Jr.

271

MAGNOLIA CAKE

Serves 12 to 14

Delicious blend of flavors.

1 18-oz. pkg. yellow
  cake mix
1 cup brown sugar
1 to 2 T. instant coffee
  powder
3/4 cup water
2 T. light rum
2 3-1/4-oz. boxes vanilla
  pudding (not instant)
3 cups milk
2 T. light rum
1 cup whipping cream,
  whipped
shaved chocolate for
  garnish

Bake cake in 2 layers according to package directions. Cool. Combine sugar, coffee and water in saucepan. Boil for 5 minutes. Cool and add 2 tablespoons rum. Remove cooled cake layers from pans, and spoon rum mixture slowly over both layers, allowing time for it to absorb. Cook pudding according to package directions, using only 1-1/2 cups milk per package. Cool and add 2 tablespoons rum. Set aside 1 cup of pudding and spread remaining pudding between the layers. Refrigerate until 2 hours before serving time. Frost cake with mixture of whipped cream and reserved 1 cup pudding. Sprinkle with shaved chocolate. Chill.

Mrs. Thomas M. Ritchie, Jr.

MOCHA ANGEL FOOD CAKE

Serves 8 to 10

This is an easy and elegant dessert.

1 pkg. angel food cake
  mix
1/4 cup cocoa
1/4 cup granulated sugar
2 tsp. vanilla

Preheat oven to 350 degrees. Prepare cake batter according to directions on the package. Mix cocoa and sugar. Fold cocoa/sugar and vanilla into cake batter. Pour into tube pan and bake as directed on the box. Cool. Chill cake in refrigerator at least one hour before frosting.

FROSTING
1 pint whipping cream
5 tsp. instant coffee
6 T. granulated sugar
1 tsp. vanilla
chocolate curls

Whip together coffee and whipping cream. Add sugar and vanilla. Frost cake. Grate chocolate curls on top and chill.

Kenilworth Union Church

GRANDMOTHER'S BIRTHDAY FROSTING

Makes 2 cups

Old-fashioned penuche with panache!

1/2 cup butter
1-1/3 cups lightly
  packed brown sugar
2/3 cup granulated sugar
2/3 cup whipping cream

Cream butter, add sugars and mix well. Add cream. Bring to a full rolling boil and let boil for 13 minutes over VERY low flame. Remove from stove and beat by hand with a wooden spoon until the right spreading consistency ("until it builds a castle of its own") is achieved. Spread immediately on white or spice cake. Enough frosting for two 9-inch round layers or 9 x 13-inch sheet cake.

NOTE: If frosting is too soft, place bowl over pan of cold water and continue to beat. If too hard, add dash of cream.

Edrita F. Braun

CREME DE MENTHE CAKE

Serves 9

A Leprechaun's delight!

1 oz. unsweetened
  chocolate
1/2 cup water
4 T. butter
3/4 cup granulated sugar
1/2 cup sour cream
1 egg
4 T. crème de menthe
1 cup flour
1 tsp. baking soda

Butter and flour an 8 x 8-inch pan. Preheat oven to 350 degrees. In a 2-quart saucepan melt chocolate, water and butter together. Beat in sugar, sour cream, egg and crème de menthe until thoroughly mixed. Sift in flour and soda. Stir to combine. Bake 30 to 35 minutes. Whip cream; mix in crème de menthe. Serve at room temperature or slightly warm with a dollop of flavored whipped cream.

Mrs. Carroll G. Wells

TOPPING
1 cup whipping cream
2 T. crème de menthe

CARROT CAKE

Serves 12

Looks spectacular and tastes so, too!

1-3/4 cups granulated
  sugar
1-1/4 cups oil
4 eggs, lightly beaten
2 cups cake flour
2 tsp. baking powder
1 tsp. salt
2 tsp. baking soda
2 tsp. cinnamon
3 cups grated carrots
1/4 cup chopped pecans
1/3 cup raisins

Preheat oven to 350 degrees. Cream together sugar and oil. Add eggs, cake flour, baking powder, salt, soda and cinnamon. Mix well. Fold in carrots, pecans, and raisins. Bake in three 9-inch greased and floured cake pans, until done (about 40 to 45 minutes; test center with a toothpick). When cool, assemble layers with frosting.

FROSTING
1 8-oz. pkg. cream
  cheese, softened
1/4 cup butter
2 tsp. vanilla
1 lb. confectioners sugar
1 cup crushed pineapple,
  very well drained

Mix all ingredients until well blended.

Mrs. Peter T. Haverkampf

GRATED APPLE SNACK CAKE

Serves 9

Wonderful when served warm...

1/4 cup butter
1 cup granulated sugar
1 large egg, beaten
3 large apples, peeled
  and grated
1 cup sifted flour
1 tsp. baking soda
1/2 tsp. cinnamon
1/4 tsp. nutmeg
1/4 tsp. cloves
1/4 tsp. salt
1/2 cup chopped walnuts
  or raisins

Preheat oven to 350 degrees. Cream butter and sugar. Add egg, blend in apples. Add flour, soda, spices and salt. Add nuts or raisins. Bake for 45 minutes in a greased 8 x 8-inch pan.

NOTE: May be topped with whipped cream, if desired.

Mrs. Julien H. Collins, Jr.

ORANGE SURPRISE CAKE

Serves 9

A layer of raisins and chocolate chips add flavor....

BATTER
1/2 cup milk
1/2 cup orange juice
1 cup raisins
1/2 cup butter
1 cup granulated sugar
2 eggs
2 cups sifted flour
1/2 tsp. salt
1 tsp. baking powder
1 tsp. baking soda
grated rind of one orange
1 cup chocolate chips

GLAZE
1/2 cup granulated sugar
1/2 cup orange juice

Preheat oven to 350 degrees. Mix milk and orange juice together and let stand. Grease and flour a deep 9-inch square cake pan or 9-inch springform pan. Place raisins in a shallow pan, barely cover with water and heat until water is completely evaporated. Beat butter, sugar and eggs together until thick and creamy in electric mixer. Mix dry ingredients together. On low speed, add one half of the dry ingredients, all of the orange-milk mixture and the orange rind, then the rest of the dry ingredients. Fold in raisins and chocolate chips. Turn batter into prepared pan and bake for 45 to 50 minutes. Pour glaze ingredients over the baked cake. Return to the oven for 5 minutes. Cool in pan. Cake can be frozen. If desired, top with a dollop of whipped cream when serving.

VARIATION: The raisins may be soaked in Cointreau or brandy before simmering with water.

Paula Nordhem

MANDARIN CAKE

Serves 9

Super easy, moist cake...

CAKE

1 cup granulated sugar
1 tsp. baking soda
1 cup flour
1/2 tsp. salt
1 egg
1 tsp. vanilla
1 11-oz. can Mandarin
  oranges, drained
1/2 cup chopped nuts

Preheat oven to 350 degrees. In large bowl, mix sugar, soda, flour and salt. Add egg, vanilla and oranges; beat for 2 to 3 minutes with electric mixer. Add nuts. Bake in a greased 8-inch square pan for 30 to 35 minutes. While cake is still warm, prick with a fork and top with frosting. Serve plain or top with whipped cream.

FROSTING

3/4 cup brown sugar
3 T. milk
3 T. butter

While cake is baking, mix frosting ingredients. Bring to a full boil and set aside.

Kenilworth Union Church

WHITE FRUIT CAKE

Makes 2 loaves

Distinctive lemon flavor makes this cake special...

1-1/2 cups butter or
  margarine
2 cups granulated sugar
6 eggs
1/2 cup lemon extract
2 tsp. vanilla
4 cups flour
2 T. baking powder
1 lb. coarsley chopped
  pecans
1 lb. chopped candied
  red cherries
1/2 lb. chopped candied
  green cherries
1/2 lb. chopped candied
  pineapple

Preheat oven to 325 degrees. Lightly grease two 9 x 5-inch loaf pans. Line with waxed paper, and grease waxed paper. Mix butter, sugar, eggs, lemon extract and vanilla well in a large mixing bowl. Reserve 1/4 cup flour. Mix remaining flour and baking powder together; gradually add to sugar mixture. Stir in pecans. Mix reserved flour with candied fruits; add to batter and stir to distribute. Bake for 1-1/4 hours or until tests done. Cool, then wrap securely. Keeps for several weeks in refrigerator.

Mrs. H. Thomas Griffith

BOUNTIFUL BUNDT CAKE

Serves 12

A State Fair winner!

2 cups unbleached flour
1 T. cinnamon
2 tsp. baking soda
2 tsp. baking powder
1 tsp. salt
1/4 tsp. nutmeg
1/4 tsp. allspice
5 medium carrots
  (3 cups shredded)
7 pitted prunes
3/4 cup chopped pecans
3/4 cup golden raisins
4 eggs
2 cups granulated sugar
1-1/2 cups oil

Preheat oven to 350 degrees. Grease and flour a 12-cup Bundt pan. Combine first 7 ingredients in large bowl and set aside. Shred carrots and chop prunes coarsely. Combine carrots, prunes, pecans and raisins in bowl and toss gently to mix. Beat eggs slightly. Add sugar and oil and mix *well*. Add dry ingredients and mix only until blended. Add to carrot mixture and blend thoroughly. Pour batter into prepared pan and bake about 50 minutes in center of oven or until tests done. Cool 5 minutes in pan. Invert. Sift confectioners sugar over top when cool if desired.

Mrs. Donald J. Ross

SPICED APPLE POUND CAKE

Serves 12 to 14

Excellent with cinnamon ice cream....

CAKE
2-1/4 cups flour
2 cups granulated sugar
1/2 tsp. salt
1/2 tsp. baking soda
1 tsp. vanilla
1 cup softened butter or
  margarine
8 oz. apple yogurt
3 eggs

Preheat oven to 325 degrees. Grease and flour a Bundt pan. Combine all cake ingredients in large mixing bowl. Blend at low speed to moisten, then increase speed to medium for 3 minutes, scraping bowl occasionally. Pour batter into prepared pan and bake for 60-65 minutes. Cool 15 minutes before removing from pan. To prepare glaze, combine confectioners sugar, milk and cinnamon, beating until smooth. Drizzle over cake and sprinkle with chopped pecans.

Mrs. James E. Sullivan

GLAZE
1 cup confectioners
  sugar
2 T. milk
1 tsp. cinnamon
chopped pecans

277

CRANBERRY CAKE WITH BUTTER SAUCE

Serves 9

A favorite holiday dessert...

CAKE
2 cups sifted flour
1 cup granulated sugar
1 T. baking powder
1/2 tsp. salt
2 cups whole raw
  cranberries
1 cup milk
3 T. melted butter

Preheat oven to 375 degrees while preparing cake. Sift together flour, sugar, baking powder and salt. Stir in cranberries, milk and melted butter. Pour into a greased 8-inch square pan. Bake for 45 minutes. Serve warm with hot sauce on top.

BUTTER SAUCE
1/2 cup butter
1 cup brown sugar,
  packed
3/4 cup half and half

Melt butter, then add sugar and cream. Bring to a boil, stirring. Cover and set aside for 10 minutes to cook on stored heat.

Mrs. Alfred F. Buckman

INDIANA STATE FAIR PRIZE GINGERBREAD

Serves 9

Awarded first prize three years in a row!

1/2 cup boiling water
1/2 cup margarine at
  room temperature
1/2 cup dark brown sugar
1/2 cup dark molasses
1 beaten egg
1-1/2 cups sifted flour
1/2 tsp. baking soda
1/2 tsp. baking powder
1/2 tsp. salt
1/2 tsp. ginger
1 tsp. cinnamon

Preheat oven to 350 degrees. Pour water over margarine; add sugar, molasses and egg. Beat well. Sift dry ingredients together. Add to sugar mixture and beat until smooth. Pour into a greased and floured 8-inch square cake pan. Bake for 35 to 40 minutes. Serve warm with whipped cream or applesauce.

Mrs. John S. Stiles

POUND CAKE SUPREME

Makes 2 cakes

Orange-glazed delight!

1 lb. butter or margarine
3 cups granulated sugar
8 eggs, separated
2 cups flour
2 tsp. vanilla extract
2 tsp. grated orange rind
1/3 cup orange juice
1/2 cup chopped pecans

Preheat oven to 350 degrees. Cream butter and 2 cups sugar until light and fluffy. Add egg yolks one at a time, beating well after each addition. Add flour in thirds, alternately with juice and rind, beating until smooth after each addition. In a large bowl beat egg whites until stiff peaks form. Gradually add remaining sugar and continue beating until stiff but not dry. Gently fold batter into meringue. Sprinkle pecans in two well-greased Bundt cake pans. Carefully turn batter into pans. Bake for one hour or until done. Meanwhile, make glaze. When cake is done, remove from oven, cool 15 minutes and remove from pans. While still warm, poke many holes in cake with skewer. Cover with 1/2 to 2/3 of orange glaze. Let cool. Glaze with remaining orange glaze. Dust with confectioners' sugar. Serve with flavored whipped cream. Recipe may be halved for one cake.

GLAZE
1 cup granulated sugar
1/2 cup orange juice
1/2 cup orange liqueur

Mix sugar, orange juice and liqueur and boil for 5 minutes.

Mrs. Donald J. Ross

TOPPING
1 cup whipping cream,
  whipped
2 T. orange liqueur,
  or to taste

PERFECT SPICE CAKE WITH
SEA FOAM FROSTING

Serves 12 to 16

Our family's favorite birthday cake...

CAKE BATTER
1 cup milk
1 T. lemon juice
2-1/2 cups sifted
   cake flour
1 tsp. baking powder
1 tsp. salt
1 tsp. cinnamon
3/4 tsp. baking soda
1/4 tsp. cloves
1/16 tsp. black pepper
3/4 cup shortening
1 cup granulated sugar
3/4 cup firmly packed
   dark brown sugar
3 eggs
1 tsp. vanilla

Preheat oven to 350 degrees. Sour the milk by adding lemon juice: stir well and set aside. Sift flour, baking powder, salt, cinnamon, soda, cloves and pepper together. Cream shortening and sugars until light and fluffy. Add eggs, one at a time, beating after each addition. Beat in vanilla. Add dry ingredients alternately with sour milk, beating after each addition. Pour batter into three greased and floured 9-inch round cake pans. Bake for 25 minutes or until done. Cool in pans on rack for 10 minutes. Remove from pans and cool completely on rack.

SEA FOAM FROSTING
2 egg whites
1-1/2 cups firmly packed
   brown sugar
1/3 cup water
1 tsp. vanilla

Mix egg whites, brown sugar, water and vanilla in top of double boiler over simmering water. Beat for 7 minutes with an electric mixer, or until soft peaks form. Remove from heat and cool. Spread top of one cake layer generously with frosting. Top with second layer and repeat. Top with third layer; frost sides and top with remaining frosting.

Mrs. Donald J. Ross

COUNTRY APPLE NUT CAKE

Serves 16 to 20

Brandy custard sauce makes this cake extra special...

CAKE

2 cups granulated sugar
2 eggs
1-1/2 cups corn oil
3 cups peeled, diced
    apples
3 cups flour
1/2 tsp. salt
1 tsp. soda
1 tsp. cinnamon
2 tsp. vanilla
1 cup chopped nuts

Preheat oven to 300 degrees. To prepare cake, cream sugar, eggs, oil and apples. Sift together flour, salt, soda and cinnamon. Add to oil mixture. Blend in vanilla and nuts. Bake in greased and floured 15 x 10-inch sheet cake pan for 45 to 50 minutes. While cake is baking, make sauce. Serve sauce warm over cake.

SAUCE

1/3 cup butter
1 cup sifted confectioners
    sugar
3 T. brandy or orange
    liqueur
3 egg yolks
1 cup half and half, at
    room temperature

Cream butter until soft in top of double boiler but do not place over heat. Add confectioners sugar and beat until creamy. Place over simmering water and beat in brandy slowly. Beat in egg yolks, one at a time. Add cream, stirring constantly. Cook until slightly thickened.

NOTE: Sauce may be prepared ahead of time, refrigerated and reheated in top of double boiler.

Mrs. James R. McClamroch

FROZEN LEMON PIE

Serves 6 to 8

Light and refreshing...

1/3 cup crushed
  vanilla wafers
3 eggs, separated
1/2 cup granulated sugar
1 cup whipping cream
1/3 cup fresh lemon juice
1 T. grated lemon rind

Butter a 9-inch pie pan and sprinkle with 1/4 cup wafer crumbs. Beat egg whites until foamy. Continue beating and add sugar, 1 T. at a time, until mixture is stiff and glossy. Beat egg yolks until thick and lemon colored. Fold in egg white mixture. Beat cream, lemon juice and lemon rind together until stiff; fold into egg mixture. Pour into prepared pie plate. Sprinkle with remaining crumbs and freeze until solid. Serve directly from the freezer.

NOTE: Pie may be prepared 48 hours before serving. Be sure to cover with foil or plastic wrap after initially frozen.

Mrs. Ted Payseur

COFFEE ICE CREAM PIE

Serves 8 to 10

Crunchy chocolate crust...

CRUST
1 12-oz. pkg. semisweet
  chocolate bits
1/4 cup butter
2-1/2 cups Rice Krispies
  cereal

Melt together chocolate bits and butter; add Rice Krispies. Press mixture into a 9-inch pie pan to form shell. Refrigerate for several hours or up to 2 days. Just before serving, spoon ice cream over crust. Top with grated bitter chocolate.

TOPPING
1 qt. coffee ice cream,
  softened
bitter chocolate, grated

NOTE: A 6-oz. pkg. chocolate bits may be used for a thinner crust.

VARIATIONS: Substitute peppermint ice cream and top with 1/2 cup shredded coconut. Cornflakes may be substituted for Rice Krispies in the crust.

Mrs. Fred L. Stone

RANDY'S KEY LIME PIE

Serves 6 to 8

Tart and light...

5 eggs, separated
3/4 cup granulated sugar
2/3 cup unsweetened
  fresh lime juice
2 tsp. grated lime rind
1/8 tsp. salt
1 9-inch graham cracker
  crust
strawberries

Preheat oven to 350 degrees. Beat egg yolks in top of double boiler until very thick. Gradually beat in 1/2 cup sugar until pale yellow and beat until mixture forms a drop when dropped from beater. Stir in lime juice and grated rind. Place over simmering water; cook and stir until mixture coats a spoon. Cool to room temperature. Beat egg whites with salt until soft peaks form. Gradually add remaining sugar and beat until stiff and glossy. Stir one third meringue into cooled yolks; fold in remaining meringue. Turn into crust. Bake for 15 minutes or until lightly browned. Cool. Cover with plastic wrap and freeze. Remove one half hour before serving. Garnish with strawberries.

Mrs. Donald J. Ross

DERBY TOWN PIE

Serves 6

Bourbon adds a nice touch...

1/4 cup butter
1 cup granulated sugar
3 eggs
3/4 cup light corn syrup
1 tsp. vanilla
1/4 tsp. salt
1/2 cup chocolate chips
1/2 cup chopped pecans
2 T. bourbon
1 10-inch pie shell,
  unbaked
whipped cream

Preheat oven to 375 degrees. Cream butter. Gradually beat in sugar. Add eggs, syrup, vanilla and salt; blend well. Stir in chips, nuts and bourbon. Pour into shell. Bake 40 to 45 minutes. Serve warm or reheat in oven. Garnish with a dollop of whipped cream.

Casey Bohnstedt

LEMON MERINGUE PIE

Serves 6 to 8

Absolute perfection!

1 baked 9-inch pie shell

FILLING
1/3 cup cornstarch
1/8 tsp. salt
**1-1/2 cups granulated
    sugar**
1-1/2 cups water
grated peel of 1 lemon
1/2 cup lemon juice
4 egg yolks
1 T. butter

In saucepan, stir together cornstarch, salt and sugar. Add water, lemon peel and lemon juice. Cook over medium heat, stirring constantly, until mixture thickens and boils. Remove from heat. In small bowl, beat egg yolks with wire whisk. Stir in small amount of the hot mixture. *Slowly* pour yolk mixture back into lemon mixture, stirring rapidly to avoid lumps. Return to heat and cook, stirring constantly, until thick. *Do not boil.* Stir in butter. Pour filling into pie crust. Cool 10 minutes.

MERINGUE
4 egg whites
1/4 tsp. cream of tartar
1/2 cup granulated sugar

Preheat oven to 400 degrees. Beat egg whites and cream of tartar in small bowl at high speed until soft peaks form. Gradually sprinkle sugar into whites and beat until peaks stand stiff and glossy. Spread meringue over filling to edge of crust. Swirl meringue with spatula or spoon to make decorative top. Bake 10 minutes or until peaks are golden. Cool on wire rack, then refrigerate if necessary. Do not refrigerate until cool, however, or meringue may "weep."

Mrs. Dane F. Hahn

LEPRECHAUN PIE

Serves 6 to 8

Special for St. Patrick's Day—on through summer!

CRUST

1-1/2 cups finely crushed
   chocolate wafers
6 T. margarine, melted

Combine ingredients and press firmly on bottom and sides of a 9-inch pie pan. Chill.

FILLING

1-1/4 cups granulated
   sugar
1/2 cup sifted flour
1/4 tsp. salt
1-3/4 cups water
1/2 cup frozen limeade
   concentrate, thawed
1 to 2 drops green food
   coloring
3 egg yolks, slightly
   beaten
3 T. margarine

In saucepan, mix granulated sugar, flour and salt. Stir in water. Add limeade concentrate and food coloring. Cook and stir until mixture thickens and boils, then cook 2 minutes more. Stir a small amount of hot mixture into beaten egg yolks. Return to the hot mixture. Cook and stir until mixture boils. Stir in margarine. Pour into crust. Cool.

TOPPING

1/2 cup whipping cream
1/4 cup granulated sugar

Whip cream with granulated sugar and spread on pie. Chill.

VARIATION: Use a meringue top instead of whipped cream.

Mrs. Lee Osborne

MARVELOUS MOCHA PIE

Serves 8

Forget about dieting until tomorrow!

CRUST
20 chocolate Oreo
  cookies, crushed
1/4 cup melted butter
1 qt. coffee ice cream

Thoroughly mix melted butter and cookies and press into a 9-inch pie pan. Spread ice cream over crust and freeze.

CHOCOLATE SAUCE
3 1-oz. squares baking
  chocolate, melted
1/4 cup butter
2/3 cup granulated sugar
2/3 cup evaporated milk
1 tsp. vanilla
1 cup whipping cream,
  whipped
toasted slivered or sliced
  almonds
Kahlua

Bring chocolate, butter and sugar to a boil. Gradually add evaporated milk. Let cool completely and add vanilla. Spread over ice cream and return to freezer. When set, top pie with whipped cream and garnish with nuts. Drizzle a small amount of Kahlua over pie before serving.

Mrs. Donald J. Ross

CHOCOLATE NUT PIE

Serves 6

Dark and divine...

CRUST
1-1/2 cups graham
  cracker crumbs
1/3 cup sugar
6 T. melted butter

Preheat oven to 300 degrees. Mix crust ingredients and press into a 9-inch Pyrex pie pan. Bake 15 minutes. Cool.

FILLING
1/4 cup butter
3/4 cup superfine sugar
3 squares unsweetened
  chocolate, melted
2 eggs
1 cup chopped nuts
1 tsp. vanilla
pinch salt
whipped cream
shaved chocolate

Cream butter. Add sugar and stir in melted chocolate. Add eggs, one at a time and mix. Stir in nuts, vanilla and salt. When smooth, pour into crust and chill several hours. Top with whipped cream and shaved chocolate.

Mrs. Adolph Pifko

CHERRY CREAM PIE

Serves 6 to 8

George W. would love it, too...

**1 9-inch graham cracker
or pastry pie shell,
baked**

FILLING
3/4 cup granulated sugar
1/3 cup flour
1/8 tsp. salt
2 cups milk, scalded
**3 egg yolks, slightly
beaten**
2 T. butter
1/2 tsp. vanilla

**1 16-oz. can pitted sour
cherries, well drained**

Combine sugar, flour and salt in top of double boiler. Add milk slowly; cook and stir until thickened, about 10 minutes. Add small amount of mixture to egg yolks, then very slowly add yolks to pudding, stirring constantly. Cook 5 minutes; blend in butter and vanilla. Remove from heat and cool to room temperature. Pour filling into prepared pie shell. Carefully distribute cherries on top.

MERINGUE
3 egg whites
few grains salt
3 T. granulated sugar
1/4 tsp. vanilla

Preheat oven to 375 degrees. Whip egg whites with salt until foamy. Gradually add sugar. Beat until stiff peaks form; add vanilla. Pile meringue on pie and bake 10 to 15 minutes. Best when chilled before serving.

Mrs. Julien H. Collins, Jr.

FROZEN PUMPKIN PIE WITH NUT CRUST

Serves 6 to 8

Very refreshing after a holiday meal.

CRUST
1/2 cup soft butter
1/4 cup brown sugar
1 cup flour
1 3-to 4-oz. pkg. finely
   chopped pecans

Preheat oven to 400 degrees. Mix crust ingredients together and spread in 9-inch Pyrex pie pan. Bake 15 minutes. Remove from oven. While warm, press into pan and up sides. Let cool.

FILLING
3/4 cup canned pumpkin
   (no spices)
1/4 cup honey
1/2 tsp. cinnamon
1/4 tsp. each: ginger,
   cloves, salt
1 quart softened vanilla
   ice cream
1/4 cup pecan halves for
   decoration (optional)
whipped cream (optional)

Mix pumpkin, honey, spices and salt in heavy pan. Cook to boiling stirring constantly. Cool. Fold mixture into softened ice cream. Pour into crust, cover and freeze overnight or up to one month. Remove from freezer one hour before serving and set in refrigerator. Garnish with pecan halves if desired. Nice to serve with whipped cream.

Mrs. R. Scott Stratton

ANGEL DELIGHT

Fabulous and fun...a giant meringue!

MERINGUE
6 egg whites
1/2 tsp. cream of tartar
1/4 tsp. salt
1-1/2 cups granulated
  sugar

Preheat oven to 400 degrees. To prepare meringue, cover cookie sheet with brown paper. Beat egg whites until foamy; add cream of tartar and salt. Continue beating until whites form soft peaks. Add sugar very gradually, beating until whites are stiff. Spoon mixture onto brown paper, forming a circle approximately 12 inches in diameter with sides 3 inches high. Place in oven; turn off heat immediately; leave for 6 hours.

FILLING
1 cup whipping cream
2 T. granulated sugar
2-1/2 T. rum or to taste
6 7/8-oz. Heath bars
1 qt. coffee ice cream,
  softened

Whip cream, add sugar and rum. Reserve one-half cup of mixture. Crumble Heath bars, reserving one-sixth. Mix whipped cream with rest of Heath bar crumbs and ice the meringue. Fill center with ice cream. Top with small dollops of reserved whipped cream. Garnish with reserved Heath bar shavings. Freeze until ready to serve.

VARIATIONS: Meringue may be formed into a heart or other desired shape. Make individual meringues rather than one large shell. For a torte-like appearance, fill meringue with ice cream, then coat the meringue on sides *and* top with whipped cream. Sprinkle with Heath bar shavings.

Mrs. Philip A. VanVlack III

GLAZED APPLES

Cinnamon coated...

8 large baking apples,
   Rome Beauty or
   Granny Smith preferred
2 cups granulated sugar
1/2 orange, sliced
1/2 lemon, sliced
10 whole cloves
1-1/2 cups water
1/4 cup cinnamon
   red-hot candies, or
   to taste

Wash apples, cut thin slice from bottom but do not discard. Core; peel upper 1/3 of skin. Sprinkle half the sugar in bottom of electric fry pan or oven-proof skillet. Place apples, top side down, on sugar. Add clove-studded orange and lemon slices. Pour in water. Cover pan and cook over low heat about 10 to 15 minutes, or until peeled ends are soft but not mushy. Turn apples right side up. Add cinnamon candies to pan. Cover and continue cooking over low heat until just tender, about 8 to 10 mintues. Meanwhile, preheat broiler to 425 degrees. If using electric fry pan, transfer apples to Pyrex pan. Sprinkle some of the remaining sugar on top of apples. Place uncovered pan in broiler about 5 inches from heat. When sugar has bubbled and formed a crust, remove pan from broiler. Baste apples with pan juices and sprinkle with more sugar; then broil until sugar bubbles again. Repeat process until all sugar is used. Cover with raw apple slices if they brown too quickly. Serve apples hot or cold with remaining syrup in pan.

NOTE: Apples freeze well and can be served with cream, if desired.

Mrs. John S. Stiles

VENETIAN TORTE

Royal rum-flavored dessert...

**2 3-oz. pkgs. ladyfingers,
  split in half**
2 T. unflavored gelatin
1/4 cup water
1 T. cornstarch
1/2 cup granulated sugar
1-1/2 cups milk
4 egg yolks
1 tsp. rum extract
**3/4 cup semisweet
  chocolate pieces**
**1 tsp. instant coffee
  powder**
1 tsp. vanilla
4 egg whites
1/2 cup granulated sugar
**1 cup whipping cream,
  whipped**
**2 oz. toasted sliced
  almonds**
**3 7/8-oz. Heath bars,
  crushed**

Line sides of an 8 or 9-inch springform pan with ladyfingers. Crumble remaining ladyfingers; pat in bottom of pan. Soften gelatin in water; set aside. In saucepan, thoroughly combine cornstarch and sugar. Beat together milk and egg yolks; stir into sugar/cornstarch mixture. Heat over low heat, stirring frequently, until mixture thickens. Add softened gelatin and stir until gelatin dissolves. Pour one half of custard into a small bowl; stir in rum extract.

To remaining custard in saucepan, add chocolate pieces and coffee powder. Stir until chocolate is melted. Add vanilla and set aside to cool. Beat egg whites until soft peaks form; gradually add 1/2 cup sugar and beat until stiff. Fold half of the egg white/sugar mixture into chocolate custard. Turn into springform pan. *Chill until partially set.* Meanwhile, fold remaining egg white/sugar mixture into rum custard. When chocolate layer is ready, spoon rum layer on top. Chill until firm (several hours or overnight). To serve, remove pan sides. Spread torte with whipped cream; garnish with almonds and crushed Heath bars.

Mrs. James R. McClamroch

MERINGUE NESTS

Makes 12 party/dessert size or 40 to 50 tea/buffet size

Filled with lemon or chocolate a glamorous finale!

6 egg whites, at room
  temperature
dash of salt
2 cups granulated sugar
1 tsp. vinegar
1 tsp. vanilla

Preheat oven to 225 degrees. Beat egg whites and salt until foamy. Add sugar, 2 tablespoons at a time, beating after each addition until the sugar is blended; continue beating until mixture stands in stiff peaks. Add vinegar and beat well. Using a spoon or a pastry tube shape into rounds, making sure each shape is uniform, on unglazed paper or foil-lined cookie sheet. Cook for 1 hour and cool before removing from paper.

LEMON FILLING
1-1/2 cups granulated
  sugar
3 T. cornstarch
3 T. flour
dash of salt
1-1/2 cups hot water
3 egg yolks, slightly
  beaten
1/2 tsp. lemon peel,
  grated
2 T. butter or margarine
1/3 cup lemon juice

In saucepan, mix sugar, cornstarch, flour and salt. Gradually blend in water. Bring to a boil over high heat, stirring constantly. Reduce heat to medium, cook and stir for 8 minutes. Stir small amount of hot mixture into egg yolks, return to hot mixture. Bring to boil over high heat, stirring constantly. Reduce heat to low, cook and stir 4 minutes longer. Remove from heat. Add lemon peel and butter. Gradually stir in lemon juice. Cover surface with plastic wrap, cool to room temperature.

CHOCOLATE FILLING
3 T. flour
1 cup granulated sugar
1 T. cocoa
pinch of salt
1 cup milk
3 egg yolks, beaten
1 T. butter
1 T. vanilla

Mix flour, sugar, cocoa and salt. Add half of milk, beaten egg yolks, then remaining milk. Cook in double boiler until thick. Add the butter and vanilla. Beat until creamy, then cool. Cover so crust doesn't develop. Pour into baked meringue shells. May be garnished with whipped cream and chocolate curls or toasted chopped nuts.

Mrs. Philip A. VanVlack III

AMARETTO SAUCE WITH FRESH FRUIT

Serves 4

Beautiful way to serve fresh fruit!

**3 cups fresh berries
and/or peaches
1/4 cup Amaretto liqueur
1/4 cup confectioners
sugar**

Toss berries and peaches with Amaretto and confectioners sugar. Set aside and chill. To serve, place chilled fruit in serving dishes. Pass sauce separately.

**SAUCE
8 oz. ricotta cheese
8 oz. cream cheese
1/2 cup granulated sugar
4 egg yolks
2 T. whipping cream
3 T. Amaretto liqueur**

Mix cheeses together using a blender or food processor. Add sugar, egg yolks, cream and Amaretto. Continue beating until smooth. Pour into serving dish and chill. Makes enough sauce for 9 cups of fruit.

Mrs. Stanton R. Cook

MINT SPONGE

Serves 8

Enticingly easy...

**1 T. unflavored gelatin
1/4 cup water
1/2 cup half and half
1/2 cup granulated sugar
1 pt. whipping cream
1/2 tsp. peppermint
extract
1/4 tsp. green
food coloring
chocolate sauce or
fresh strawberries**

Moisten gelatin in water. Scald half and half with sugar. Add gelatin. Beat whipping cream until stiff. Add flavoring and coloring. Mix all together. Put in a 6-cup ring mold and refrigerate for 3 hours. Serve with chocolate sauce or fresh strawberries.

Mrs. Harvey Scribner

TARTES
AUX POMMES

Makes 2 tarts

Cookie-like crust, spicy apple filling...

CRUSTS
2 cups flour
3/4 cup confectioners
  sugar
1 egg yolk
1 cup softened butter
1 tsp. vanilla (or lemon
  rind to taste)

To prepare crusts, gently handmix all ingredients together. Chill dough overnight in refrigerator. Let dough sit at room temperature for 30 to 60 minutes. Preheat oven to 350 degrees. Gently press dough into two 9-inch tart pans with removable bottoms. Bake for 5 minutes, until crusts are set. Peel and core apples. Slice and sprinkle with lemon juice. Arrange apples on top of prebaked crusts. Mix sugar with desired amount of cinnamon and sprinkle over apples. Bake until crusts are light brown, about 45 to 60 minutes.

FILLING
10 medium apples
2 tsp. lemon juice
6 T. granulated sugar
cinnamon to taste

Mrs. Sibrand Jurriaans

PINEAPPLE PECAN CREME

Serves 12

An elegant party dessert for that very special occasion.

1 lb. vanilla wafers
3 cups confectioners
  sugar
1 cup butter, softened
4 eggs, beaten until light
2 cups whipping cream
2 cups crushed pineapple,
  drained
1 cup chopped pecans

Roll wafers into crumbs or use blender to make 4 cups of crumbs. Cream butter and sugar and add beaten eggs. Butter a 13 x 8-inch Pyrex pan. Sprinkle one cup of wafer crumbs in the bottom and top with butter/sugar/egg mixture. Sprinkle another cup of crumbs, then whipped cream, crumbs, pineapple and top with remaining cup of crumbs and chopped pecans. Refrigerate overnight.

Mrs. Lyman Missimer

FRAISES AUX NUAGES

Serves 12 to 16

Luscious, light dessert...

MERINGUE
6 egg whites
1/2 tsp. cream of tartar
1/4 tsp. salt
1-3/4 cups granulated
   sugar

Preheat oven to 275 degrees. Beat egg whites with cream of tartar and salt until foamy. Gradually add sugar, beating until stiff peaks form. Spread on bottom of 13 x 9-inch baking pan, mounding mixture slightly at the center. Bake one hour. Turn off heat; leave in oven to cool.

FILLING
2 3-oz. pkgs. cream
   cheese, softened
1 cup granulated sugar
1 tsp. lemon juice
1 tsp. vanilla
1 cup whipping cream,
   whipped
2 cups miniature
   marshmallows
1 pt. fresh strawberries,
   sliced

Beat cream cheese until light. Add sugar, lemon juice and vanilla; beat well until very smooth. Fold in whipped cream and marshmallows. Spread on cooled meringue. Refrigerate several hours or overnight. To serve, top each piece with sliced strawberries.

NOTE: Frozen strawberries may be substituted for fresh strawberries. Also, sliced fresh peaches may be used.

Mrs. Richard P. McClamroch

RHUBARB CRISP

Serves 6

Deliciously different!

3 cups frozen rhubarb,
   thawed
1/4 cup granulated sugar
1/3 cup butter
1/2 cup quick-cooking
   oatmeal
1/2 cup flour
1/4 cup brown sugar

Preheat oven to 350 degrees. Mix together rhubarb and granulated sugar and put in 9 x 9-inch pan. Mix butter, oats, flour and brown sugar with a pastry fork until crumbly; sprinkle over rhubarb. Bake uncovered for 50 minutes. Serve with ice cream or whipped cream.

Paula Nordhem

TODAY'S TRIFLE

Serves 12

Chicago's 1980 version...

CUSTARD
2 eggs
3/4 cup granulated sugar
2 cups milk
1 tsp. vanilla

Beat eggs until light in top of double boiler. Gradually add sugar. Slowly add milk, stirring constantly. Cook, stirring frequently, over simmering water until mixture coats the back of a wooden spoon—about 5 to 7 minutes. Add vanilla. Cool to room temperature.

CAKE LAYER
2 3-oz. pkgs. ladyfingers
1 12-oz. jar raspberry or strawberry jam
1/2 cup sherry or to taste

Split one package of ladyfingers into halves; spread generously with jam. Arrange in bottom of a cut glass bowl. Sprinkle with 1/4 cup sherry; cover with half of custard sauce. Repeat the layers. Refrigerate, covered, for 24 hours.

TOPPING
1 cup whipping cream
2 T. granulated sugar
2 tsp. light rum

Before serving, whip the cream, gradually adding sugar and rum. Spread cream on trifle and serve.

Mrs. Donald G. Andrews

ENGLISH TARTS

Makes 12

Individual pies, perfect for luncheon!

1 cup granulated sugar
1/2 cup butter
2 eggs, well beaten
1 cup currants
1/2 cup diced dates
1 tsp. vanilla
pie crust dough
whipped cream

Preheat oven to 375 degrees. Cream sugar, butter and eggs together. Mix currants, dates and vanilla and add to egg mixture. Line cupcake tins with dough. Fill tins 2/3 full. Bake for 30 minutes. Serve warm with whipped cream.

Mrs. Edith Michell

CRANBERRY SORBET

Serves 6 to 8

Refreshing finale to a festive dinner...

**1 quart cranberries,
  rinsed well
2 cups boiling water
3 cups granulated sugar
juice of 2 small lemons
1/2 cup orange juice
1 cup raspberry juice
  or water**

Put cranberries in boiling water and cook 10 minutes (skins will break). Drain and reserve juice. Mix together sugar, lemon juice, orange juice, raspberry juice and cranberry juice in a big bowl. Stir until sugar dissolves. Grind cranberries in a food mill to make a smooth pulp. Pour cranberry pulp into sugar mixture and stir. Put in a bowl and place in freezer. When mixture begins to freeze, remove and whip with electric mixer. Freeze until firm in bowl or ice cream mold. Serve in small cups or sherbet glasses.

NOTE: Recipe may be doubled.

Mrs. James R. McClamroch

GLACE AU CHOCOLATE FRANÇAISE

Serves 6

A delicious, rich chocolate dessert that can be made in a hurry.

**1/4 cup granulated sugar
1/3 cup water
6 oz. chocolate bits
3 egg yolks
1-1/2 cups whipping
  cream, whipped**

Boil sugar and water for 3 minutes. Put chocolate in food processor and add hot sugar syrup. Blend until smooth. Add yolks, blend 10 seconds. Fold into whipped cream. Chill 2 hours. Can be frozen.

VARIATIONS: Add 2 to 3 tablespoons rum or cointreau to chocolate mixture before folding it into whipped cream. Leave some of the chocolate chips in tiny chunks for added texture.

Mrs. David Schafer

LOUISIANA ICE BOX DESSERT

Serves 8 to 12

Serve in a glass bowl so layers can be seen...

1/2 cup butter
1-1/2 cups confectioners
 sugar
4 egg yolks
2 ounces rum
2 tsp. instant coffee
1 tsp. vanilla
2 cups whipping cream
24 ladyfingers
24 almond macaroons,
 crumbled
1/2 cup toasted slivered
 almonds

Cream butter; gradually add confectioners sugar. Add egg yolks, one at a time, and beat until light. Add rum, coffee and vanilla. Whip one cup cream until stiff and fold into rum mixture. Place 1/5 of cream mixture in bottom of 3-quart bowl. Add a layer of 12 ladyfingers; then 1/5 of cream mixture. Add layer of 12 crumbled macaroons; then 1/5 of cream mixture. Add rest of ladyfingers, 1/5 of cream mixture, 12 crumbled macaroons, remaining cream mixture. Dessert may be frozen at this point. Top with one cup cream, whipped, and toasted almonds. Chill several hours before serving.

Mrs. Howard R. Hayes

FROZEN RASPBERRY SOUFFLE

Serves 6 to 8

Elegant dessert with little effort.

2 10-oz. pkgs. frozen
 raspberries, thawed
5 eggs
3/4 cup granulated sugar
2 T. unflavored gelatin
1/4 cup water
2 cups whipping cream,
 whipped

Purée raspberries in blender, then strain to remove seeds. Beat eggs and sugar well. Dissolve gelatin in water and stir into egg/sugar mixture. Stir in raspberry purée slowly. Fold in whipped cream. Pour into souffle dish with waxed paper collar. Freeze 3 hours or longer. Remove to refrigerator 2 hours before serving.

Mrs. David M. Stone

MOUSSE EXTRAORDINAIRE

Serves 12

Chocoholic's dream...

CHOCOLATE CUPS
**2 4-oz. pkgs. German
  sweet chocolate
4 T. butter**

Partially melt one 4-ounce package German chocolate with 2 tablespoons butter over boiling water. Remove from water and stir rapidly until completely melted. Using a teaspoon, swirl chocolate around insides of 6 large paper baking cups, coating entire surface with a thin layer. Place in muffin pans. Repeat with remaining German chocolate and butter in 6 more baking cups. Chill baking cups in muffin pan until firm (about one hour).

FILLING
**6 T. strong coffee
4 T. cognac
8 oz. semi-sweet
  chocolate bits
1/4 cup superfine
  granulated sugar
1/4 tsp. vanilla
2 cups whipping cream
1 T. superfine granulated
  sugar**

Heat coffee and cognac in top of double boiler. Add chocolate bits and 1/4 cup sugar. Stir over hot water until glossy; add the vanilla and cool. Whip cream; fold in tablespoon of sugar. Fold cooled chocolate mixture into whipped cream. After the cups have been chilled, peel off paper carefully. Fill cups with chocolate mousse and chill until serving time.

NOTE: Garnish with whipped cream and candied violets.

Mrs. James R. McClamroch

FROZEN STRAWBERRY – MINT RING

Serves 8 to 10

Easy to make, pretty to serve and low in calories.

3 pts. lemon sherbet
1/3 cup green crème de menthe
2 pts. freshly hulled strawberries
shredded fresh or canned coconut
mint sprigs for garnish

Early in the day or the day before, in a large bowl quickly combine lemon sherbet and crème de menthe – use electric mixer. Pack into a 5-1/2-cup ring mold, and freeze. At serving time, invert sherbet ring onto a large serving platter. If the mold does not slip out, place a hot cloth over the ring for a few minutes, and run a knife around the edge. Fill center of the ring with strawberries, and sprinkle lightly with coconut. Top with mint for garnish, and serve immediately.

Mrs. Ellwood G. Peterson

LEMON CHIFFON TORTE

Serves 12

Lovely and light...

2 T. unflavored gelatin
1/3 cup cold water
7 egg yolks, slightly beaten
juice of 3 lemons
1/4 tsp. salt
2 cups granulated sugar
grated rind of 3 lemons
7 egg whites
1 cup whipping cream, whipped
2 3-oz. pkgs. ladyfingers, split
strawberries
mint sprigs

Soften gelatin in cold water. Mix egg yolks, lemon juice, salt and 1 cup sugar in top of double boiler. Cook, stirring constantly, until mixture coats the back of a spoon. Add gelatin and lemon rind; cool. Beat egg whites until stiff but not dry; gradually beat in 1 cup sugar. Gently fold lemon mixture into egg whites. Fold in whipped cream. Line bottom and sides of a 9-inch springform pan with ladyfingers; add filling. Chill until firm, at least 8 hours. Garnish with fresh strawberries and mint sprigs. Pass additional whipped cream, if desired.

Mrs. Julien H. Collins

ALMOND MERINGUE TORTE

Serves 8 to 10

Spectacular appearance and luscious taste!

CAKE
1/4 cup butter
1/2 cup granulated
  sugar, sifted
4 egg yolks
1/2 tsp. vanilla
1 cup cake flour, sifted
1 tsp. baking powder
1/8 tsp. salt
5 T. whipping cream

Cream butter; add sugar and blend until light and creamy. Beat in egg yolks, one at a time. Add vanilla. Resift cake flour with baking powder and salt. Alternately add flour and cream to butter mixture, one third at a time, blending well after each addition. Spread batter in two greased 8 or 9-inch round cake pans. Preheat oven to 325 degrees. Prepare meringue and spread on top of cake batter in both pans. Cover one meringue with almonds. Bake for 30 to 40 minutes. Let cakes cool in pans. To assemble torte, remove layer without almonds from pan and place, meringue side down, on cake plate. Spread with whipped cream topping, reserving 1/4 cup. Remove other layer from pan and place, meringue side up, on top of whipped cream. Spoon reserved whipped cream topping in center of cake.

MERINGUE
4 egg whites
1/8 tsp. salt
1 cup granulated sugar,
  sifted
1 tsp. vanilla
1-1/2 oz. sliced blanched
  almonds

Whip egg whites and salt until soft peaks form. Add sugar, one tablespoon at a time, beating well after each addition. Continue beating for several minutes after all the sugar has been added. Beat in vanilla.

TOPPING
11 T. whipping cream
3/4 cup top-quality
  apricot jam

Whip cream until stiff. Purée jam in blender or food processor until smooth; fold into whipped cream until well mixed.

Paula Nordhem

CRUSTLESS CHEESE CAKE

Serves 12

Light and lemony...

1 lb. small curd cottage
   cheese or pot cheese
1 lb. cream cheese
1-1/2 cups granulated
   sugar
4 eggs, lightly beaten
1-1/2 T. lemon juice
1 tsp. vanilla
3 T. cornstarch
3 T. flour
1/2 cup butter, melted
1 pint sour cream

Preheat oven to 325 degrees. Cream cottage cheese and cream cheese in a large bowl. Gradually add sugar, stirring. Add eggs and beat well. Stir in lemon juice, vanilla and mixed cornstarch and flour. Add melted butter; then sour cream. Pour into a greased 9-inch spring form or angel food cake pan. Bake for one hour or until firm. Turn off heat, leave door closed and let cake remain in the oven for 2 hours. Serve cold.

Patricia Palmer

MERINGUE DESSERT

Serves 12 to 16

Topping choices are endless!

CAKE
1/4 cup margarine
1/4 cup Crisco
1/2 cup granulated sugar
4 egg yolks, beaten
5 T. milk
1 tsp. baking powder
1 cup flour
1/2 tsp. vanilla

Preheat oven to 325 degrees. Cream shortenings and sugar; add eggs and milk. Mix baking powder with flour and add to egg mixture; stir in vanilla. Spread on a greased 15 x 12-inch jellyroll pan. Spread meringue on UNBAKED crust. Bake for 30 to 35 minutes. Serve with ice cream or whipped cream and top with sliced fresh strawberries or peaches.

MERINGUE
4 egg whites
1 cup granulated sugar
1/2 tsp. baking powder
1 tsp. vanilla

Beat egg whites until foamy. Mix sugar and baking powder together; gradually add to egg whites, beating until stiff. Add vanilla.

Mrs. Stanton R. Cook

BANANAS HANALEI PLANTATION

Serves 4

Impressive and easy!

1/4 cup butter
1/4 cup dark brown
  sugar
1/4 unpeeled large lime
  or lemon
1/4 unpeeled orange
4 large, firm, ripe
  bananas
1/4 cup curaçao
3 oz. brandy or rum
coffee ice cream or
  pineapple sherbet

Heat butter in frypan directly over heat. Mix in brown sugar. Hold quarters of lime and orange over pan and squeeze out juice, pressing to extract a little of the aromatic oil from the peels. Peel bananas and slice in bite-size pieces into butter mixture. Add curaçao. Heat until sauce is bubbly and hot and bananas have absorbed flavor of sauce. Warm brandy or rum and pour over top and flame. Spoon flaming sauce over fruit for one minute. Spoon hot mixture over individual servings of ice cream or sherbet.

NOTE: Can be a chafing dish classic!

Mrs. Edwin B. Bosler

PEACHY BLUEBERRY CRISP

Serves 8

Great summer dessert!

1 cup sifted flour
3/4 cup granulated sugar
1 tsp. baking powder
1/2 tsp. salt
1 egg
2 cups fresh blueberries
3 cups fresh peaches,
  peeled and sliced
1/4 cup melted butter
  or margarine
2 T. granulated sugar
1/2 tsp. cinnamon

Preheat oven to 375 degrees. Combine first four ingredients in a medium bowl. Stir in unbeaten egg and mix with fork until mixture is crumbly. Place fruit in 2-qt. buttered baking dish; sprinkle with flour mixture. Drizzle on melted butter. Combine sugar and cinnamon. Sprinkle on top. Bake about 40 minutes, or until browned. Serve at room temperature, with ice cream or whipped cream.

Mrs. Charles Shaw

BLUEBERRY BUCKLE

Serves 9 to 12

Terrific dessert for a summer luncheon, especially when you've picked the blueberries yourself.

BATTER
1/2 cup butter
1/2 cup granulated sugar
1 egg
2 cups flour
2-1/2 tsp. baking powder
1/4 tsp. salt
1/2 cup milk
1 pt. blueberries,
  washed and drained

Preheat oven to 375 degrees. Cream butter and sugar; add egg and beat well. Add sifted dry ingredients alternately in thirds with milk, beating well after each addition. Spread batter in greased 9-inch square pan. Cover with blueberries, then topping. Bake for 45 minutes. Serve warm with whipped cream or vanilla ice cream.

TOPPING
1/2 cup flour
1/2 cup granulated sugar
1/4 cup butter
1/2 tsp. cinnamon

Blend ingredients until crumbly. Sprinkle over blueberries.

Mrs. Julien H. Collins

MIDSUMMER BERRIES

Serves 9 to 12

Splendid summer confection...

1 10-oz. pkg. Lorna
  Doone cookies,
  crushed
3/4 cup butter
1 cup confectioners
  sugar
2 eggs
1/3 cup chopped walnuts
1 qt. fresh raspberries
  or blueberries
1 cup whipping cream,
  whipped

Press cookie crumbs into bottom of 9-inch square cake pan, reserving 1/3 cup crumbs. Cream butter and sugar. Add eggs one at a time, beating after each addition. Carefully spread butter mixture over crumbs; sprinkle with nuts; top with berries. Spread on whipped cream and top with remaining crumbs. Chill 2 or more hours. Cut into squares.

Mrs. Lyman Missimer

306

NUBIAN CHOCOLATE ROLL

Serves 6

Elegant!

ROLL
3 eggs, separated
5 T. granulated sugar
3 T. Droste cocoa
1 tsp. vanilla
1/2 tsp. almond flavoring
**1/4 tsp. ground
  anise seed**
1/2 tsp. cinnamon

Preheat oven to 350 degrees. Grease a 9-inch pan and line with waxed paper which is also greased. Beat egg yolks until light. Beat in sugar 1 tablespoon at a time. Mixture should be creamy. Stir in cocoa, vanilla, almond flavoring and spices. Beat egg whites until stiff. Fold gently into cocoa mixture. Spoon into pan. Bake 25 minutes. Cool 5 minutes. Turn onto tea towel that has been dusted lightly with sifted confectioners sugar. Peel off paper. Roll, bringing sides together in towel. Cool.

FILLING
1 cup whipping cream
2 T. granulated sugar
1 T. Droste cocoa
1/2 tsp. vanilla

Blend cream, sugar, cocoa and vanilla. Chill 2 hours in refrigerator (or 10 minutes in freezer and 10 minutes in refrigerator). Whip. Spread one half filling in middle of cooled cake. Roll or bring sides together. At serving time, cover with the remaining filling.

TOPPING
toasted almond slices

Sprinkle on top at serving time.

Mrs. Wilfred H. Heitmann

PINEAPPLE BRIDGE DESSERT

Serves 9

Delicate appearance, refreshing flavor!

1 20-oz. can crushed
  pineapple
1 3-oz. pkg. lemon jello
1-1/2 cups crushed
  vanilla wafers
1/3 cup melted
  margarine
1/2 cup granulated sugar
1/3 cup margarine
3 egg yolks
1/2 cup chopped walnuts
3 egg whites
1/4 cup granulated sugar

Drain pineapple, reserving liquid. Heat liquid to boiling; remove from heat and dissolve jello. Cool to room temperature. Mix wafers and melted margarine. Reserve 1/2 cup of crumb mixture for topping. Line bottom of a greased 9 x 9-inch pan with rest of crumb mixture. Cream 1/2 cup sugar and 1/3 cup margarine. Add egg yolks and beat well. Stir in jello, pineapple, and nuts. Beat egg whites until soft peaks form and then gradually add 1/4 cup sugar and beat until stiff. Fold into gelatin/pineapple mixture. Let set in refrigerator until it starts to thicken. Pour into wafer lined pan. Top with reserved crumbs.

Mrs. H. H. Hanlon

FROZEN CHOCOLATE GRAHAM CRACKER DESSERT

Serves 9 to 12

Rich!

6 oz. chocolate chips
2 T. water
1/2 cup white corn syrup
20 graham crackers
1 cup whipping cream
1 tsp. vanilla

Melt chocolate chips in water; stir in syrup. Reserve 1/4 cup mixture. Cut graham crackers into 1/2-inch squares. Whip cream; add vanilla. Fold in chocolate mixture. Place 1/3 of graham cracker squares in an 8 x 8-inch pan, then 1/3 chocolate cream mixture. Repeat twice more. Drizzle reserved chocolate on top and freeze.

NOTE: Mixture may be placed in miniature paper muffin cups (foil lined).

Mrs. Julien H. Collins

CRUNCHY ICE CREAM TORTE

Serves 12 to 15

Chocolate sauce laces this fix-ahead dessert...

CHOCOLATE SAUCE
1 13-oz. can evaporated milk
1 10-1/2-oz. pkg. miniature marshmallows
1 6-oz. pkg. chocolate chips

CRUMB MIXTURE
1/2 cup melted butter
1 3-oz. can shredded coconut
2 cups graham cracker crumbs
1 cup chopped walnuts

1/2 gallon vanilla ice cream

Heat sauce ingredients together until melted; set aside to cool. Mix crumb ingredients together. Pat three-fourths of mixture into a 9 x 13-inch pan to form a crust. Slice half of the ice cream and place on top of crumb crust to form single layer. Top with half of chocolate sauce. Repeat layers. Sprinkle rest of crumbs on top. Freeze.

Mrs. Julien H. Collins, Jr.

PEANUT BRITTLE ICE BOX CAKE

Serves 10 to 12

Rich and crackly...

1/2 cup butter
2 cups confectioners sugar
3 egg yolks
2 cups whipping cream, whipped
1 lb. commercial or homemade pound cake
1-1/2 cups crushed peanut brittle

Cream butter and sugar; add egg yolks and mix well. Fold mixture gently into whipped cream. Thinly slice pound cake. Alternate layers of pound cake and cream mixture in a 9 x 5-inch loaf pan or square cake pan, topping each layer with peanut brittle. Chill well or freeze. Turn out into serving platter and slice.

Mrs. Ellwood G. Peterson

CHOCOLATE TORTE

Serves 12

Perfect end to a special meal...

2 T. fine fresh
  bread crumbs
2 cups finely ground
  pecans
6 oz. Maillards sweet
  chocolate, finely
  ground
1 T. baking powder
1/2 cup unsalted butter
1 cup granulated sugar
7 large eggs, separated
2 tsp. Myers dark rum
pinch of salt

Preheat oven to 350 degrees. Butter an 8-inch spring form pan. Combine bread crumbs, pecans and chocolate in a large bowl. Add baking powder. Cream butter, sugar, egg yolks, rum and salt. Mix thoroughly with the dry ingredients. Beat egg whites until stiff, and fold gently into the chocolate mixture. Pour into prepared pan and bake for 60 minutes. Cool in pan.

GLAZE
3 oz. Maillards sweet
  chocolate
2 T. water
2 T. butter
4 T. confectioners sugar
1 T. Myers dark rum

Combine chocolate, water, butter, confectioners sugar and rum in a small double boiler. Heat until mixture is smooth. Gently glaze over the top of the torte.

Mrs. Peter T. Haverkampf

CHOCOLATE ANGEL CAKE DESSERT

Serves 12 to 14

This yummy concoction can be fixed ahead and frozen...

1 12-oz. pkg. chocolate
  chips
2 T. granulated sugar
3 eggs, separated, room
  temperature
2 cups whipping cream,
  whipped
1 tsp. vanilla
1 angel food cake
1 cup slivered toasted
  almonds

Melt chocolate chips in top of double boiler; add sugar. Beat egg yolks well; add gradually to chocolate, beating continuously. Mixture will be very stiff. Remove from heat and cool 5 minutes. Beat egg whites until stiff; fold into chocolate mixture until no lumps of chocolate remain. Fold in whipped cream and vanilla. Tear cake into small pieces and place half in the bottom of a buttered 9 x 13-inch pan or 9-inch spring form pan. Cover cake with half of chocolate mixture. Dot with remaining cake, then remaining chocolate mixture. Top with almonds, patting gently. Refrigerate overnight. Cut into small squares or wedges to serve. If desired, garnish each serving with a dab of whipped cream and a strawberry.

NOTE: Recipe can be doubled.

VARIATION: Liqueur such as Kahlua, crème de menthe or rum or almond extract can be added to taste.

Mrs. John R. Lee

311

CHEESE CAKE

Serves 8 to 10

A dash of cinnamon adds delicious flavor...

CRUST
20 graham cracker
  squares, crushed
4 T. melted butter
2 T. granulated sugar

FILLING
12 oz. cream cheese
1/2 cup granulated sugar
2 eggs
1 tsp. vanilla
1/2 tsp. cinnamon
  (reserve)

TOPPING
1/2 pint sour cream
1/2 tsp. vanilla
2 T. granulated sugar

To prepare crust, mix ingredients together and pat into a 9-inch pie pan or square cake pan. Preheat oven to 375 degrees.

To prepare filling, beat the cream cheese until light in a bowl. Add sugar. Beat in eggs, one at a time. Beat well—until very thin and smooth. Add vanilla. Pour filling into prepared pan. Bake 20 minutes. Remove from oven and sprinkle with cinnamon. Cool to room temperature.

Mix topping ingredients together and carefully spread on cake. Bake 5 minutes at 375 degrees. Refrigerate cake before serving.

VARIATION: Cinnamon may be mixed with filling ingredients before baking for color.

Mrs. Edwin B. Bosler

ICE CREAM CRISP

Serves 9

Easy family dessert.

2-1/2 cups Rice Krispies
1/2 cup melted butter
  or margarine
1 cup brown sugar
1 cup flaked coconut
1/2 cup chopped walnuts
1 qt. vanilla ice cream,
  slightly thawed

Preheat oven to 350 degrees. Place Rice Krispies in shallow pan and toast about 10 minutes. Combine with remaining ingredients except ice cream. Place half of mixture in bottom of lightly greased 9 x 9-inch pan. Spread ice cream on top. Cover with remaining mixture. Freeze 2 hours or until firm. Cut in squares to serve.

Mrs. Robert Balsley

CHILLED BUTTERSCOTCH DESSERT

Serves 9

Mouthwatering!

CRUST
1/2 cup butter
  or margarine
1 cup flour
1/2 cup finely chopped
  walnuts or pecans

Preheat oven to 350 degrees. Cut butter into flour, using pastry blender. Stir in nuts. Press mixture into a 9 x 9-inch pan. Bake for 15 minutes; cool thoroughly.

FILLING:
1 3-5/8-oz. pkg.
  butterscotch pudding
  mix (not instant)
1 3-1/8-oz. pkg.
  vanilla pudding mix
  (not instant)
3 cups milk
1 8-oz. pkg. cream
  cheese, softened
1 cup confectioners
  sugar
1 cup whipping cream,
  whipped
1/3 cup chopped walnuts
  or pecans

Prepare pudding mixes together, using 3 cups milk and following package directions. Turn into non-metal bowl. Place wax paper or plastic wrap directly on top of pudding. Cool completely. Beat cream cheese with confectioners sugar until light and fluffy. Fold in half of whipped cream. Spread over crust. Spoon pudding over cheese layer. Cover with remaining whipped cream. Top with nuts. Chill for several hours or overnight.

NOTE: One 9-oz. carton Cool Whip may be substituted for whipped cream.

Mrs. James E. Sullivan

DATE-OATMEAL CRISP

Serves 9 to 12

Rich date filling, toasted topping...

CRUST
1-1/2 cups
  quick-cooking oatmeal
1-1/2 cups flour
1/2 tsp. salt
1 cup brown sugar
1 tsp. vanilla
3/4 cup melted butter

Preheat oven to 350 degrees. Stir together oatmeal, flour and salt. Add sugar and stir well. Add vanilla and melted butter. Pat 1/2 of the crust in the bottom of an 8 x 8-inch pan. Top with date filling. Sprinkle with remaining crust. Bake 20 to 30 minutes.

FILLING
1/2 lb. dates, diced
1 cup cold water
1/2 cup brown sugar

Combine ingredients in saucepan and cook over low heat until thick.

Mrs. R. E. Carlson

L'ABRICOT ET AMONDE DESSERT

Serves 12

Refreshing...

1-1/2 cups crushed
  vanilla wafers
1/3 cup melted butter
2/3 cup toasted almonds
1 tsp. almond flavoring
2 qts. vanilla ice cream,
  softened
1 20-oz. jar apricot jam

Mix wafer crumbs, butter, almonds and flavoring together. Reserve 1/3 cup of this mixture for topping. Press half of the remaining crumb mixture into the bottom of a 9 x 13-inch pan. Spread one quart softened ice cream smoothly on top of crumbs. Freeze to firm. Coat with half the apricot jam. Sprinkle with remaining crumb mixture. Spread on second quart of ice cream. Freeze until firm. Repeat layer of jam. Top with reserved crumb mixture. Store in freezer. Cut in squares to serve. May be made ahead. Remove from freezer 15 minutes before serving.

Mrs. L. Steven Minkel

Chicago Entertaining

Ten of Chicago's most creative hosts and hostesses have been generous enough to share their entertaining ideas with us— for you.

Biggs Restaurant, located in a lovely Victorian mansion on Chicago's North Side, was built in 1874 for the deKoven's, an important name in Chicago history. In 1884 it was taken over by the Biggs family who developed a catering business in the coach house of the mansion. Biggs has been one of Chicago's outstanding dining establishments since it opened as a restaurant in 1964. It is our pleasure to provide you with three of their most requested and famous recipes.

FILET MIGNON WELLINGTON   *Serves 2*

1/4 lb. frozen pastry
   dough
flour
2 6-oz. beef tenderloins
salt and pepper
2-oz. liver paté
2 egg yolks

BORDELAISE SAUCE
1 shallot, chopped fine
2 T. butter
1/2 lb. mushrooms,
   chopped fine
1/2 cup burgundy wine
roux, made of 1/4 stick
   butter and 3 T. flour,
   stirred over medium
   heat for 3 to 4 minutes
2 cups beef stock
dash of thyme
salt and pepper

Roll out pastry dough to 1/4-inch thickness, flouring generously as you roll. Press out 2 round pieces about the size of a silver dollar and 2 pieces about 6 inches in diameter. Salt and pepper the filets to taste and broil quickly on both sides—keeping meat rare (this seals in the juices). Let the filets cool for 15 minutes. Place the cooled filets on each 6-inch piece of dough and brush around the dough with egg yolk. Place one tsp. of liver paté on each filet and seal with dough. Brush egg yolk over the outside and top with the dough medallion. Brush again with egg yolk. Bake the Wellingtons in a 400 degree oven for 15 minutes or until golden brown. Serve on top of Bordelaise Sauce.

Sauté shallot in butter for about 30 seconds. Add mushrooms and sauté for another minute. Add burgundy wine and simmer 2 to 3 minutes. Add roux and 2 cups beef stock and bring to boil. Add thyme and boil for at least 5 minutes. Season to taste with salt and pepper. Serve remaining Bordelaise Sauce on the side.

Peter H. Salchow
Biggs Restaurant

RACK OF LAMB WITH CREAM GARLIC SAUCE

Serves 2

1 8-rib rack of lamb
  (2-1/2 to 3 lbs. double
  set of connected ribs)
salt
pepper

Remove fell from lamb. Place roast, fat side up, in shallow roasting pan; sprinkle with salt and pepper. Roast, uncovered in 400 degree oven, for 45 to 50 minutes or until meat thermometer registers 175 degrees. Spoon off fat as it accumulates.

BROTH
4 oz. lamb bones
1 stalk celery,
  cut up (1/2 cup)
1 small carrot,
  cut up (1/3 cup)
1/2 small onion,
  cut up (2 T.)
2 cloves garlic, minced
1 cup water
2 T. dry sherry
1 small bay leaf
1/8 tsp. rosemary

In 1-1/2-qt. saucepan, combine lamb bones, celery, carrot, onion, garlic, water, sherry, bay leaf and rosemary. Boil gently, uncovered, for 15 to 20 minutes or until liquid is reduced by about 2/3. Strain, reserving liquid (should have 1/3 cup broth). Place broth in small saucepan.

CREAM GARLIC SAUCE
1 T. butter, softened
1 T. flour
reserved lamb broth
1/4 cup whipping cream
1/8 tsp. salt

Stir together softened butter and flour until smooth. Add to broth in saucepan. Cook and stir until thickened and bubbly. Stir in whipping cream and salt; heat through. Serve with roast.

Peter H. Salchow
Biggs Restaurant

QUICHE

Makes 2

4 eggs
2 cups whipping cream
1 tsp. nutmeg
salt and pepper
1 T. Dijon mustard
1 medium onion, diced
2 T. butter
1/2 cup chives
2 cups grated Swiss,
  Gruyère, mozzarella
  cheese (one cheese or
  any combination)
2 unsweetened, unbaked
  pie shells

Preheat oven to 325 degrees. Mix eggs, cream, nutmeg, salt, pepper and Dijon mustard together to make custard filling. Sauté onion in butter until clear; cool. Layer onions, chives and grated cheese in unbaked pie shells. Pour custard over onions and cheese, filling the shells. Bake for 45 to 60 minutes, until knife inserted in center comes out clean.

VARIATIONS: Sauté cooked crabmeat or shrimp with onions, then layer with cheese.

Peter H. Salchow
Biggs Restaurant

DATE TORTE

Serves 9

From Washington, D.C., Lorraine Percy has sent us her date torte recipe, the perfect ending to a light meal. Her husband, Charles, is Senior United States Senator from Illinois.

3 eggs
1 cup granulated sugar
3 rounded tsp. flour
1/2 tsp. baking powder
1 8-oz. pkg. chopped
  dates
1 cup chopped pecans
whipped cream

Preheat oven to 300 degrees. Separate eggs, beat yolks well and add sugar. Mix flour, baking powder, dates and nuts and fold into egg yolk mixture. Fold in beaten egg whites. Pour into a greased 9 x 9-inch pan. Bake for 40 minutes. Cool. Cut into squares and top with whipped cream.

Mrs. Charles H. Percy

BILL KURTIS'S VEGETABLE TEMPURA WITH BEARNAISE SAUCE
Serves 24

Chicago's loss is the nation's gain! Popular television newscaster Bill Kurtis was recently named co-anchor of the CBS Morning News. Before moving to The Big Apple, Bill shared his crispy appetizer recipe with us.

BEARNAISE SAUCE
6 green onions,
  coarsely chopped
1/4 cup wine vinegar
4 egg yolks
1/4 tsp. dry mustard
2 tsp. tarragon
drop red pepper sauce
1 cup butter, melted

To prepare sauce, sauté onions in vinegar over medium high heat until all liquid is absorbed and onions are tender. Combine first six ingredients in blender; process for 30 seconds at high speed. Add butter slowly, blending constantly. Pour into a bowl and keep warm by placing in a larger bowl of warm water.

BATTER
4 eggs
1-1/4 cups flour
2 cups milk
1/2 tsp. salt
1/4 tsp. pepper

Combine all ingredients and beat until smooth. Batter will be thin.

VEGETABLES
2 lbs. fresh mushrooms
2 14-oz. cans artichoke
  hearts
corn oil

Wipe mushrooms but do not wash. Cut artichokes in half and drain thoroughly. Pat dry. Heat oil in deep fryer. Dip vegetables in batter; fry in oil until golden brown. Drain on paper towels. Serve with warm bearnaise sauce.

Bill Kurtis

STAN'S BARBECUED SALMON WITH BOBBIE'S FISH SAUCE

Makes 1 pint sauce, Serves 12

Mr. and Mrs. Stanton R. Cook are residents of Kenilworth and members of the Kenilworth Union Church. Stan, who is publisher of **The Chicago Tribune,** *likes to relax in his yard, cooking on his barbecue grill. Here is one of his specialties which he serves with a tasty sauce his wife, Bobbie, whips up in her kitchen.*

BOBBIE'S FISH SAUCE

1 cup sour cream
1 cup mayonnaise
1/2 tsp. dry mustard
1 T. white vinegar
chopped chives or scallions to taste

To prepare sauce, combine all ingredients in blender. Chill. Sauce will keep about 2 weeks in a covered jar in refrigerator.

STAN'S BARBECUED SALMON

1 whole fresh salmon (8 to 10 lbs.)
heavy aluminum foil
softened butter or margarine
1/2 cup lemon juice
1 T. Worcestershire sauce
1 T. prepared mustard
1/2 tsp. basil
1/2 tsp. garlic salt
1/2 tsp. salt
1 medium onion, thinly sliced
1 lemon, thinly sliced

Clean and scale fish, removing head, tail and fins. Wash gently in cold water and pat dry between paper towels. Form foil into a roasting pan to fit fish. Grease foil well with butter or margarine. Combine lemon juice with seasonings. Brush cavity of fish with lemon juice mixture. Put half of the sliced onion and lemon into fish cavity. Brush outside of fish generously with butter or margarine. Place remaining onion and lemon slices on top. Pour remainder of lemon juice mixture over fish. Place foil roasting pan on rack of outdoor grill when coals are ready. Cover grill and roast fish one hour and 30 minutes. Do not turn fish. Serve at once with Bobbie's Fish sauce.

Mr. and Mrs. Stanton R. Cook

CHICKEN BREAST ROULADES, CHASSEUR

Serves 4

French Chef Julia Child delighted TV Talk Show Host Phil Donahue and his audience when she prepared this recipe for them. Phil forwarded the recipe to us, noting that he's used it when entertaining friends.

4 chicken breast halves, boned and skinned
salt and pepper
2 T. Dijon mustard
1 tsp. herb mixture, such as Provençal or Italian seasoning
4 slices mozzarella cheese
1 cup flour
2 to 3 T. olive oil or fresh peanut oil
2 T. minced shallots or scallions
1 clove minced garlic (optional)
1 cup sliced fresh mushrooms
2 fresh ripe tomatoes, peeled, seeded, juiced and chopped
1 T. fresh parsley

To prepare chicken, lift inner flap of meat from center of each half breast and fold outward. Pound pieces, one at a time, between two sheets of wax paper to flatten and enlarge them. Season top sides lightly with salt and pepper. With a rubber spatula, spread 1/2 tablespoon mustard over top side of each breast; sprinkle lightly with herb mixture. Arrange a slice of mozzarella on each. Roll up breast from one of its short sides, making a tight, neat package. Press the meat into place with your fingers, as necessary. Film heavy frying pan (non-stick preferred) with 1/16-inch oil. Pan should be just large enough to hold chicken in single layer. Sprinkle breasts lightly with salt and pepper; roll in flour and shake off excess. Heat oil until very hot but not smoking. Add chicken and sauté, turning several times, for 6 to 8 minutes. Regulate heat so chicken browns nicely without burning. Chicken is done when just springy to touch. Remove to side dish. Add shallots and garlic to frying pan; cook for a few minutes. Add mushrooms; sauté for 2 minutes. Stir in tomato; sauté for 2 minutes more while shaking and tossing pan. Season with salt, pepper and herbs to taste. Return chicken to pan and boil rapidly, basting the chicken until the sauce has thickened lightly. Carefully correct seasoning, sprinkle with fresh parsley and serve.

SUMMER DINNER FOR SIX

Filet of Sole with Basil Sauce
French Cut Green Beans
Buttered Baby Carrots
Belgian Endive Salad
Peach Mousse Espresso

BELGIAN ENDIVE SALAD

6 medium sized Belgian
　Endive
3/4 cup French Dressing
　with Dijon mustard
1/2 cup chopped walnuts
1 apple peeled, cored and
　chopped
salt and pepper to taste

Separate Endive leaves and toss with remaining ingredients.

FILET OF SOLE WITH BASIL SAUCE

3 or 4 egg yolks
1/2 cup melted butter
1 tsp. basil
1 T. sherry
1/2 cup whipping cream,
　whipped
2 lbs. lemon or gray sole
　filets

To prepare sauce, place egg yolks in blender. Add hot butter while mixing. Blend until smooth, then add basil and sherry. Add whipped cream just before serving. Broil fish quickly in butter. Serve with sauce.

PEACH MOUSSE ESPRESSO

1 qt. coffee ice cream
1 pkg. peach jello
1 cup boiling water
red raspberries or
　strawberries

Bring ice cream to room temperature. Dissolve jello in hot water and combine with melted ice cream. Mix thoroughly. Refrigerate at least 3 to 4 hours before serving. Serve in large red wine glasses garnished with raspberries or strawberries.

Mrs. Marshall Field IV

DINNER FOR EIGHT

Tomato Clam Bouillon
Cold Crabmeat with Sauce on Bibb Lettuce
Rack of Lamb
Wild Rice Artichoke Casserole
Fresh Green Beans
Strawberries Suisse

TOMATO CLAM BOUILLON

To be served in the living room...

2-2/3 cups canned or
  bottled clam juice
3 cups tomato juice
1/3 cup celery tops
lemon slice
bay leaf
8 thin cucumber slices

Combine all ingredients except cucumber slices. Bring to a boil. Simmer 5 minutes and strain. Serve hot, garnishing each serving with cucumber.

CRABMEAT SAUCE

1 cup mayonnaise
1/8 to 1/4 cup
  horseradish
1/8 to 1/4 cup chili sauce
1 or 2 shakes Tabasco
1/2 tsp. Sauce Diable
1/2 tsp. Worcestershire
  sauce
1 tsp. granulated sugar
2 shakes salt
3 or 4 grinds pepper
1 oz. brandy
crabmeat
bibb lettuce
parsley sprigs

Combine all sauce ingredients. Arrange crabmeat on top of bibb lettuce. Spoon sauce over crabmeat. Garnish with parsley.

RACK OF LAMB

5-lb. rack of lamb
soy sauce
thyme

Preheat oven to 400 degrees. Slather rack of lamb with soy sauce. Sprinkle generously with thyme and bake for one hour.

WILD RICE ARTICHOKE CASSEROLE

1 cup wild rice
2-1/4 cups water
1 T. instant chicken
    bouillon
1-1/2 cups sliced fresh
    mushrooms
1-1/2 cups sliced celery
2 T. butter
1 10-oz. pkg. frozen
    artichoke hearts
1/4 cup sliced green
    onion
2 T. chopped pimiento
1 T. fresh lemon juice
1 tsp. grated lemon peel
1/2 tsp. thyme
salt and pepper to taste

Rinse rice. Mix bouillon and rice with water and bring to a boil. Simmer 30 minutes, covered. Do not drain. Preheat oven to 350 degrees. Sauté mushrooms and celery in butter until tender but not brown, about 5 minutes. Add artichokes, onion, pimiento, lemon juice and peel and spices. Combine rice and artichoke mixture and put in a shallow 2-quart casserole. Cook, covered, until rice is tender, about 45 minutes.

STRAWBERRIES SUISSE

3 3-oz. pkgs. cream
    cheese
1-1/3 cups confectioners
    sugar
1/2 cup whipping cream
1 tsp. vanilla or
    Cointreau
2 qts. strawberries,
    washed and hulled

Blend cream cheese, sugar, cream and vanilla together with electric mixer until smooth and thick. Gently fold in strawberries and chill.

Mrs. Donald S. Perkins

LUNCHEON FOR EIGHT
Rice Salad Niçoise
Hot French Bread
Lemon Squares

RICE SALAD NIÇOISE

Serves 8

1-1/2 cups raw rice
3/4 cup olive oil
1/4 cup red wine vinegar
2 cloves garlic, minced
1 tsp. salt
1/4 tsp. pepper
1/4 tsp. thyme
2 T. chopped pimiento
Romaine, chilled
2 large tomatoes,
  cut into wedges
1 large Bermuda onion
  or red onion, sliced
3 hard cooked eggs,
  sliced
1 2-oz. can rolled
  anchovies, drained
2 6-1/2-oz. cans tuna,
  in chunks
1 4-oz. can pitted
  ripe olives
2 cups marinated
  green beans

Cook rice according to package directions. Combine oil, vinegar, garlic, seasonings and pimiento, then toss with rice. Chill several hours, mixing occasionally. Put rice mixture in 9-inch mold. On a large cake plate, arrange chilled Romaine and rice mold. Arrange chilled tomatoes, onion, eggs, anchovies, tuna chunks, ripe olives and green beans attractively around rice mold.

LEMON SQUARES

Makes 12

BOTTOM LAYER
1 cup flour
1/2 cup butter
1/4 cup granulated sugar

Preheat oven to 325 degrees. Blend flour, butter and sugar together. Pat in 9 x 9-inch pan. Bake for 20 minutes. Pour top layer mixture carefully over bottom layer. Bake 20 minutes more. Cool; cut into squares.

TOP LAYER
2 eggs
1 cup granulated sugar
juice of 1 lemon
rind of 1 lemon
2 T. flour
1/2 tsp. baking powder

Beat eggs; mix in sugar, juice and rind. Stir in flour and baking powder.

Mrs. Donald S. Perkins

SCANDINAVIAN DINNER FOR EIGHT

Gravlax with Mustard Sauce
Cucumber Salat
Chilled White Wine

Roast Venison with Goat Cheese Sauce
Steamed Green Beans and Cauliflower
Tiny Buttered Potatoes with Dill
Hot Rolls
Lingonberry Jelly
Red Wine

Arctic Cloudberry Cream
Pirouettes
Coffee

Signe Marie Kilens contributed an authentic Scandinavian menu. She and her husband, Arve, own Scandinavian Design, a national chain of stores noted for their array of fine imported furniture and accessories.

GRAVLAX

4 lbs. *fresh* salmon,
  center cut, cleaned
  and scaled
1 extra large bunch dill
1/3 cup kosher salt
  (coarse salt)
1/4 cup granulated
  sugar
2 T. white peppercorns,
  crushed
buttered toast
lemon wedges

The fish should be cut lengthwise and the backbone and small bones removed. Place half of the fish, skin-side down in a glass dish. Wash and dry the dill and place it on the fish. Combine the salt, sugar and crushed peppercorns and sprinkle this mixture evenly over the dill. Top with the other half of the fish, skin-side up. Cover with aluminum foil and set a heavy platter on top of the salmon. Pile 5 to 6 cans of food on top of the platter so the weight is evenly distributed over the fish. Refrigerate for 2 to 3 days. Turn the fish evenly every 12 hours, basting with the liquid marinade that accumulates, separating the halves a little to baste the salmon inside. Replace the platter and weights every time. When the gravlax is ready, remove the fish from its marinade, scrape away the seasonings and dry with paper towels. Place the

MUSTARD SAUCE

4 T. highly seasoned
   prepared mustard
1 tsp. dry mustard
3 T. granulated sugar
2 T. white vinegar
1/3 cup vegetable oil
3 T. fresh chopped dill

CUCUMBER SALAT

2 large cucumbers
   (European style
   cucumbers)
1 T. salt
3/4 cup white vinegar
1 T. granulated sugar
1 tsp. salt
1/4 tsp. white pepper
2 T. fresh chopped dill

ROAST VENISON (OR REINDEER) WITH GOAT-CHEESE SAUCE

4 lbs. boneless venison
   (or reindeer ordered in
   advance from the
   butcher)
4 T. butter, softened
salt
freshly ground pepper
2 cups beef stock
2 T. butter
2 to 3 T. flour

separated halves, skin-side down, on a carving board and slice the salmon halves thinly on the diagonal, thereby detaching each slice from the skin. Gravlax is served on a buttered piece of toast, garnished with lemon wedges and a mustard sauce. A touch of cucumber salat is placed next to the gravlax and some dill sprinkled on top. Serve with chilled white wine.

Mix the 2 mustards, sugar and vinegar to a paste. Slowly beat in the oil until it forms a thick emulsion. Stir in dill. Refrigerate.

Cut the cucumbers into thinnest possible slices; the slices should be almost translucent (use a Norwegian cheese cutter if available). Arrange them in a thin layer in shallow glass dish and sprinkle with salt. Allow the salat to refrigerate under weight (place 2 to 3 plates on top of the cucumbers) for a few hours. Mix vinegar, sugar, salt, and pepper and pour it over the cucumbers. Sprinkle with dill. Again refrigerate for 2 to 3 hours. Drain away nearly all the liquid before serving it with the gravlax.

Ask the butcher to tie up the roast so it will hold its shape while cooking. Preheat oven to 475 degrees. Spread the softened butter evenly over the meat with a brush and place it in oven for 20 minutes. When the meat is quite brown and "sealed," reduce the heat to 375 degrees and sprinkle the roast generously with salt and pepper. Baste the meat with beef stock and pour the remaining beef stock into

1 oz. brown Norwegian
   goat cheese,
   finely diced
   (Ski Queen Asjetost)
2 T. red currant jelly
1/2 cup sour cream
4 T. cream sherry wine

the pan. Cook the roast uncovered for 1 to 1-1/2 hours, while basting it every 15 to 20 minutes with the pan juices. The interior of the meat, when finished, should be slightly rare (150 degrees on a meat thermometer). Skim and discard the fat from the pan juices and add some hot water to it. In a small, heavy saucepan, melt 2 T. butter and stir in the flour. Stirring continuously with a wooden spoon, cook this roux for 8 to 10 minutes over low heat until light brown. Carefully and slowly add the pan juices while beating the roux with a wire whisk. Next, whisk in the cheese and finally the jelly. Beat until they dissolve and the sauce is smooth. Carefully stir in the sour cream. Do *not* let the sauce boil. Finally, add the sherry wine. Let the sauce "settle" for 5 to 10 minutes. Taste for seasoning. Remove the strings from the roast, carve the meat in thin slices. The sauce is served separately.

ARCTIC CLOUD – BERRIES STIRRED WITH CREAM

18-oz. jar of cloudberry
   preserves
1 pint whipping cream
1 T. granulated sugar

The orange-yellow Arctic cloudberries are a fruit of the far North belonging to the raspberry family. Any Scandinavian store will sell cloudberry preserves. It is delicious. This dessert always becomes a topic of conversation. Whip the cream with the sugar and carefully spoon in the cloudberry preserves.

Signe Marie Kilens
Scandinavian Design

JANE YLVISAKER'S SPRING DINNER FOR EIGHT

Curried Melon and Seafood
White Wine

Roast Duck
Spinach Soufflé
Soufflé Potatoes
Carrots with Parsley
Red Wine

Hazelnut Meringue
Raspberries in Melba Sauce
Champagne or White Wine

Espresso and Liqueurs

Lots of fresh flowers, place cards and careful seating are important. I really like to try new recipes and ideas, using fresh, seasonal foods. Theme menus are a favorite, such as a Chinese Night or Mexican Night, with drinks, decor and menu carefully planned. My favorite number is 12 around one table, but we're usually 20!!

CURRIED MELON AND SEAFOOD

1/2 to 1 lb. seafood—
  shrimp, scallops,
  lobster or mixture of
  your choice
court bouillon
1 fresh cantaloupe or
  honeydew melon
1 T. wine vinegar
salt and pepper
paprika
1 T. olive oil
3 T. mayonnaise
1 T. whipping cream
2 tsp. curry powder or
  more to taste
melon halves or lettuce
chopped pimiento

Boil seafood briefly in court bouillon; drain and set aside. Cut melon into small balls, reserving shells, if desired. Put vinegar in salad bowl; stir in salt, pepper and paprika to taste. Blend in olive oil, then mayonnaise. Ensure smoothness by stirring in cream. Add enough curry powder to establish a strong curry taste, bearing in mind that the juice from the melon will tone it down. Toss the melon pieces in the dressing; add seafood. Chill in refrigerator. Serve in melon halves or on lettuce bed, adding chopped pimiento for color.

HAZELNUT MERINGUE

FILLING

4 oz. dried apricots
1/2 cup water
1 strip lemon rind
1/2 cup granulated sugar
1-1/2 T. fresh lemon juice

Soak apricots overnight in water. Then stew gently with lemon rind. When tender, purée in food processor. Add sugar and lemon juice. Cool.

MERINGUE

4 egg whites
1 cup superfine sugar
1 tsp. vanilla
1/2 tsp. vinegar
4-1/2 oz. toasted
   ground hazelnuts
1/4 pint whipping cream
confectioners sugar

Butter bottom and sides of two 8-inch round cake pans; dust with flour and line bottom with wax paper. Preheat oven to 375 degrees. Whisk egg whites until stiff; beat in sugar, 2 tablespoons at a time. Continue beating until very stiff, adding vanilla and vinegar. Fold in nuts. Pour into prepared pans and bake for 30 to 40 minutes. Cool. Whip cream until stiff. Fold in apricot purée. Place one meringue layer on serving plate; top with whipped cream mixture. Place other layer on top; dust with confectioners sugar. Pass raspberries in Melba sauce separately.

Jane Ylvisaker

LADIES LUNCHEON FOR SIX

Chilled Pea and Lettuce Soup
Moussaka in Eggplant Skins
Tossed Escarole with Vinaigrette Dressing
Homemade Rolls
Cabernet Sauvignon

This way of serving Moussaka is especially colorful in its purple shell. When combined with the red tomato sauce and the pale yellow cheese sauce, it resembles an artist's pallet. It should be served on a platter before it is individually sliced.

MOUSSAKA

Can be prepared a day ahead...

2 medium eggplants
olive oil
1 large onion, chopped
4 T. butter
2 lbs. cold cooked lamb,
  ground or chopped
1/2 lb. mushrooms, finely
  chopped
4 or 5 T. bread crumbs
1 clove garlic,
  finely chopped
2 T. chopped fresh
  parsley
salt and pepper to taste
dash nutmeg
3/4 cup tomato purée
3 eggs, slightly beaten
6 oz. plain yogurt

Preheat oven to 400 degrees. Bake quartered eggplants for 30 to 40 minutes. Peel off the skins; line a buttered 2-quart casserole with the skins, purple side next to the dish. Cut the eggplant into cubes; sauté in oil. Sauté the onions in butter. Combine the eggplant cubes, lamb, mushrooms, onions, bread crumbs, garlic, parsley, salt, pepper and nutmeg. Mix in the tomato purée. Mix the eggs and yogurt together, then fold it into the eggplant mixture. Pour into the prepared casserole dish. Bake in a preheated 350-degree oven for 1 to 1-1/4 hours. Remove from oven and let casserole rest for a few minutes. Then unmold on a hot platter. Serve with tomato sauce and Mornay sauce.

Makes 1-1/3 cups

MORNAY SAUCE

2 T. butter
2 T. flour
1 cup hot milk
salt and white pepper
  to taste
1/2 cup grated Swiss
  cheese

Melt butter, stir in flour. Gradually stir in hot milk. Cook, stirring constantly, until thickened. Add cheese and simmer slowly for 5 minutes.

TOMATO SAUCE

Makes 4 cups

1 onion, chopped
2 T. butter
1 28-oz. can Italian
  tomatoes, undrained
1 cup red wine
2 cloves garlic, chopped
1/4 cup chopped fresh
  parsley
1 tsp. fresh lemon juice
grated rind of 1 lemon
salt and pepper to taste

Sauté onion in butter until transparent. Add tomatoes, wine, garlic and parsley. Add lemon juice and rind and simmer for 1/2 to 3/4 hour. Purée in food processor. Add salt and pepper to taste.

Mrs. James Hemphill

INDEX

CHICAGO ENTERTAINS
P.O. Box 145
Kenilworth, Illinois 60043

Please send me _____ copies of CHICAGO ENTERTAINS at $11.95
each, plus $1.75 each for postage and handling (Illinois residents add 84¢
state sales tax for each book purchased).

NAME_____

ADDRESS_____

CITY_____ STATE_____ ZIP_____

Please make checks payable to CHICAGO ENTERTAINS

CHICAGO ENTERTAINS
P.O. Box 145
Kenilworth, Illinois 60043

Please send me _____ copies of CHICAGO ENTERTAINS at $11.95
each, plus $1.75 each for postage and handling (Illinois residents add 84¢
state sales tax for each book purchased).

NAME_____

ADDRESS_____

CITY_____ STATE_____ ZIP_____

Please make checks payable to CHICAGO ENTERTAINS

CHICAGO ENTERTAINS
P.O. Box 145
Kenilworth, Illinois 60043

Please send me _____ copies of CHICAGO ENTERTAINS at $11.95
each, plus $1.75 each for postage and handling (Illinois residents add 84¢
state sales tax for each book purchased).

NAME_____

ADDRESS_____

CITY_____ STATE_____ ZIP_____

Please make checks payable to CHICAGO ENTERTAINS

CHICAGO ENTERTAINS
P.O. Box 145
Kenilworth, Illinois 60043

Please send me _____ copies of CHICAGO ENTERTAINS at $11.95 each, plus $1.75 each for postage and handling (Illinois residents add 84¢ state sales tax for each book purchased).

NAME_____

ADDRESS_____

CITY_____ STATE_____ ZIP_____

Please make checks payable to CHICAGO ENTERTAINS

CHICAGO ENTERTAINS
P.O. Box 145
Kenilworth, Illinois 60043

Please send me _____ copies of CHICAGO ENTERTAINS at $11.95 each, plus $1.75 each for postage and handling (Illinois residents add 84¢ state sales tax for each book purchased).

NAME_____

ADDRESS_____

CITY_____ STATE_____ ZIP_____

Please make checks payable to CHICAGO ENTERTAINS

CHICAGO ENTERTAINS
P.O. Box 145
Kenilworth, Illinois 60043

Please send me _____ copies of CHICAGO ENTERTAINS at $11.95 each, plus $1.75 each for postage and handling (Illinois residents add 84¢ state sales tax for each book purchased).

NAME_____

ADDRESS_____

CITY_____ STATE_____ ZIP_____

Please make checks payable to CHICAGO ENTERTAINS